UV-B RADIATION and OZONE DEPLETION

Effects on Humans, Animals, Plants, Microorganisms, and Materials

Edited by

MANFRED TEVINI

LEWIS PUBLISHERS

Boca Raton   Ann Arbor   London   Tokyo

Library of Congress Cataloging-in-Publication Data

UV-B radiation and ozone depletion : effects on humans, animals, plants, microorganisms,
  and materials / edited by Manfred Tevini.
    p.   cm.
  Includes bibliographical references and index.
  ISBN 0-87371-911-5
  1. Ultraviolet radiation--Physiological effect. I. Tevini,
Manfred, 1939-   .
  QP82.2.U4U8 1993
  574.19'154--dc20
                                           92-36185
                                             CIP

PRINTED IN THE UNITED STATES OF AMERICA
1 2 3 4 5 6 7 8 9 0

Printed on acid-free paper

Preface

Ultraviolet radiation damaging to our biosphere is generally absorbed by the ozone layer. Since we know that this protective sheath is being depleted, UV-B radiation has become a global interest. UV-B, which is the most important wave band (according to CIE publication no. 17.4, 1987), is defined as 280 to 315 nm, but is often extended to 320 nm in the scientific literature.

UV radiation can be divided into four wave bands:

Vacuum UV	<200 nm
UV-C	200–280 nm
UV-B	280–315 (320) nm
UV-A	315 (320)–400 nm

At the earth's surface, vacuum UV and UV-C radiation are not present due to their absorption by oxygen, ozone, and other gases. The development of atmospheric oxygen and the ozone layer was a prerequisite for the evolution of life on our planet, protecting life from radiation damage.

However, through anthropogenic emission of chlorofluorocarbons (CFCs) and some other gases affecting the ozone layer adversely, the manifestation of this damage has been the development of "holes" within this layer, the first of which was detected over Antarctica in 1985, again increasing the concern of a global danger which had been recognized much earlier. Rowland and Molina hypothesized the catalytic effect of CFCs on the ozone layer in 1974. In the same year, the United Nations Environment Program (UNEP) was laying the foundation for international action. In 1977 the Coordinating Committee on the Ozone Layer (CCOL) was founded with representatives of governments, concerned organizations, and chemical manufacturers. This committee layed the milestones for the Vienna convention in 1985 and the Montreal Protocol of 1987. By July 1990, 62 countries and the European Economic Community (EEC) had joined the Montreal Protocol, which specifies large cuts in the consumption and production of five CFCs and three halons.

For revision of the Montreal Protocol several groups in the international scientific community were selected to prepare UNEP panel reports, which were divided into three parts guided by leading scientists:

1. the report of the Ozone Scientific Assessment Panel (Dr. Watson, Dr. Albritton)
2. the report of the Environmental Effects Assessment Panel (Dr. van der Leun, Dr. Tevini)
3. the report of the Technology and Economic Assessment Panel (Dr. Anderson, Mr. Lee Bapty)

New experimental results, which were summarized in the UNEP reports of 1989 and 1991 (update), showed that the protocol assessments had not been sufficient with respect to a drastic reduction of the ozone depletion trend in the near future. Numerous conferences and workshops all over the world were also necessary to integrate the developing countries into plans for a further cut in CFC production and emission. The UNEP Environmental Panel Reports from 1989 and 1991 (update), together with the other reports, were the main background for the working groups to evaluate the need to amend the control measures of the Montreal Protocol.

With a decrease in total ozone and the resulting increase of UV-B at ground level, adverse effects on man, animals, plants, and materials are expected. For humans, induction of skin cancer and immunosuppression are not the only concerns. Impacts on the marine phytoplankton will be propagated throughout the food chain, resulting in a decrease of the total biomass, diminishing the main CO_2 sink.

We must also be aware of the potential consequences following impaired growth and photosynthesis of plants as our primary food source. One step has been taken with the Montreal Protocol, but in my opinion this is only the very first step toward protecting life on earth. I would like to conclude with a remarkable sentence written by my colleague Jan van der Leun which excellently summarizes the problem. "The deleterious effects that we recognize are serious enough to plea for action by the nations of the world to protect the ozone layer."

This book presents the newest results and will help inform people about environmental effects on the geo- and biosphere resulting from depletion of the ozone layer. Finally, I thank Jon Lewis for his great interest in the preparation of this book, my colleagues for their kind willingness to contribute, and all those who helped prepare the final version of this book.

Manfred Tevini

The Editor

Manfred Tevini was born in East Germany in 1939. He is currently Professor of Botany at the University of Karlsruhe, Germany. In 1968 he received his doctorate in Natural Sciences after having studied Biology and Chemistry at the University of Münster. He then spent four years as Assistant to Professor Reznik, University of Cologne, and in 1972 became a Lecturer (Habilitation) at the University of Karlsruhe. From 1990 to 1992 he was Dean of the Faculty for Biological and Geological Sciences at the University of Karlsruhe.

In the first part of Dr. Tevini's scientific career his research interest was on lipid physiology of plants. In this topic he edited (together with H. K. Lichtenthaler) the book *Lipid and Lipid Polymers in Higher Plants*, published by Springer in 1977. From that time on he switched his research area to environmental physiology with special interest in biological effects of UV radiation following ozone depletion by anthropogenic gases. In 1980 Dr. Tevini became a member of the Coordinating Committee for the Protection of the Ozone Layer (CCOL), where he co-chaired the biological effects group. Subsequently, he co-chaired the UNEP-Environmental Effects Panel, which assisted decisionmakers in developing and progressing the Montreal Protocol. Two UNEP reports appeared in 1989 and 1991 on the environmental effects of ozone depletion under Jan van der Leun's (Netherlands) and Manfred Tevini's chairmanship. In 1989 he was awarded by UNEP for his excellent activities in this respect.

Research in UV radiation effects is part of his general interest in photobiology. In 1987 Donat Häder and Manfred Tevini wrote the textbook *General Photobiology*, published by Pergamon Press.

Dr. Tevini is a member of the German Botanical Society and the American Society of Photobiology.

Contributors

Anthony L. Andrady
Department of Polymer Science
Research Triangle Institute
Research Triangle Park,
  North Carolina

Mario Blumthaler
Institute of Medical Physics
University of Innsbruck
Innsbruck, Austria

Michael W. Gery
Atmospheric Research Associates
Boston, Massachusetts

Frank R. de Gruijl
Dermatology, Academic Hospital
University of Utrecht
Utrecht, Netherlands

Donat-P. Häder
Institute for Botanical and
  Pharmacological Biology
Friedrich-Alexander University
Erlangen, Germany

Sasha Madronich
Atmospheric Chemistry Division
National Center for Atmospheric
  Research
Boulder, Colorado

Manfred Tevini
Botanik II
University of Karlsruhe
Karlsruhe, Germany

Jan C. van der Leun
Dermatology, Academic Hospital
University of Utrecht
Utrecht, Netherlands

Contents

1

Molecular Biological Effects of Ultraviolet Radiation

Manfred Tevini

INTRODUCTION

Due to space limitations this chapter is intended to be a limited overview, far from being exhaustive, but focussing on UV damage and damage repair.

The damaging effect of ultraviolet radiation is very obvious from sunburn. It is UV-B radiation, which begins at about 285 nm in the natural global radiation, that causes the skin damage also known as the erythema response.[1-3] (For the action spectrum, see Figure 1 in Chapter 4 in this volume.)

UV-C radiation, emitted by artificial UV sources, was often used to kill microorganisms and induce mutations with high effectiveness.[4,5] UV-B radiation from the sun can also induce these damages, as shown for example in yeast or human fibroplasts.[6,7] The nucleic acids DNA and RNA are the main targets of UV radiation, and their damage causes these genetic responses.[8,9] A well-known damage induced by UV radiation from the sun is skin cancer, which is also (but not exclusively) related to DNA damage.[2,10-16] In addition to DNA, structural and enzyme proteins absorb in the UV range (Figure 1) and are inactivated by UV radiation.[17] However, not all UV-absorbing biomolecules need to be the primary effector sites. Energy transfer to other molecules makes the distinction between primary and secondary effects difficult. A UV effect

0-87371-911-5/93/$0.00 + $.50
© 1993 by Lewis Publishers

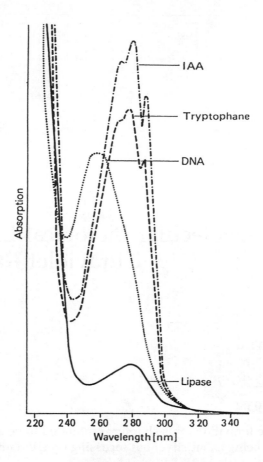

Figure 1 Absorption spectra for some biologically important substances in the UV range.

can also be caused by photosensitizers which absorb the UV radiation; it is the photochemically generated product which then damages the organisms.[18,19] Many organisms have repair mechanisms to remove the products of primary radiation damage to the genetic material.[20] This also makes the identification of primary UV effects difficult.

EFFECTS OF UV RADIATION AT THE MOLECULAR LEVEL

Because of the aromatic π-electron system of pyrimidine and purine bases, nucleic acids have a strong absorbance near 260 nm. Proteins have an absorbance maximum at about 280 nm due to the absorption by the aromatic amino acids phenylalanine, tyrosine and tryptophane (Figure 1).

Numerous lipids also absorb in the UV range due to their isolated or conjugated π-electron systems — for example, the highly unsaturated

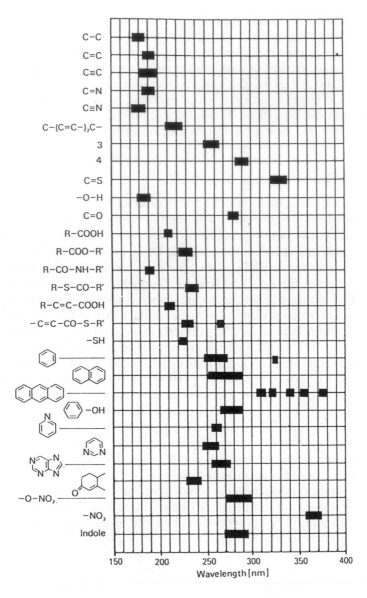

Figure 2 Absorbance range of some chromophoric groups of biologically important molecules.

fatty acids (e.g., linolenic acid) contained in complex membrane lipids. The phytohormone abscisic acid and the plant growth regulator indoleacetic acid (IAA, auxin) also absorb in the UV range. Figure 2 summarizes the absorbance range of some chromophoric groups of biologically important molecules.

The primary photoreceptors can be characterized by measuring action spectra, which have been developed in the UV wave band for many biological responses.[21-25] The action spectrum for inactivation of bacteria and also degeneration of mammalian cells has a maximum near 265 nm and strongly resembles the absorbance spectrum of DNA, indicating that the UV target is located in the genome.[26-28] Depending on the organism and the experimental conditions, different DNA photoproducts which cause the biological effects can be formed by high-energy UV radiation.

Photoreactions of Nucleic Acids

The biologically most effective UV-induced photoreactions occur at the pyrimidine base thymine. The following photoproducts can mainly be found: cyclobutane-type dimers of thymine, cytosine and uracil, pyrimidine adducts, photohydrates, and DNA-protein cross-links.[29-33]

Thymine dimers of the cyclobutane type contain two thymine molecules connected by a cyclobutane ring, which can result in several isomers. This dimer formation occurs in vitro and in vivo with a high quantum efficiency and may be responsible for most UV-induced damage of the DNA (and RNA). The dimerization in vitro is photoreversible: UV radiation at a wavelength of 280 nm predominantly induces dimers, while at 240 nm monomers are mainly produced. In vivo the dimers can be split to monomers by a DNA photolyase working between 300 and 450 nm.[34,35] In the presence of special photosensitizers the dimer production of thymine in the DNA, normally induced in the UV-B and UV-C wave band, can also be induced in the UV-A wave band.[36]

Recently, another UV-induced photodamage in DNA, the pyrimidine (6-4) pyrimidone photoproduct, was discussed to play a significant role in the induction of human skin cancer.[37]

In pyrimidine adducts either two thymine monomers or a thymine and a cytosine monomer form a dimer. In *Bacillus subtilis* spores, one finds a 5-thyminyl-5,6-dihydrothyminyl photoproduct. Pyrimidine adducts cannot be separated into monomers by a simple photochemical reaction like dimers of the cyclobutane type. Inactivation of microorganisms or cells by adducts may contribute 5–15% compared to 85–95% due to dimer formation.[27]

Pyrimidine photohydrates are formed by addition of water to a double bond, especially in uracil and cytosine. These pyrimidine hydrates may play a role in the induction of mutations. In addition to pyrimidine photoproducts, those of purine bases are known; their biological relevance, however, is far smaller.

A DNA-protein cross-link is formed after UV irradiation between a pyrimidine base and an amino acid. The bond between cysteine and thymine is especially reactive. Uracil preferentially binds to cysteine, phenylalanine and tyrosine. DNA-protein cross-links induce irreversible cell damage. The biological importance of strand breaks is being debated, although they have been demonstrated in bacteria.

Photoreactions in Proteins, Lipids and Membranes[33,38,39]

The photochemistry of proteins mainly involves the amino acids phenylalanine, tyrosine and tryptophane, with their aromatic π-electron systems, as well as histidine, cystine and cysteine. The disulfide group of cystine can be split by UV radiation into reactive sulfhydryl groups. Since the covalent bonds of sulfur atoms are important for the tertiary structure of many proteins, the effects of UV on these bonds strongly influence the structure and function of proteins. The disulfide groups can also be split indirectly by singlet energy from tryptophane, which absorbs above 280 nm. Since the energy transfer to reactive centers is possible over considerable distances, the longer wavelengths in the UV range are equally important.

Tryptophane can be excited either directly by UV or by energy transfer from neighboring amino acids such as phenylalanine or tyrosine. The end product is N-formyl kynurenine. After absorption of long-wavelength UV-A radiation this photoproduct can react with nucleic acids, which damages the cell or disturbs its functions. Another possible end product following irradiation of tryptophane with UV is tryptamine. Photochemical reaction products of tyrosine are bityrosine and 4,4-dihydrophenylalanine (DOPA), which can also be produced in plants by a phenol oxidase. Photochemical reactions of amino acids usually deactivate the protein. In some enzymes the deactivation is due to an energy migration to the functionally important amino acids of the active center.

Lipids with isolated or conjugated double bonds can also be photochemically modified by UV absorbance. Phospho- and glycolipids, which are the main components in animal and plant cell membranes, contain unsaturated fatty acids which react under UV radiation and in the presence of oxygen to form lipohydroperoxides via radicals. In keratinocytes and fibroblast membranes it has been shown that fatty acids are released by the action of phospholipase A_1 and A_2, the action of which might be induced by UV-B.[40,41] Either radicals or singlet oxygen can be produced by photosensitization with dyes, aromatic carbohydrates or porphyrins. In the presence of protoporphyrin, a photosensitizer (precursor of hemoglobin and chlorophylls), the singlet oxygen which is produced reacts with cholesterin to form hydroperoxide, which in turn destroys the membrane fatty acids. UV-induced damage to membranes is mainly focussed on transport phenomena. High fluences accelerate molecule flow by producing large breaks. Low UV fluences inactivate membrane function like electrogenic pumps, transport systems, ATPase and photosynthetic activity.

Effects of UV Radiation on Cellular Systems

UV-induced changes in molecular structure most probably decrease the survival probability of an organism. However, during evolution organisms have developed repair mechanisms for radiation damage, so that more UV-resistant species have evolved. The repair mechanisms do not always operate error-free, so that mutations and defects still occur in microorganisms, plants, humans and animals.

The sensitivity of an organism to damaging radiation can be defined by its survival curve. The survival rate is usually an exponential function of radiation doses. The dose-response curves can be single-hit, shoulder and stimulation curves or biphasic curves.

Survival Curves[4,42]

Single-Hit Curves. When a cell is deactivated by a single hit of a photon the survival can be defined by the equation

$$N = N_0 \times e^{-kD}$$

where N is the number of surviving cells
N_0 is the number of initial cells
D is the radiation dose
k is a species-specific constant

Due to the exponential function a semilogarithmic plot shows a linear curve. This type of response is usually found in viruses, phages and enzyme deactivation curves.

Shoulder Curves. At higher radiation doses the curves are also exponential. Lower doses, however, cause less damage than expected. The curve can be interpreted to represent multiple hits. The extrapolation of the exponential part indicates the number of hits. The shoulder may be due to a repair effect which increases the survival at lower doses and causes a deviation from a single-hit curve. An extremely large shoulder is characteristic of *Micrococcus radiodurans*.

Stimulation Curves. These curves show a stimulation at low doses before damage becomes manifest at higher doses. These survival curves are often found in higher plants and are not easily explained by the hit theory.

Bi- or Multiphasic Curves. These curves indicate that a population consists of several subpopulations with different sensitivities. This situation can occur during aging of a population. During their exponential growth, bacteria are usually very UV sensitive, while they are less sensitive in their stationary stage.

Repair Mechanisms[28-31]

The shoulder curves indicate that bacteria can possible repair UV-radiation damage, especially when the cells are not in the logarithmic growth phase. This can be experimentally induced by nutrition deficiency. During this resting period the repair enzymes can remove the damage to the DNA. This process is known as liquid holding recovery. There are basically three different repair mechanisms: excision repair, photoreactivation and post-replication repair.

Excision repair is found from viruses through bacteria, mammalian cells and plants in most organisms and is independent of light.[43] When DNA damage is detected the damaged site (such as a thymine dimer) is cleaved by an endonuclease and excised by an exonuclease.[44] This gap is closed by a local de novo synthesis of the DNA strand by means of a DNA polymerase and a ligase. The excision repair seems to decrease the amount of damage that could cause mutations or cancer.

Photoreactivation is promoted by the DNA photolyase, which is capable of binding and splitting dimers when activated by long-wavelength UV radiation or visible light. However, this radiation has to occur immediately after the UV damage. The DNA photolyase has been found in microorganisms, plants, humans and animals.

In contrast to the excision repair, where the UV-induced DNA damage is recognized and removed immediately by the enzyme, post-replication repair is carried out after replication.[44-46] During replication either a gap is left opposite to the damaged strand or the gap is closed by insertion of false bases. The gap is closed by recombination with the correct parental DNA sequence. In the second case the false bases are removed by an SOS repair: the presence of the damage (for example dimers) is detected and functions as a trigger for the repair mechanism, which is usually blocked. This repair after replication often operates erroneously, so that the mutation rate is relatively high.

UV Effects in Microorganisms, Invertebrates and Mammalian Cells

Viruses, Phages, Bacteria

UV-induced DNA damage in viruses and phages can often be repaired by the host cell if it possesses the necessary excision repair mechanisms. The host cell also does not distinguish between its own and foreign DNA during photoreactivation. Reactivations by the host cell have been found for example in *Escherichia coli*, *Salmonella typhimurium*, and *Haemophilus influenza*. *Micrococcus radiodurans* has an exceptional position among bacteria because of its high UV resistance. It has a perfectly operating system which constantly removes the dimers even when produced in large numbers by high UV doses. In bacteria spores, which are normally less UV sensitive than the vegetative bacteria, hardly any dimers are produced. Instead a spore photoproduct, which cannot be photoreactivated, accumulates. Recently it was reported that sunlight can activate the human immunodeficiency virus (HIV).[52]

Simple Eukaryotes

As in bacteria, we also find dimer formation and photoreactivation in yeast, algae and protozoa. In yeast a UV-induced mutant (petite mutant) which has lost the ability to respire is of interest. The sensitivity for induction of this mutation is localized both in the nucleus and in the mitochondrial DNA.

Insects

The UV effects on insects are interesting for two reasons. First, a number of nocturnal species are attracted by UV radiation. Second, the solar UV radiation influences the biological clock of arthropods. The removal of radiation damage by photoreactivation and other repair mechanisms has also been demonstrated in insects. Aquatic organisms like corals and crustaceae also have photoreactivation capacities, as shown for example in hermatypic corals (*Scleractinia*) and *Daphnia* species, respectively.[53,54]

Mammalian Cells[55]

Mammalian cells such as HeLa cells (cancerogenous human cells) kept in a synthetic medium have a much higher UV sensitivity than bacteria. The action spectrum indicates that DNA and proteins are possible targets.

In addition to pyrimidine dimers, DNA protein cross-links have been found.[56] Photoreactivation has been observed in human leukocytes and mouse cells, but excision repair and post-replication repair mechanisms seem to dominate.

UV Effects on Vertebrates

The uncovered epidermis of many vertebrates is the main target of UV radiation. Short-term UV radiation can induce erythema, melanin pigmentation (tanning) and vitamin D synthesis. Long-term radiation, however, often induces degenerative skin disease known as photoaging or elastosis, which was extensively described by Kligman.[57] Furthermore, pigmented (melanoma) and nonpigmented (non-melanoma) tumors, eye disease and immune suppression can be developed after longer exposure to increased UV-B radiation.[58-61] (Further details are presented in Chapter 4.)

Erythemal Activity[62]

The human skin consists of several layers; the outermost, the *stratum corneum*, has a high absorbance for radiation below 300 nm. Therefore only UV radiation at longer wavelengths penetrates into the lower layers of the epidermis and the *corium*. The skin responds to increased UV-B radiation with well-known sunburn (erythema) (for action spectrum see Chapter 4, Figure 1). The visible indication of a sunburn is the red skin due to increased blood circulation in the epidermis.

Melanin pigmentation is a protective mechanism of the skin against increased UV radiation. It is induced by suberythemal fluence rates and usually becomes manifest a few hours after UV application. The tanning is induced by migration of a previously synthesized chromophore, melanin, into the outer cell layers. Melanins seem to be complex polymers of DOPA-quinone, 5-6-dihydroxyindole and its 2-carboxylic acid, at various oxidation levels, synthesized in melanocytes. A de novo formation of melanocytes by cell division or melanin synthesis in amelanogenous cells is also possible.

Vitamin D$_3$

A positive effect of UV radiation is the formation of the essential vitamin D$_3$ from 7-dehydrocholesterol. Vitamin D$_3$ regulates calcium and phosphate metabolism and prevents rachitis.

UV Effects in Plants[63-65]

As soon as a seedling breaks through the soil surface it is exposed to natural UV radiation. The continuous growth, however, indicates that plants can tolerate or adapt to UV radiation. When plants are grown in a greenhouse without UV radiation they experience a UV shock when planted outside; this can kill the plant. Even plants adapted to UV radiation are impaired in their development, structure and function by increased UV radiation. (Further details are presented in Chapter 5.)

The molecular effects and targets in plants are very heterogeneous. The UV-induced decrease in the mitosis frequency in *Rumex* indicates that DNA is the target. In addition, effects on phytohormones are feasible. Photolytic degradation of indoleacetic acid (IAA) is also possible, especially when growth responses are involved.[66] Continuous UV-B irradiation of barley seedlings disturbs the vertical growth; this may be due to destruction of IAA in the leaf tips. The action spectra measured so far do not allow identification of a photoreceptor, since most of the effects detected after long-term irradiation are secondary effects. However, it was shown in parsley cell cultures that a UV-B receptor must exist, since the synthesis of flavonoid is strictly induced by UV-B, not by red light which normally works in higher plants via the phytochrome system. A coaction of blue light and/or phytochrome, however, has been demonstrated.[67-70] A general rule for these coactions cannot be recognized, since flavonoid synthesis even in corn varieties is regulated differently.[71] Plants possibly protect themselves against increased UV irradiation by an increased synthesis of pigments in the epidermis. It has been shown that UV-B radiation at about 300 nm effectively stimulates the synthesis of flavone glycosides and anthocyanins. The regulation of this process in rye seedlings is possibly due to cis-trans isomerization of cinnamic acids and their derivatives. It was shown that *trans*-cinnamic acid, the primary product of phenylalanine deamination by the key enzyme of the phenylpropanoid metabolism, can be changed to the cis form, which does not inhibit the L-phenylalanine ammonia lyase (PAL) as the trans form does. Through this mechanism rye seedlings accumulate UV-absorbing phenylpropanoids of the flavonoid type in the epidermal layer.[72] It is not yet clear whether cis-trans phenylpropanoids can also regulate mRNA synthesis for the key enzymes of the flavonoid metabolism.

Photoreactivation of DNA dimer products was demonstrated in different plant systems.[73-77] The efficient wave band is 300–500 nm, with high quantum yield around 400 nm. In solar radiation, where UV-B and longer wavelengths are present simultaneously, DNA damage may be small except when the photoreactivating enzyme is destroyed by UV-B.

UV Radiation and Evolution[78,79]

The earth is about 4.6×10^9 years old. The oldest sedimentary rocks with bacteria-like microfossils are about 3.4×10^9 years old. The prebiotic phase, with the chemical evolution of organic compounds from inorganic gases such as water vapor, methane, nitrogen, ammonia and hydrogen sulfide as well as carbon monoxide and dioxide, preceded this, forming an environment capable of producing life. During the prebiotic phase 2.2×10^9 years ago oxygen evolved by photodissociation of water vapor by means of short-wavelength solar UV radiation.

During the chemical evolution short-wavelength UV radiation was probably also the main energy source for photoreactions. It has been demonstrated in laboratory experiments that UV irradiation of typical gases of the primeval atmosphere produces amino acids, formaldehyde and hydrogen cyanide. In aqueous solutions intensive UV radiation formed di- and tripeptides from amino acids, sugars from formaldehydes, and the purine bases adenine and guanine from hydrogen cyanide. Even nucleosides and nucleotides could be produced under UV-C irradiation from their precursors in aqueous solutions.

Principally similar photochemical reactions may have occurred during the prebiotic phase. It is not clear how self-reproducing nucleic acids have evolved from nucleotides, but it seems probable that prebiotic life has developed in the depth of the oceans protected from UV radiation. After the development of repair mechanisms primitive bacteria may have migrated into shallower waters where species developed with the capability of evolving oxygen. The biotically produced oxygen accumulated slowly in the atmosphere and was converted into ozone in the upper layers by solar UV radiation. The gradually forming ozone layer effectively protected life from short-wavelength UV radiation. Under these conditions life could have mastered the transition from marine to terrestrial habitats about 400 million years ago. Within very few years man is going to disturb the protecting ozone layer, but the biological consequences cannot be assessed fully at the moment.

ACKNOWLEDGMENTS

I am grateful to Thomas Hietzker for his help in preparing the manuscript.

REFERENCES

1. Johnson, B. E., F. Daniels, Jr., and I. A. Magnus. "Response of Human Skin to Ultraviolet Light," in *Photophysiology, Vol. 4,* A. C. Giese, Ed., (New York: Academic Press, 1968), pp. 139–202.
2. Urbach, F., Ed. *The Biological Effects of Ultraviolet Radiation,* (New York: Pergamon Press, 1969).
3. Epstein, J. H. "Photomedicine," in *The Science of Photobiology,* K. C. Smith, Ed., (New York: Plenum Press, 1989), pp. 155–192.
4. Harm, W. *Biological Effects of Ultraviolet Radiation,* (London: Cambridge University Press, 1980).
5. Witkin, E. M. "Ultraviolet Mutagenesis and Inducible DNA Repair in *Escherichia Coli,*" *Bacteriol. Rev.* 40:869–907 (1976).
6. Resnick, M. A. "Sunlight-Induced Killing in *Saccaromyces cerevisiae,*" *Nature* 226:377–378 (1970).
7. Parson, P. G. and P. Gross. "DNA Damage and Repair in Human Cells Exposed to Sunlight," *Photochem. Photobiol.* 32:635–641 (1980).
8. Smith, K. C. "Physical and Chemical Changes Induced in Nucleic Acids by Ultraviolet Light," *Radiat. Res. Suppl.* 6:54–79 (1966).
9. Rahn, R. O. "Ultraviolet Irradiation of DNA," in *Concepts in Radiation Cell Biology,* G. L. Whitson, Ed. (New York: Academic Press, 1972), pp. 1–56.
10. Setlow R. B. "The Wavelength in Sunlight Effective in Producing Skin Cancer: Theoretical Analysis," *Proc. Natl. Acad. Sci. U.S.A.* 71:3363–3369 (1974).
11. De Gruijl, F. R. and J. C. van der Leun. "A Dose-Response Model for Skin Cancer Induction by Chronic UV Exposure of a Human Population," *J. Theor. Biol.* 83:487–504 (1980).

12. Epstein, J. H. "Photocarcinogenesis, Skin Cancer and Aging," *J. Am. Acad. Dermatol.* 9:487–506 (1983).
13. van der Leun, J. C. "UV-Carcinogenesis," *Photochem. Photobiol.* 39:861–868 (1984).
14. Urbach, F. "Potential Effects of Altered Solar Ultraviolet Radiation on Human Skin Cancer," *Photochem. Photobiol.* 50:507–514 (1989).
15. Lee, J. A. H. "The Relationship Between Melanoma of Skin and Exposure to Sunlight," *Photochem. Photobiol.* 50:493–496 (1989).
16. Ananthaswamy, H. and W. E. Pierceall. "Molecular Mechanisms of Ultraviolet Carcinogenesis," *Photochem. Photobiol.* 52:1119–1136 (1990).
17. Grossweiner, L. I. "Photochemical Inactivation of Enzymes," *Curr. Top. Radiat. Res. Q.* 11:141–199 (1976).
18. Spikes, J. D. "Photosensitization," in *The Science of Photobiology*, H. C. Smith, Ed. (New York: Plenum Press, 1989), pp. 79–110.
19. Averbeck, D. "Recent Advances in Psoralens Phototoxicity Mechanism," *Photochem. Photobiol.* 50:859–882 (1989).
20. Smith, K. C. "UV Radiation Effects," in *The Science of Photobiology*, H. C. Smith, Ed. (New York: Plenum Press, 1989), pp. 111–133.
21. Coohill, T. P. "Action Spectra for Mammalian Cells in Vitro," in *Topics in Photomedicine*, K. C. Smith, Ed. (New York: Plenum Press, 1984), pp. 1–37.
22. Caldwell, M. M., L. B. Camp, C. W. Warner, and S. D. Flint. "Action Spectra and Their Key Role in Assessing Biological Consequences of Solar UV-B-Radiation Change," in *Stratospheric Ozone Reduction, Solar Ultraviolet Radiation and Plant Life, Vol. 8*, NATO ASI Series G: Ecological Sciences, R. C. Worrest and M. M. Caldwell, Eds. (Berlin: Springer-Verlag, 1986), pp. 87–112.
23. Coohill, T. P. "Ultraviolet Action Spectra (280–380 μm) and Solar Effectiveness Spectra in Higher Plants," *Photochem. Photobiol.* 50:451–457 (1989).
24. Peak, J. J. and J. G. Peak. "Use of Action Spectra for Identifying Molecular Targets and Mechanisms of Action of Solar Ultraviolet Light," *Physiol. Plant.* 58:367–372 (1983).
25. Rundel, R. D. "Action Spectra and Estimation of Biologically Effective UV Radiation," *Physiol. Plant.* 58:360–366 (1983).
26. Zölzer, F. and J. Kiefer. "Action Spectra for Inactivation and Mutagenesis in Chinese Hamster Cells and Their Use in Predicting the Effects of Polychromatic Radiation," in *Stratospheric Ozone Reduction, Solar Ultraviolet Radiation and Plant Life*, R. C. Worrest and M. M. Caldwell, Eds. (Berlin: Springer-Verlag, 1988), pp. 131–118.
27. Jagger, J. "Ultraviolet Inactivation of Biological Systems," in *Photochemistry and Photobiology of Nucleic Acids, Vol. 2*, S. Y. Wang, Ed. (New York: Academic Press, 1976), pp. 147–186.
28. Sutherland, J. C. and K. P. Griffin. "Absorption Spectrum of DNA for Wavelengths Greater than 300 nm," *Radiat. Res.* 86:399–409 (1981).
29. Wang, S. Y. "Pyrimidine Bimolecular Photoproducts," in *Photochemistry and Photobiology of Nucleic Acids, Vol. 3*, S. Y. Wang, Ed. (New York: Academic Press, 1976), pp. 295–356.

30. Patrick, M. H. and R. O. Rahn. "Photochemistry of DNA and Polynucleotides: Photoproducts," in *Photochemistry and Photobiology of Nucleic Acids, Vol. 2*, S. Y. Wang, Ed. (New York: Academic Press, 1976), pp. 35–95.

31. Smith, K. C., Ed. *Aging, Carcinogenesis and Radiation Biology: The Role of Nucleic Acid Addition Reactions* (New York: Plenum Press, 1976).

32. Shetlar, M. D. "Cross-Linking of Protein to Nucleic Acids by Ultraviolet Light," in *Photochemical and Photobiological Reviews, Vol. 5*, K. C. Smith, Ed. (New York: Plenum Press, 1980), pp. 187–218.

33. Grossweiner, L. I. and K. C. Smith. "Photochemistry," in *The Science of Photobiology*, K. C. Smith, Ed. (New York: Plenum Press, 1989), pp. 47–78.

34. Teramura, A. H., L. H. Ziska, and A. E. Szetin. "Changes in Growth and Photosynthetic Capacity of Rice with Increased UV-B Radiation," *Physiol. Plant.* 83:373–380 (1991).

35. Wang, S. Y., Ed. *Photochemistry and Photobiology of Nucleic Acids* (New York: Academic Press, 1976).

36. Costalat, R., J. Blais, J. P. Ballini, A. Moysan, and J. Cadet. "Formation of Cyclobutane Dimers Photosensitized by Pyrodopsoralens: A Triple-Triplet Energy Transfer Mechanism," *Photochem. Photobiol.* 51:255–262 (1990).

37. Mitchell, D. L. and R. S. Nairu. "The Biology of the (6-4) Photoproduct," *Photochem. Photobiol.* 49:805–819 (1989).

38. Murphy, T. M. "Membranes as Targets of Ultraviolet Radiation," *Physiol. Plant.* 58:381–388 (1983).

39. Kochevar, J. E. "UV-Induced Protein Alterations and Lipid Oxidation in Erythrocyte Membranes," *Photochem. Photobiol.* 52:795–800 (1990).

40. DeLeo, V. A., D. Hanson, J. B. Weinstein, and L. C. Harber. "Ultraviolet Radiation Stimulates the Release of Arachidonic Acid from Mammalian Cells in Culture," *Photochem. Photobiol.* 41:51–56 (1985).

41. Punnonen, K. and C. T. Jansen. "UV-B Irradiation and Distribution of Arachidonic Acid and Stearic Acid in Human Keratinocytes," *J. Invest. Dermatol.* 92:503a (1989).

42. Niemann, E.-G. "Strahlenbiophysik," in *Biophysik*, W. Hoppe, W. Lohmann, H. Markl, and H. Ziegler, Eds. (Berlin: Springer-Verlag, 1982), pp. 300–312.

43. Soyfer, V. N. and K. G. Ceminis. "Excision of Thymine Dimers from the DNA of UV Irradiated Plant Seedlings," *Environ. Exp. Bot.* 17:135–143 (1977).

44. Frieberg, E. C. *DNA Repair* (New York: W. H. Freeman, 1985).

45. Degain, N., E. Ben-Hur, and E. Riklis. "DNA Damage and Repair: Induction and Removal of Thymine Dimers in Ultraviolet Light Irradiated Intact Water Plants," *Photochem. Photobiol.* 31:31–36 (1980).

46. Sancar, A. and G. B. Sancar. "DNA Repair Enzymes," *Annu. Rev. Biochem.* 57:29–67 (1988).

47. Hsiao, D. "Impact of Climatic Change on the Biosphere," CiAP Monograph No. 5, (Springfield, VA: National Technical Information Service, 1975).

48. Sutherland, B. M., P. Runge, and J. C. Sutherland. "DNA Photoreactivating Enzyme from Placental Mammals. Origin and Characteristics," *Biochemistry* 13:4710–4715 (1974).

49. Sutherland, B. M., L. C. Harber, and I. E. Kochevar. "Pyrimidine Dimer Formation and Repair in Human Skin," *Cancer Res.* 40:3181–3185 (1980).
50. D'Amrosio, S. M., J. W. Whetstone, L. Slazinski, and E. Lowney. "Photorepair of Pyrimidine Dimers in Human Skin In Vivo," *Photochem. Photobiol.* 34:461–464 (1981).
51. World Health Organization, "Ultraviolet Radiation," Environmental Health Criteria 14, Kirjapaino, Vammala (1979).
52. Zumdzka, B. Z. and J. Z. Beer. "Activation of Human Immunodeficiency Virus by Ultraviolet Radiation," *Photochem. Photobiol.* 52:1153–1162 (1990).
53. Siebeck, O. "Experimental Investigation of UV-Tolerance in Hermatypic Corals (*Scleractinia*)," *Mar. Ecol. Prog. Ser.* 43:95–103 (1988).
54. Siebeck, O. and U. Böhm. *Untersuchungen zur Wirkung der UV-B-Strahlung auf kleine Wassertiere* (Müchen: BPT-Bericht 1/87, Gsf, 1987).
55. Kaina, B., B. Stein, A. Schönthal, H. J. Rahmsdorf, H. Ponta, and P. Herrlich. "An Update on the Mammalian UV Response: Gene Regulation and Induction of a Protective Function," in *DNA Repair Mechanisms and Their Biological Implications in Mammalian Cells,* M. W. Lambert and J. Laval, Eds. (New York: Plenum Press, 1990).
56. Shetlar, M. D. "Cross-Linking of Proteins to Nucleic Acids by Ultraviolet Light," *Photochem. Photobiol. Rev.* 5:107–197 (1980).
57. Kligman, L. H. "The Hairless Mouse and Photoaging," *Photochem. Photobiol.* 54:1109–1118 (1991).
58. Koh, H. K., B. E. Kligler, and R. A. Lew. "Sunlight and Cutaneous Malignant Melanoma: Evidence for and against Causation," *Photochem. Photobiol.* 51:765–779 (1990).
59. Dekter, M. "Photobiology of the Skin and Eye," E. M. Jackson, Ed. (New York: 1986).
60. Kripke, M. L. "Photoimmunology," *Photochem. Photobiol.* 52:919–924 (1990).
61. Noonan, T. P. and E. C. De Fabo. "Ultraviolet-B Dose-Response Curves for Local and Systemic Immunosuppression Are Identical," *Photochem. Photobiol.* 52:801–812 (1990).
62. McKinley, A. F. and B. J. Diffey. "A Reference Action Spectrum for Ultraviolet Induced Erythema in Human Skin," in *Human Exposure to Ultraviolet Radiation: "Risks and Regulations,"* W. F. Passchier and B. F. M. Bosnajokovic, Eds. (Amsterdam: Elsevier, 1987), pp. 83–86.
63. Caldwell, M. M. "Plant Response to Solar Ultraviolet Radiation," in *Encyclopedia of Plant Physiology.* New Series, Vol. 12A: Physiological Plant Ecology, O. L. Lange, P. S. Nobel, C. B. Osmond, and H. Ziegler, Eds. (Berlin: Springer-Verlag, 1981).
64. Wellmann, E. "UV Radiation in Photomorphogenesis," in *Encyclopedia of Plant Physiology.* New Series, Vol. 16 B: Photomorphogenesis, W. Shropshire and H. Mohr, Eds. (Berlin: Springer-Verlag, 1983).
65. Tevini, M. and A. Teramura. "UV-B Effects on Terrestrial Plants," *Photochem. Photobiol.* 50:479–487 (1989).
66. Tevini, M., J. Braun, P. Grusemann, and J. Ros. "UV-Wirkungen auf Nutzpflanzen," in *Wirkungen von UV-B-Strahlung auf Pflanzen und Tiere* (Laufener Seminarbeiträge 3/88, 1989), pp. 38–52.
67. Duell-Pfaff, N. and E. Wellmann. "Involvement of Phytochrome and Blue Light Photoreceptor in UV-B Induced Flavonoid Synthesis in Parsley (*Petroselinum hortense* Hoffm.)," *Planta* 156:213–217 (1982).

68. Beggs, C. J., A. Stolzer-Jehle, and E. Wellmann. "Isoflavonoid Formation as an Indicator of UV Stress in Bean (*Phaseolus vulgaris* L.) Leaves. The Significance of Photorepair in Assessing Potential Damage by Increased Solar UV-B Radiation," *Plant Physiol.* 79:630–634 (1985).

69. Mohr, H. and H. Drumm-Herrel. "Coaction between Phytochrome and Blue/UV Light in Anthocyanin Synthesis in Seedlings," *Physiol. Plant.* 58:408–414 (1983).

70. Ohl, S., K. Hahlbrock, and E. Schäfer. "A Stable Blue-Light Derived Signal Modulates Ultraviolet Light Induced Activation of Chalkon-Synthase Gene in Cultured Parsley Cells," *Planta* 177:228–236 (1989).

71. Beggs, C. J. and E. Wellmann. "Analysis of Light Controlled Anthocyanin Formation in Coleoptiles of *Zea mays* L.: The Role of UV-B, Blue, Red and Far-Red Light," *Photochem. Photobiol.* 41:481–486 (1985).

72. Tevini, M. and U. Mark. "Effects of Enhanced UV-B and Temperature on Growth and Function in Crop Plants," International Congress on Photobiology, Kyoto, Japan (September 1992).

73. Saito, N. and H. Werbin. "Evidence for a DNA-Photoreactivating Enzyme in Higher Plants," *Photochem. Photobiol.* 9:389–393 (1969).

74. Ikenaga, M. and S. Kondo. "Action Spectrum for Enzymatic Photoreactivation in Maize," *Photochem. Photobiol.* 19:109–113 (1974).

75. McLennan, A. "The Repair of UV Light-Induced DNA Damage in Plant Cells," *Mutat. Res.* 181:1–7 (1987).

76. Langer, B. and E. Wellmann. "Phytochrome Induction of Photoreactivating Enzyme in *Phaseolus vulgaris* L. Seedlings," *Photochem. Photobiol.* 52:861–863 (1990).

77. Pang, Q. and J. B. Hays. "UV-B-Inducible and Temperature-Sensitive Photoreactivation of Cyclobutane Pyrimidine Dimers in *Arabidopsis thalina*," *Plant Physiol.* 95:536–543 (1991).

78. Canuto, V. M., J. S. Levine, T. R. Augustsson, C. L. Imhoff, and M. S. Giampapa. "The Young Sun and the Atmosphere and Photochemistry of the Early Earth," *Nature* 305:281–286 (1983).

79. Rao, K. K., R. Cammack, and D. O. Hall. "Evolution of Light Energy Conversion," in *Evolution of Prokaryotes*, FEMS Symp., K. H. Schleifer and E. Stackebrandt, Eds. (London: Academic Press, 1985), pp. 143–173.

2

UV Radiation in the Natural and Perturbed Atmosphere

Sasha Madronich

OVERVIEW

The ultraviolet (UV) radiation reaching the biosphere varies with time and location. Some of this variation is regular and due to well-determined geometric factors such as the position of the sun in the sky and the yearly change in the earth-sun distance. Other variations are due to changes in atmospheric constituents which determine the transmission of the radiation from the top of the atmosphere to the surface; ozone, clouds, and aerosols are the most important among these, but minor trace gases (e.g., nitrogen dioxide and sulfur dioxide) can also contribute in highly polluted areas. The atmospheric constituents exhibit geographic and seasonal patterns, as well as day-to-day fluctuations which are largely unpredictable. A possibility of most serious concern is that these constituents may also be changing over time periods of years and decades as a result of human activity. In particular, the introduction of man-made chlorofluorocarbons (CFCs) to the atmosphere has resulted in significant global and localized changes in atmospheric ozone since the late 1970s.[1] Cloudiness, aerosols, and local pollutant gases may have also been changing since the pre-industrial days.

The natural variability of UV radiation makes direct measurement of human-induced changes extremely difficult. The temporal variability implies that trends have to be extracted from measurements obtained

0-87371-911-5/93/$0.00 + $.50
© 1993 by Lewis Publishers

over a long period of time, e.g., decades, during which the UV monitoring instruments need to retain a constant sensitivity and calibration. The spatial variability imposes the condition of multiple measurement locations, preferably on a global scale, chosen carefully to avoid particular local biases (e.g., from increasing urban pollution). There is, at present, no UV measurement network which fulfills these conditions.

Most of our knowledge about environmental UV comes from atmospheric radiative transfer models. These models combine measurements of the extraterrestrial solar radiation and atmospheric optics to calculate the amount of UV radiation reaching the surface at any time and location. The power of such models is that they allow detailed studies of the sensitivity of surface UV to numerous different conditions, including potential future scenarios of atmospheric change. Thus, much of this chapter is based on UV levels calculated with radiative transfer models, with several sections devoted to describing the structure of commonly used radiative transfer models and the sensitivity of calculated UV levels to different atmospheric conditions. The likely response of UV levels to current trends in atmospheric composition is described in a later section. The relatively few direct measurements of UV changes due to changes in atmospheric composition are discussed in the final section.

RADIOMETRIC DEFINITIONS

The radiation reaching the earth is described by the spectral radiance (sometimes called the intensity), $I(\lambda,\theta,\phi)$, where λ is the wavelength, θ is the zenith angle measured from the local vertical, and ϕ is the azimuth angle measured horizontally from a standard direction, e.g., north. Except for polarization differences which are not considered here, the radiance contains the full specification of the radiation field: it gives the energy arriving per unit time from an infinitesimal solid angle centered around direction (θ,ϕ), per unit area perpendicular to that direction, at each wavelength. Although not shown explicitly, the radiance is a function of time (of day, of year, etc.) and location (latitude, longitude, elevation above sea level, etc.), and it varies in response to different environmental conditions (ozone, clouds, surface reflections, etc.).

The total energy impingent on a target can be obtained by integrating the spectral radiance over all directions of incidence. The result generally depends on the relative orientation of the target and the incident light. Two idealized cases should be recognized. For a spherical target, the energy per unit time received by a unit cross sectional area of the target is the scalar irradiance,

$$F_s = \int_0^{2\pi} \int_{-1}^{1} I(\theta, \phi) d(\cos \theta) d\phi = F_0 + \int_0^{2\pi} \int_0^{1} I_{\downarrow}(\theta, \phi) d(\cos \theta) d\phi$$
$$+ \int_0^{2\pi} \int_{-1}^{0} I_{\uparrow}(\theta, \phi) d(\cos \theta) d\phi$$

where the expression on the right shows possible individual contributions from parallel light with scalar irradiance F_0 (e.g., the direct solar beam), diffuse down-welling radiance $I_{\downarrow}(\theta, \phi)$ (e.g., the diffuse sky radiation), and upwelling diffuse radiance $I_{\uparrow}(\theta, \phi)$ (e.g., ground reflections). The wavelength dependence has been omitted for brevity. If, on the other hand, the target is a two-sided horizontal surface, the energy from all directions is the vector irradiance (sometimes called the flux),

$$F_v = \int_0^{2\pi} \int_{-1}^{1} I(\theta, \phi) \cos \theta d(\cos \theta) d\phi$$
$$= F_0 \cos \theta_0 + \int_0^{2\pi} \int_0^{1} I_{\downarrow}(\theta, \phi) \cos \theta d(\cos \theta) d\theta$$
$$+ \int_0^{2\pi} \int_{-1}^{0} I_{\uparrow}(\theta, \phi) \cos \theta d(\cos \theta) d\phi$$

Both scalar and vector irradiance have the same units (e.g., $W\ m^{-2}$), but the vector irradiance is reduced by cosine factors which account for the change in projected area of the receiving surface with respect to the directions of incidence. The downwelling vector irradiance is the quantity most commonly measured by radiometric instruments, while the scalar irradiance, which is much more difficult to measure, is often the more applicable quantity for the irradiation of biological systems, especially for organisms which are randomly oriented (e.g., Reference 2). Because of the measurement problems, most studies found in the literature concern the vector irradiance unless explicitly stated otherwise, a convention continued here. The irradiance can be defined at a specific wavelength (spectral irradiance) or integrated over broad wavelength bands. When the wavelength dependence is of interest, the spectral irradiance is defined as the irradiance per unit wavelength, e.g., with units of $W\ m^{-2}\ nm^{-1}$.

The biological effectiveness of UV radiation depends on the particular biological or chemical processes of interest. In many cases, the biological response is a strong function of wavelength. The relative biological effectiveness of different wavelengths is described by monochromatic action spectra, which are usually obtained from laboratory studies. Figure 1 gives actions spectra for three different biological effects and the spectral response function of a commonly used UV detector. All of the action spectra given in the figure have been normalized to unity at 300 nm.

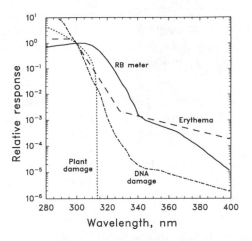

Figure 1 Action spectra for DNA damage,[3] generalized plant damage,[4] erythema induction,[5] and the Robertson-Berger UV radiometer.[6]

Given the spectral irradiance $F(\lambda)$ and an action spectrum $B(\lambda)$ for a particular biological effect, the spectral dose rate for that effect is defined by the product $F(\lambda)B(\lambda)$, with units equal to those of spectral irradiance, e.g., $W\ m^{-2}nm^{-1}$. Integration of the spectral irradiance over all wavelengths gives the dose rate,

$$\text{Dose rate} = \int B(\lambda)\ F(\lambda)\ d\lambda$$

with units of irradiance, e.g., $W\ m^{-2}$. The dose rate is a measure of the biologically effective irradiance at any given instant and is therefore a function of time. Integration of the dose rate over a time period (e.g., hour, day, or year) yields the corresponding (hourly, daily, or yearly) dose:

$$\text{Dose} = \int\int B(\lambda)\ F(\lambda)\ d\lambda\ dt$$

in units of energy area^{-1}, e.g., $J\ m^{-2}$. Action spectra specify only the relative biological response at different wavelengths, not the absolute biological effect. Thus, spectral dose rates, dose rates, and doses computed for two different biological effects cannot be compared with each other numerically. Only relative changes can be compared meaningfully, e.g., the geographical, diurnal, and seasonal distributions of each dose or the increase in each dose for a given decrease in the atmospheric ozone column.

THE CALCULATION OF SPECTRAL IRRADIANCE

Methods

The theoretical calculation of UV irradiance may be viewed as consisting of four separate components:

(1) geometrical factors which account for the daily, seasonal, and latitudinal variation of the angular position of the sun in the sky and for the seasonal variation of the earth-sun distance
(2) wavelength-dependent input data such as the extraterrestrial spectral irradiance, the absorption cross section of ozone and other gases, Rayleigh scattering cross sections for air molecules, and absorption and scattering parameters for particulates including clouds and aerosols
(3) altitude-dependent input data including vertical distributions of ozone, air density, temperature (which may alter the ozone absorption cross sections), other absorbing gases, clouds, and aerosols
(4) a radiative transfer scheme to compute the propagation of UV radiation through the atmosphere

The angular position of the sun in the sky is specified by the solar zenith angle θ_0, which is the angle between the center of the solar disk and an observer's local vertical direction (actually the local normal on a virtual celestial sphere concentric with the earth, since the earth is not perfectly spherical). The expression for θ_0 is

$$\cos \theta_0 = \sin \delta \sin \Phi + \cos \delta \cos \Phi \cos t_h$$

where δ, the solar declination, is the angle between the sun's direction and the earth's equatorial plane
Φ is the latitude (positive in the northern hemisphere, negative in the southern hemisphere)
t_h is the local hour angle

The local hour angle is given by

$$t_h = \pi(GMT/12 - 1 + \Psi/180) + EQT$$

where   GMT is the Greenwich Mean Time corresponding to the local time
of interest
Ψ is the longitude (positive east of the Greenwich meridian, negative west)
EQT is the equation of time

Both δ and EQT vary with time of year and (to a much lesser extent)
from year to year and may be calculated with great accuracy using the
expressions given, e.g., by Smart.[7] However, for most biological irradiation applications the year-to-year variation can be ignored, and
Spencer[8] has expressed δ and EQT using a Fourier expansion in terms
of the angular day θ_n,

$$\theta_n \equiv 2\pi d_n/365 \qquad \text{radians}$$

where the day number d_n is 0 for January 1 and 364 for December 31.
The expressions are

$$EQT = 0.000075 + 0.001868 \cos \theta_n - 0.032077 \sin \theta_n$$

$$- 0.014615 \cos 2\theta_n - 0.040849 \sin 2\theta_n$$

$$\delta = 0.006918 - 0.399912 \cos \theta_n + 0.070257 \sin \theta_n$$

$$- 0.006758 \cos 2\theta_n + 0.000907 \sin 2\theta_n$$

$$- 0.002697 \cos 3\theta_n + 0.001480 \sin 3\theta_n$$

The yearly averaged *earth-sun distance*, R_0, is 1 astronomical unit (au)
or 1.496×10^{11} m. The yearly variation may also be represented fairly
accurately by a Fourier expansion,[8]

$$(R_0/R_n)^2 = 1.000110 + 0.034221 \cos \theta_n + 0.001280 \sin \theta_n$$

$$+ 0.000719 \cos 2\theta_n + 0.000077 \sin 2\theta_n$$

where R_n is the earth-sun distance on day d_n.

The UV wavelengths of interest to environmental photobiology at the
earth's surface are in the range 280–400 nm. The definitions of UV-B as
the range 280–315 nm and UV-A as 315–400 nm will be used here,
although several alternative definitions have also been proposed. This
distinction is of qualitative utility only, since in practice a much finer
resolution of wavelengths is required. The high-resolution wavelength
grid is especially necessary in the UV-B range, because the transmission
of the atmosphere decreases by many orders of magnitude from 315 nm
to 280 nm, while some biological response functions increase by several
orders of magnitude. However, the use of small wavelength intervals
can be computationally costly, since the full radiative transfer calculation
must be carried out for each wavelength interval. No systematic studies

have been carried out to assess the optimum resolution needed to obtain accurate results of biologically active UV radiation. However, a similar study carried out for atmospheric photochemistry purposes[9] shows that wavelength intervals of 2 nm or smaller give errors of 4% or less for all tropospheric photodissociation processes considered, while intervals of 10 nm can induce large errors, in some cases exceeding a factor of two.

The extraterrestrial spectral irradiance at UV-A and UV-B wavelengths is fairly well established and has been reviewed recently.[10,11] Measurements were obtained from ground-based stations,[12] aircraft,[13] balloons,[14] and more recently from the solar ultraviolet spectral irradiance monitor (SUSIM)[15] aboard Spacelab 2. At any given wavelength, values obtained by different techniques can vary by as much as 15%,[11] but after some averaging the uncertainties are estimated as about 3% at 400 nm, increasing to 5–10% near 280 nm.[10] Natural fluctuations in the solar output (e.g., from the 11-year solar sunspot cycle) are minor in the 280–400 nm region (<1%), but are significant at the shorter wavelengths involved in the production and destruction of stratospheric ozone, so that they may affect indirectly the UV-B radiation transmitted through the atmosphere.[10]

Molecular ozone, O_3, absorbs strongly in the Hartley region (200–300 nm) and more weakly in the Huggins bands (300–360 nm). The weak Chappius bands begin at 410 nm and extend into the infrared, being therefore unimportant to UV considerations. Laboratory studies have determined the ozone absorption cross sections with accuracy of 1% or better, which is sufficient for most atmospheric calculations. Molina and Molina[16] give measurements at three different temperatures (226, 263, and 298 K) which can be used to interpolate to intermediate atmospheric temperatures of interest. Other atmospheric gases which may affect UV levels in certain regions (usually polluted urban environments) are nitrogen dioxide, NO_2, and sulfur dioxide, SO_2. Absorption cross sections are well known, e.g., Reference 17 for NO_2 and References 18 and 19 for SO_2.

Cross sections for Rayleigh scattering by air molecules may be calculated from the expression given by Fröhlich and Shaw,[20]

$$\sigma_r = 3.90 \times 10^{-28}/\Lambda^x \qquad cm^2$$

where Λ is the wavelength in μm, and

$$x = 3.916 + 0.074\Lambda + 0.050/\Lambda$$

or alternatively from the expression given by Nicolet,[21]

$$\sigma_r = 4.02 \times 10^{-28}/\Lambda^x \qquad cm^2$$

with

$$x = 3.677 + 0.389\Lambda + 0.09426/\Lambda \quad \text{for } 0.20 \text{ } \mu m < \Lambda < 0.55 \text{ } \mu m$$
$$x = 4.04 \qquad\qquad\qquad\qquad\quad \text{for } 0.55 \text{ } \mu m < \Lambda < 1.0 \text{ } \mu m$$

which gives values about 3–4% higher in the UV-A and UV-B regions. The difference is not significant for most biological effects applications.

Clouds and aerosols are generally difficult to represent realistically in a model because they tend to be highly variable, and detailed information about their microphysical properties is usually unavailable for a particular atmospheric situation of interest. Factors which affect their optical characteristic include particle shape and size distribution, chemical composition, the bulk morphology of individual clouds, broken cloud fields and aerosol plumes, and their geometric placement in relation to the sun and the observer. Summaries of approximate methods for representing clouds may be found in the treatises by Stephens,[22,23] Stephens et al.,[24] and Feigelson.[25] A characteristic of clouds important to UV studies is that the transmission is relatively independent of wavelength, at least over the limited UV-A and UV-B ranges. Several standard aerosol models have been proposed.[26,27] For sulfate aerosols, most common in urban and rural locations of industrialized regions, the attenuation generally increases with decreasing wavelengths, although not as strongly as for Rayleigh scattering.

The UV transmission of the atmosphere depends sensitively on the vertical amounts and distributions of gases and particles which scatter and absorb radiation. Because these atmospheric constituents fluctuate widely with time and location, it is convenient to first calculate the UV radiation levels for an idealized atmosphere and then to examine separately the dependence of the UV transmission on variations in the individual environmental factors. One model which has been frequently used for this purpose is the *U.S. Standard Atmosphere*,[28] which specifies the vertical distribution of the temperature and the number density of air and ozone molecules for typical mid-latitude northern hemisphere conditions. The total vertical ozone column for this model atmosphere is 348 DU (Dobson units, 1 DU = 2.69×10^{20} molecules m^{-2}).

Radiative transfer schemes are used to compute the propagation of radiation through the atmosphere. This calculation requires the solution, at each wavelength, of the equation of radiative transfer (e.g., Reference 29) for the spectral radiance $I(\tau,\theta,\phi)$,

$$\cos\theta[dI(\tau,\theta,\phi)/d\tau] = -I(\tau,\theta,\phi) + (\omega_0/4\pi)F_\infty e^{-\tau/\cos\theta_0} P(\theta,\phi;\theta_0,\phi_0)$$
$$+ (\omega_0/4\pi)\int_0^{2\pi}\int_{-1}^{+1} I(\tau,\theta',\phi') P(\theta,\phi;\theta',\phi')d\cos\theta'd\phi'$$

where θ and ϕ are the usual angular coordinates (θ_0 and ϕ_0 for the direct solar beam) τ is the vertical coordinate measured in optical depth units

F_∞ is the extraterrestrial spectral irradiance

$P(\theta,\phi,\theta',\phi')$ is the scattering phase function, defined as the probability that a photon incoming from the direction defined by the angles θ',ϕ' will be scattered into angles θ,ϕ

ω_0 is the single scattering albedo, defined as the ratio of scattering probability to total attenuation (scattering plus absorption) probability

Values of $\tau, P(\theta,\phi,\theta',\phi')$, and ω_0 depend on wavelength and altitude and are computed from the absorption and scattering properties of the atmospheric gases and particles. Once a solution for $I(\tau,\theta,\phi)$ is obtained, the spectral irradiance is computed by integration over all angular directions as discussed previously.

No analytical solution of the radiative transfer equation exists for the realistic atmosphere. Several very accurate numerical methods have been developed, including the discrete ordinates, Feautrier, spherical harmonics, Fourier expansion, adding, successive orders, and Monte Carlo methods (see, for example, References 29–31). These methods are usually quite complex in formulation and require extensive computing resources. More efficient approximate methods have also been developed. The most important class of methods is based on the two-stream approximation and includes the hemispheric mean, quadrature, Eddington, and delta-Eddington methods (see, for example, References 32 and 33). The uncertainties induced by use of the simpler model are overall quite small when considering that the idealized environmental conditions used for the model calculations are generally never attained exactly in the real atmosphere. The results presented in the remainder of this chapter were obtained using the delta-Eddington method.[34]

Illustrative Results

Typical values of the spectral irradiance computed using a radiative transfer model are shown in Figure 2. The values were calculated using the delta-Eddington radiative transfer scheme, for clear (aerosol- and cloud-free) skies, vertical profiles from the U.S. standard atmosphere with an ozone column of 348 DU, surface albedo of 0.05, average earth-sun separation, and three different solar zenith angles. The extraterrestrial spectral irradiance is also shown for comparison. Note in particular the large reductions in surface UV radiation at wavelengths below about 320 nm, due to ozone absorption.

Figures 3 and 4 illustrate the calculation of the dose rate for erythemally weighted UV. The spectral dose rates (Figure 3) have a sharp peak between 300 and 320 nm and a significant contribution from UV-A radiation. This long-wavelength tail is not present with some other action spectra (e.g., DNA damage and plant damage). The clear sky erythemal

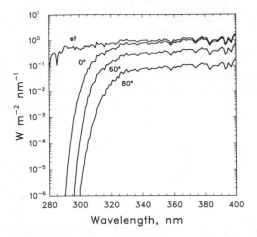

Figure 2   Spectral irradiance at the surface for clear skies, ozone column of 348 DU. Uppermost curve shows the extraterrestrial spectral irradiance. Progressively lower curves are for solar zenith angles of 0°, 60°, and 80°.

dose rate, i.e., area under the erythemal spectral dose rate curve, is shown in Figure 4 for summer solstice at several locations.

UV DISTRIBUTIONS AND SENSITIVITIES

Geographical and Seasonal Distributions

Seasonal and latitudinal variations of doses are obtained by (1) accounting for the variations in the earth-sun distance, (2) computing the appropriate zenith angle for each time and latitude of interest, and (3) estimating the ozone concentrations appropriate to the location and time of the year. The earth-sun distance varies by about 3.4% from minimum (perihelion, on about 3 January) to maximum (aphelion, on about 5 July), and the corresponding variation in the square of the distance, which is important for radiation calculations, is about 7%. The solar zenith angle varies with time of day, time of year, and latitude. Figure 5 shows the values of the solar zenith angle at local solar noon. Figure 6 shows the monthly average ozone column values for different latitudes, obtained by the total ozone mapping spectrometer (TOMS) over the years 1979–1989. Values are typically lower in the tropics (250–300 DU) throughout the year and highest during the spring at mid- and high latitudes but with clearly lower levels in the southern polar region.

The latitudinal and seasonal dependence of daily doses computed for clear skies is shown in Figure 7 and was obtained by integration of dose rates computed at 15-minute intervals at each latitude. Highest values

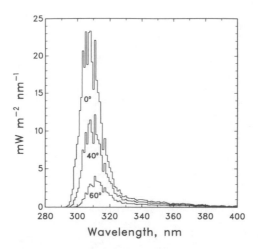

Figure 3 Spectral dose rate for erythema induction, for clear skies, ozone column of 348 DU. Values of the solar zenith angle are indicated.

track the subsolar point between the tropics of Capricorn and Cancer, and lowest values occur in the polar regions with the usual 6-month offset between the hemispheres. Doses in the tropics are due mostly to irradiation during a few hours about noon, while in the polar regions the daily doses are accumulated over a much longer period of time. Table 1 illustrates the width of the diurnal distributions, expressed as the time about noon needed to accumulate 75% of the daily dose, γ in hours (i.e., 75% of the daily dose is due to exposure between the hours $12 - \gamma/2$ and $12 + \gamma/2$). Note that the effective times are much shorter than the total hours of sunlight, especially for DNA-damaging radiation, as may be expected from the high UV-B sensitivity of its action spectrum. The effective times for scalar, rather than vector, irradiance are longer by about 0.5 hours in June and less during the other months. The width of the distribution can also be used for some rough estimates of the daily variation of doses and dose rates. For example, if the daily variation of dose rates at tropical and middle latitudes is approximated as a triangle (quite roughly — see Figure 4), γ is simply the full width at half maximum. The noon-time dose rate is then the daily dose (from Figure 7) divided by γ (from Table 1), and it is also straightforward to estimate the dose attained between any two times of the day. For example, the fraction of the daily dose incurred between times t_1 and t_2 (where both times are in the morning sunlit hours) is

$$(1/2\gamma^2)[(t_2 - 12 + \gamma)^2 - (t_1 - 12 + \gamma)^2]$$

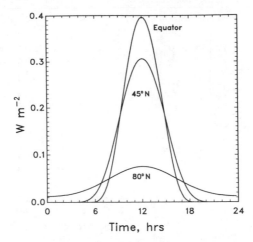

Figure 4 Diurnal dependence of erythema induction dose rate on 21 June at three different latitudes. Calculations with ozone column of 267 DU at equator, 337 DU at 45°N, and 364 DU at 80°N.

e.g., at 45°N in June the period 10:00–11:00 a.m. accounts for 12% of the daily erythema dose, or about 860 J m^{-2}. The formulae for triangular distributions are inappropriate for the long days of high latitudes, as is clear from the 80°N curve of Figure 4.

Annual clear sky doses are shown in Figure 8. As may be expected, maximum values are found at the equator. The decrease toward the poles is most rapid for DNA damage and plant damage doses, which are sensitive primarily to UV-B radiation, while erythema doses fall more slowly due to their non-negligible sensitivity to UV-A wavelengths. The asymmetry between hemispheres, only slightly apparent in this figure, is shown more clearly in Figure 9. Values are consistently larger in the southern hemisphere, due partly to the smaller earth-sun separation during the southern hemisphere summer, but in larger proportion to the lower values of southern hemispheric ozone.[36,37] This is further evidenced by the fact that the greatest interhemispheric differences occur for DNA and plant damage, which are most sensitive to ozone as discussed in more detail in the next section.

Sensitivity to Atmospheric Ozone

The sensitivity of a specific biological dose to ozone changes is in large part determined by its action spectrum. Spectra with high UV-B sensitivity and rapid fall-off at longer wavelengths are very sensitive to ozone changes, while spectra with significant contributions in the UV-A range can be quite insensitive. A common measure used to compare the sen-

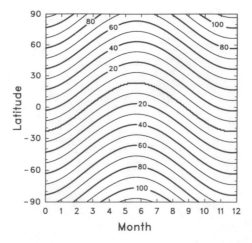

Figure 5 Solar zenith angle at local solar noon, for different latitudes and times of the year.

sitivities of different biological effects is the radiation amplification factor (RAF), which is computed for each biological response function using a full radiative transfer calculation of the dose change for a small (usually 1%) decrease in ozone. RAFs are defined by the expression

$$\Delta D/D = RAF \, (-\Delta N/N) \qquad \text{(percent rule)}$$

where D and ΔD are the dose and the dose change, respectively
        N and ΔN are the ozone column and its change, respectively

A compilation of RAFs for different biological effects is given in Table 2. The simple proportionality is accurate only for small changes in the ozone column (a few percent), but is quite useful in comparing the sensitivity of different biological processes to ozone depletion. A somewhat wider range of ozone changes can be described by the integral form of the percent rule,

$$D_1/D_2 = (N_2/N_1)^{RAF} \qquad \text{(power rule)}$$

where D_1 and D_2 are the doses corresponding to ozone amounts N_1 and N_2, respectively. Figure 10 illustrates the range of validity of the percent and the power rules.

The use of RAFs has several serious limitations. First, if non-negligible response is likely to exist but has not been measured at longer wavelengths (where radiation levels are usually greater), the RAFs can be grossly overestimated. This is illustrated in Table 2 by the values given in brackets, which were obtained by extrapolating the measured action

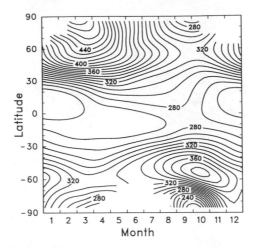

Figure 6 Latitudinal and seasonal variation of total ozone, in Dobson units. Values are averages for the years 1979–1989, measured by the total ozone mapping spectrometer (TOMS) aboard the Nimbus-7 satellite. (Version 6 data courtesy of R. Stolarski.)

spectra with an exponential tail to 400 nm. Second, different RAF values may be appropriate for different conditions, particularly solar zenith angle and total ozone column. The effect is quite strong for generalized plant damage, as shown in Figure 11, while for DNA damage and erythema induction the variations are much smaller (see also Reference 59). Several other environmental factors, listed in Table 3, do not affect the RAFs to any significant extent, since they affect primarily the total dose, not its wavelength dependence.

One additional consideration about the RAFs, and about doses in general, is the dependence on the altitude of the perturbation to the ozone. Even if the total ozone column is maintained at a constant value, changes in the vertical distribution of the ozone concentration can result in significant changes in the dose, as shown in Figure 12. For high sun (ca. $\theta_0 < 60°$), tropospheric ozone is more effective in absorbing UV-B radiation than stratospheric ozone,[61] while the opposite is true at low sun.[62,63] The effect is due to the different photon path lengths in the troposphere, where most of the UV-B radiation is diffuse, and in the stratosphere, where most of the light is direct. The net effect on daily dose rates depends on the (dose-weighted) prevailing solar zenith angle at any given latitude, as shown in Figure 13. In equatorial regions and at mid-latitudes of the summer hemisphere, a shift of the ozone distribution towards the troposphere results in a net reduction of daily doses, while a net dose increase occurs in polar regions and during mid-latitude

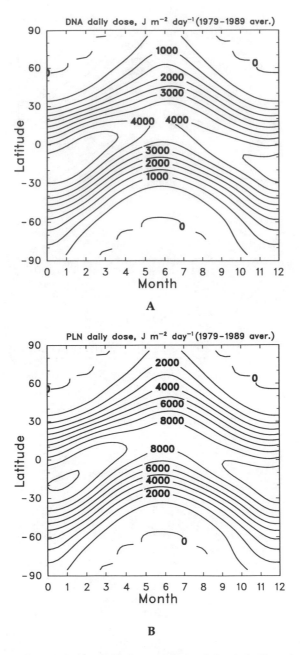

Figure 7 Latitudinal and seasonal dependence of the daily doses calculated for clear skies and low surface albedo (0.05) using measured ozone column averages over 1979–1989. (A) DNA damage; (B) generalized plant damage; (C) erythema induction; (D) relative response of the Robertson-Berger UV meter. Units of contours are J m⁻², with action spectra normalized to unity at 300 nm. (Adapted from Reference 35.)

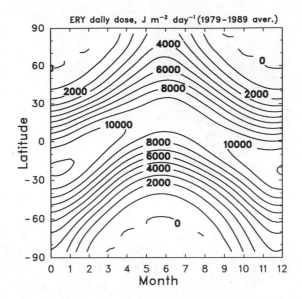

Figure 7C

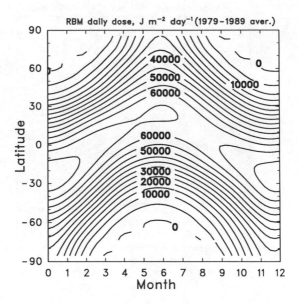

Figure 7D

winter. Note, however, that to maintain the same total column the relative increase in stratospheric ozone must be much greater than the relative reduction in stratospheric ozone, e.g., 78% compared to 12% in the example given in Figures 12 and 13.

Table 1 Duration of Illumination for Different Latitudes and Seasons

Latitude	January	February	March	April	May	June
	Mid-day hours for 75% of daily dose for DNA damage					
85°	—	—	6.7	11.3	13.0	13.8
75°	—	3.6	5.2	6.4	7.4	8.0
65°	3.1	4.0	4.6	5.4	6.0	6.4
55°	3.6	4.0	4.4	5.0	5.4	5.8
45°	3.6	4.0	4.4	4.8	5.2	5.4
35°	3.8	4.0	4.4	4.6	4.9	5.0
25°	4.0	4.1	4.4	4.6	4.8	4.8
15°	4.2	4.2	4.4	4.4	4.6	4.6
5°	4.3	4.3	4.4	4.4	4.4	4.4
	Mid-day hours for 75% of daily dose for erythema induction					
85°	—	—	6.6	12.8	14.6	15.0
75°	—	3.5	5.6	7.4	9.0	9.6
65°	3.1	4.2	5.3	6.2	7.0	7.4
55°	3.8	4.4	5.0	5.8	6.3	6.6
45°	4.2	4.6	5.0	5.4	5.8	6.0
35°	4.3	4.6	5.0	5.2	5.6	5.6
25°	4.4	4.6	4.8	5.1	5.3	5.4
15°	4.6	4.7	4.8	5.0	5.1	5.3
5°	4.8	4.8	4.8	5.0	5.0	5.0
	Total hours of sunlight (sunrise to sunset)					
85°	0.0	0.0	8.4	24.0	24.0	24.0
75°	0.0	4.3	10.9	17.3	24.0	24.0
65°	4.5	8.1	11.4	14.8	18.2	21.0
55°	7.5	9.5	11.6	13.9	15.9	17.1
45°	9.0	10.3	11.7	13.3	14.6	15.4
35°	9.9	10.8	11.8	12.9	13.8	14.4
25°	10.6	11.2	11.9	12.6	13.2	13.6
15°	11.2	11.5	11.9	12.4	12.7	12.9
5°	11.8	11.8	12.0	12.1	12.2	12.3

Note: For vector irradiance on 15th day of each month, northern hemisphere. Southern hemisphere values are similar if offset by 6 months.

Sensitivity to Surface Reflections

Reflections from water, land, vegetation or other surfaces may increase the UV radiation directly by illuminating the downward-facing side of a target and indirectly by illuminating the atmosphere from below, which can then scatter radiation back to the surface. The distinction must there-

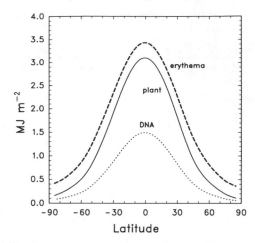

Figure 8 Yearly doses for plant damage (solid line), DNA damage (dotted line),
and erythema induction (dashed line); average over 1979–1989.

fore be made between local reflections, which are directly visible from
the target, and regional reflections, from the surrounding region of about
a 10-km radius, which may influence the sky radiation.

The albedo of a surface, defined as the ratio of reflected to incident
irradiance, is generally a function of the surface material and texture
and of the wavelength. It can also depend on the angle of incidence of
the incoming radiation, which is a particularly severe problem at visible
wavelengths for different solar zenith angles, but causes less variability
in the UV range since much of the incoming radiation is diffuse. Many
measurements of the albedo of different surfaces are available for visible
wavelengths, and satellite imagery is adding to the knowledge of the
global surface albedo distribution. Relatively few albedo measurements
exist for the UV wavelengths; a partial compilation is given in Table 4.

The dependence of dose rates on albedo is shown in Figure 14. The
effect of albedo on vector irradiance is only weakly dependent on solar
zenith angle (because most of the incident radiation is already diffuse)
so that similar effects are expected for daily doses. Note that for high
albedo the enhancement of doses based on vector irradiance exceeds
2.0, which would be the theoretical limit in the absence of an atmosphere.
Figure 14 also shows that the effect of reflections can be considerably
greater if the scalar irradiance (or scalar dose) is of interest. The theoretical maximum enhancement of scalar irradiance due to surface reflections in the absence of an atmosphere is 3.0,[71] but atmospheric back-
scattering can increase this value considerably.

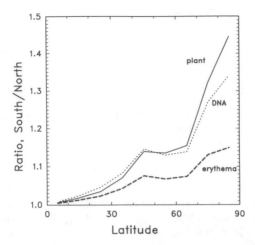

Figure 9 Interhemispheric ratio for yearly doses for plant damage (solid line), DNA damage (dotted line), and erythema induction (dashed line). For clear skies.

Sensitivity to Clouds

Clouds can change substantially the UV irradiance at the surface. Unfortunately, to date there have been no simultaneous measurements of UV transmission with detailed cloud physical properties such as particle size distributions or liquid water content. Some studies have related the transmission to cloud type, mostly at visible wavelengths, but as may be expected, a wide range of values was obtained because properties such as the cloud optical depth were not measured. A few of these empirical studies are summarized in Table 5.

Cloud droplets, which are relatively large compared to aerosols, have scattering cross sections that are essentially independent of wavelength over the UV-A and UV-B regions. Absorption by pure cloud water is negligible from the visible through most of the UV range, down to wavelengths less than 200 nm. Impurities are usually too small to cause significant absorption, except in highly polluted regions. Scattering by clouds may increase photon path lengths through absorbing gases (such as ozone) in the interstitial cloud space and below cloud, resulting in increased absorption at wavelengths absorbed by these gases.[74] Overall, clouds are expected to introduce only a weak wavelength dependence in the transmitted radiation, and the few available measurements appear to confirm this.[75]

For uniform cover, the effect of clouds is usually a reduction of the clear sky UV levels. Broken clouds can decrease or increase the radiation, but because of the tremendous difficulty in representing all possible

Table 2 Radiation Amplification Factors (RAFs) at 30°N

Effect	RAF		Reference
	January	July	
DNA related			
Mutagenicity and fibroblast killing	[1.7]2.2	[2.7]2.0	39, 40
Fibroblast killing	0.3	0.6	41
Cyclobutane pyrimidine dimer formation	[2.0]2.4	[2.1]2.3	42
(6-4) Photoproduct formation	[2.3]2.7	[2.3]2.5	42
Generalized DNA damage	1.9	1.9	3
HIV-1 activation	[0.1]4.4	[0.1]3.3	43
Plant effects			
Generalized plant spectrum	2.0	1.6	4
Inhibition of growth of cress seedlings	[3.6]3.8	3.0	44
Isoflavonoid formation in bean	[0.1]2.7	[0.1]2.3	45
Inhibition of phytochrome-induced anthocyanin synthesis in mustard	1.5	1.4	45
Anthocyanin formation in maize	0.2	0.2	46
Anthocyanin formation in sorghum	1.0	0.9	47
Photosynthetic electron transport	0.2	0.2	48
Overall photosynthesis in leaf of *Rumex patientia*	0.2	0.3	49
Membrane damage			
Glycine leakage from *Escherichia coli*	0.2	0.2	50
Alanine leakage from *Escherichia coli*	0.4	0.4	50
Membrane-bound K^+-stimulated ATPase inactivation	[0.3]2.1	[0.3]1.6	51
Skin			
Elastosis	1.1	1.2	52
Photocarcinogenesis, skin edema	1.6	1.5	53
Erythema reference	1.1	1.1	5
Skin cancer in SKH-1 hairless mice	1.4	1.3	54, 55
Eyes			
Damage to cornea	1.2	1.1	56
Damage to lens (cataract)	0.8	0.7	56
Movement			
Inhibition of motility in *Euglena gracilis*	1.9	1.5	57
Other			
Immune suppression	[0.4]1.0	[0.4]0.8	58
Robertson-Berger meter	0.8	0.7	6

Source: Adapted from reference 38.

Note: Values in brackets show effect of extrapolating original data to 400 nm with an exponential tail, for cases where the effect is larger than 0.2 RAF units.

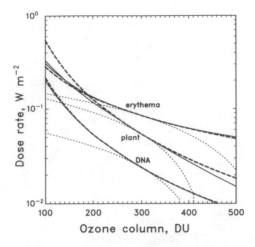

Figure 10   Sensitivity of dose rates to ozone, for three different action spectra, solar zenith angle = 60°, clear skies. Solid lines give the exact radiative transfer calculations. Dased lines are estimated using the power rule and dotted lines using the percent rule (see text), from the exact value at 300 DU and assumed RAFs of 2.0 for DNA damage, 2.1 for plant damage, and 1.1 for erythema induction. (Adapted from Reference 35.)

cloud morphologies and their position in the sky relative to the sun, partial cloud cover is usually treated as a simple linear combination of UV irradiances computed for fully overcast and fully clear sky, weighted by the estimated fraction of the sky which is covered by cloud. Estimates of cloud cover are available from ground observations (usually at airports) and are conventionally expressed in "tenths" of cloud cover, with $^0/_{10}$ for completely clear sky and $^{10}/_{10}$ for fully overcast conditions. However, such visual estimates are known to have systematic errors (usually overestimating the cloud cover) and are limited in their geographic coverage. Better cloud data are becoming available through measurements from various satellites and are being analyzed and archived through programs such as the ongoing International Satellite Cloud Climatology Project.[76] Figure 15 shows the global distribution of the frequency of occurrence of clouds for January 1990, expressed as the percent of the horizontal area which is covered by clouds at any instant. Figure 16 shows, for the same time period, the average optical depth of clouds when these are present. Frederick and Lubin[74] used satellite cloud images to estimate that, during July 1979, clouds reduced the ground-level UV-B on average by 10 to 30%, depending on latitude.

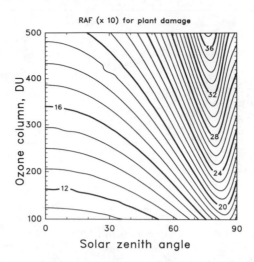

Figure 11 Dependence of Radiation Amplification Factor (RAF) for generalized
plant damage on solar zenith angle and ozone column.

**Table 3 Environmental Effects on DNA Radiation
Amplification Factor (RAF)**

Model	Solar Zenith Angle			
	0°	60°	75°	85°
Base model[a]	1.88	1.97	2.00	1.99
Surface albedo = 0.50	1.90	1.98	2.02	2.00
Aerosols[26]	1.89	1.99	2.02	2.01
Cloud, thin	1.90	2.00	2.03	2.01
Cloud, thick	1.93	2.02	2.05	2.03
Hemispherical receiver	1.92	1.98	2.00	2.00
Surface at 3 km above sea level	1.88	1.98	2.01	2.00

Source: Adapted from reference 60.

[a] Base model: surface albedo 0.05, no aerosols, no clouds,
horizontal receiver, sea level. RAF computed for ozone
column change from 300 to 303 Dobson units.

The theoretical reduction of UV doses by uniform complete cloud
cover is shown in Figure 17 and may be compared to the values given
in Table 5 — but in both cases the uncertainties are considerable due to
the usual lack of knowledge about optical depths of specific clouds and
to the variability of clouds even when nominally of the same type.
Uncertainties are even higher when under partly cloudy skies. Figure
18 illustrates average reductions due to cloud cover (relative to clear sky
values) observed at a few locations.

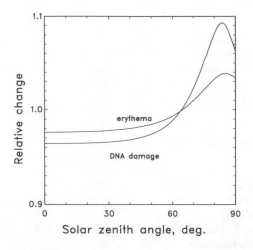

Figure 12 Differential effect of tropospheric and stratospheric ozone changes on DNA-damaging and erythemal UV radiation. Dose rate changes were computed by reducing stratospheric ozone concentrations by 12% (35 DU) while simultaneously increasing tropospheric concentrations by 78% (also 35 DU), at a constant total ozone column of 348 DU.

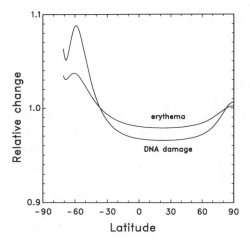

Figure 13 Differential effect of tropospheric and stratospheric ozone changes on DNA-damaging and erythemal UV radiation, as a function of latitude, for 21 June. Ozone perturbations as in Figure 12.

Table 4 Ultraviolet Albedo of Various Surfaces

Surface	Albedo,%	Reference
Liquid water	5–10[a]	64, 65, 66
Clean dry snow	30–100	64, 65, 66, 67
Dirty wet snow	20–95	64, 65
Ice	7–75	64, 65
Sudan grass	2	64
Maize	2	64
Conifer trees	4–8	64
Grass (unspecified)	1	67
Alfalfa	2–4	68
Rice	2–6	68
Sorghum	2–5	68
Pasture	2–6	65
Grassland	1–3	65
Green farmland	4	66
Brown farmland	4	66
Pine forest	1–2	66
Dry Yolo loam soil	5–8	68
Wet Yolo loam soil	5–8	68
Sacramento silt and clay	8–11	68
Black lava	1–3	69, 70
Limestone	8–12	65
Desert sand	4	70
Gypsum sand	16–30	70
White cement	17	67
Blacktop asphalt	4–11	65, 68
Plywood	7	67
Black cloth	2	67

[a] Depending on solar zenith angle and surface roughness.

UV radiation measurements have been made at several locations over extended periods of time and have been correlated with the observation of the fraction of the sky area which is covered by cloud. Fitting of rather scattered data has resulted in different representations, e.g.,

$$D_c/D_0 = 1 - 0.56c \qquad \text{(Reference 78)}$$

$$= 1 - 0.50c \qquad \text{(Reference 79)}$$

$$= 1 - 0.7c^{2.5} \qquad \text{(Reference 80)}$$

where D_0 and D_c are the UV irradiances for clear sky and for fractional cloud area coverage c, respectively. The fully overcast transmission (i.e., for c = 1) from the above expressions ranges from 0.30 to 0.50, while another study[81] resulted in values as low as 0.2, with strongly nonlinear

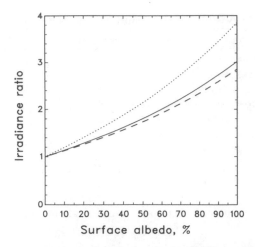

Figure 14   Effect of isotropic surface albedo on erythema dose rates, clear skies.
Solid curve give enhancement of vector irradiance at any solar zenith
angle. Enhancement of scalar irradiance is given by dotted curve for
zenith angle = 0° and by dashed line for zenith angle = 70°.

dependence on c. Obviously, the simple relationships for partial cloud
cover should be applied with great caution due to the variability of cloud
distributions and morphologies at any particular time and location.

An important additional consideration is the coupling between clouds
and surface albedo. The combination of high reflectivities for both surface and cloud can trap radiation in the intervening atmosphere and
may result in surprisingly high doses. This is shown in Figure 19. If the
surface albedo is low, clouds reduce the irradiance strongly (e.g., from
the figure, for albedo = 0, increasing cloud optical depth from 0 to 40
reduces the irradiance from 100 to 26%), while if the albedo is high, the
same clouds will cause a lesser reduction of irradiance (e.g., for albedo
= 0.8, increasing cloud optical depth from 0 to 40 reduces the irradiance
from 240 to 120%, or only a 50% reduction).

Sensitivity to Atmospheric Aerosols

Tropospheric aerosols, including mineral dust, sea-salt particles, soot,
organic aerosols, ammonium sulfate, and diluted sulfuric acid droplets,
can reduce the surface UV irradiance if present in sufficient amounts.
Sulfate aerosols, mostly of anthropogenic origin, are frequently observed
in industrialized regions as a haze which reduces the visibility in the
lowest 0.5–2 km of the atmosphere (the planetary boundary layer, PBL).
Figure 20 shows the average horizontal visual range (defined at the 2%
contrast level) for the eastern U.S. during the 1970s. Current values are
believed to be similar.[82] The relationship between the horizontal visual

Table 5a Visible Transmission of Different Cloud Types

Cloud Type	Transmission,%[a]
Ci, cirrus	84
Cs, cirrostratus	78
Ac, altocumulus	50
As, altostratus	41
Sc, stratocumulus	34
St, stratus	25
Ns, nimbostratus	19
Fog	17

Source: Modified from reference 72.

[a]   Transmissions for a solar zenith angle of 60°.

Table 5b

Solar Zenith Angle Range, Degrees	Transmission, %Mean (Range)	No. of Cases
Cirrus (Ci)		
35–45	84 (93–67)	3
45–55	80 (96–57)	6
55–65	76 (89–66)	4
65–75	68 (88–46)	7
75–85	62 (86–37)	2
Cirrostratus (Cs)		
35–45	73 (91–44)	10
45–55	63 (86–35)	13
55–65	61 (84–25)	22
65–75	53 (62–28)	6
75–85	46 (69–26)	3
Cirrus (Ci) with Cirrostratus (Cs)		
35–45	72 (89–57)	7
45–55	65 (84–40)	9
55–65	63 (77–31)	5
65–75	58 (83–40)	5
Altocumulus (Ac)		
45–55	25 (−)	1
55–65	15 (37–2)	4
65–75	13 (20–1)	4
75–85	10 (14–7)	4

Source: Modified from reference 73.

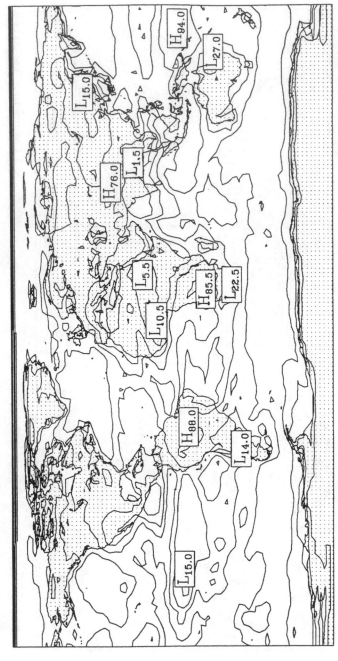

Figure 15 Monthly average frequency of cloud occurrence during January 1990. (From Reference 76.)

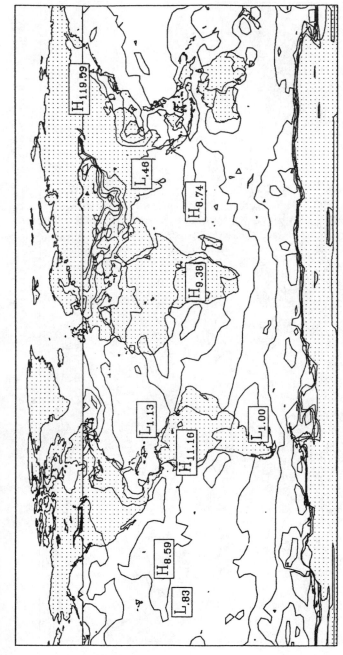

Figure 16   Monthly average optical depth of clouds during January 1990. (From Reference 76.)

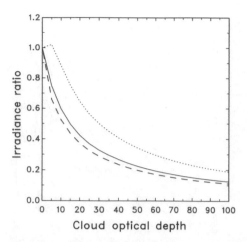

Figure 17 Effect of clouds on erythema dose rates, albedo = 0.05. Solid curve
gives reduction of vector irradiance at any solar zenith angle. Reduction of scalar irradiance is given by the dotted curve for zenith
angle = 0° and by the dashed line for zenith angle = 70°.

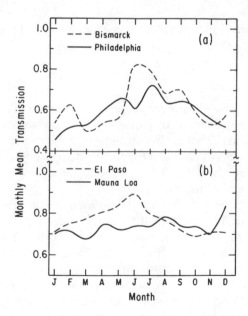

Figure 18 Monthly mean transmission (relative to cloud-free sky) measured
with Robertson-Berger meters at Bismark (North Dakota), Philadel-
phia (Pennsylvania), El Paso (Texas), and Mauna Loa (Hawaii). (Reprinted from Reference 77. With permission.)

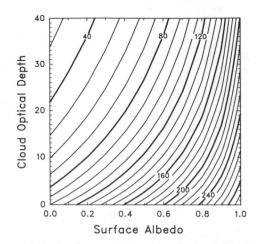

Figure 19 Coupling between cloud and surface albedo. Calculation for DNA
damage dose rates, solar zenith angle = 45°. Contours give vector
irradiance, in % relative to the value at zero albedo and no clouds
(100%).

range, R_v in km, and the attenuation coefficient at 550 nm, β_{550} in km^{-1},
is

$$R_v = 3.912/\beta_{550}$$

with the aerosol-free atmosphere corresponding to a visual range of 386
km due to Rayleigh scattering alone. The reduction in vertical transmission is related to R_v, but is also a function of the depth of the planetary
boundary layer over which the aerosols are distributed. Figure 21 shows
the effect of aerosol on DNA-damaging daily dose for a typical summer
day and at different visual ranges.

Stratospheric aerosols (e.g., the Junge layer of sulfate particles) normally have a negligible effect on surface UV radiation, but may increase
after a volcanic eruption. Enhanced levels of stratospheric aerosols are
generally expected to reduce the UV reaching the surface, but may in
some cases increase it by scattering a fraction of the radiation more
directly downward through the stratospheric ozone. This effect is significant only at wavelengths where ozone absorption is greatest[84] and
for low sun.[63] A potentially much larger effect of stratospheric sulfate
aerosols is that they may convert, via reactions occurring at their surfaces, reservoir chlorine species such as HCl and ClONO$_2$ into active
chlorine species (Cl$_2$, Cl, and ClO) which destroy ozone.[85] This effect
scales strongly with the amount of stratospheric chlorine, which has
increased in recent years probably due to CFC production, so that vol-

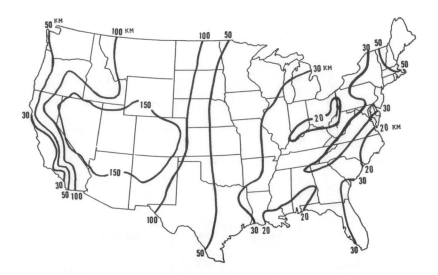

Figure 20 Average visual range (in km) in rural and suburban areas of the
United States during 1974–1976. (Reprinted from Reference 82. With
permission.)

canic eruptions may be much more effective at destroying stratospheric
ozone than in the past.[86]

Sensitivity to Urban Pollutants

Atmospheric concentrations of UV-absorbing gases such as SO_2 and
NO_2 are usually too small to affect the surface UV irradiances at the
surface, except in relatively polluted urban environments where their
values are sufficiently high that a correction for their absorption may be
necessary. For example, the absorption cross section at 310 nm is about
2.5×10^{-19} cm^2 for both NO_2[17] and SO_2.[18,19] With a 1-km boundary
height and a solar zenith angle of 60°, the transmission at 310 nm is
reduced by 10% for SO_2 or NO_2 concentrations near 170 ppb (parts per
billion). Because of the extreme variability of pollutants with location
and time, estimates of their effect on UV must be made on a case-by-
case basis.

TRENDS IN ATMOSPHERIC COMPOSITION AND IMPLICATIONS FOR UV RADIATION

Ozone

There is increasing evidence that the total atmospheric ozone column
is decreasing, probably due to the production and eventual release to
the atmosphere of compounds such as CFCs. These compounds are

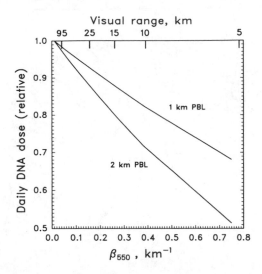

Figure 21   Effect of aerosol on DNA-damaging daily dose, relative to the aerosol-free atmosphere. The lower scale gives the extinction coefficients at 550 nm, corresponding to the visual range shown in the upper scale. Values are shown for different depths of the planetary boundary layer (PBL). (Reprinted from Reference 83. Copyright by the American Geophysical Union.)

stable in the troposphere, and thus a significant amount is transported to the stratosphere, where photodissociation by UV-C radiation releases atomic chlorine which catalyzes ozone destruction. The atmospheric chemical and transport cycles of ozone and related compounds have been reviewed recently.[1,10,60]

The clearest ozone depletion has been detected in the Antarctic regions during spring.[87] Figure 22 shows the October values measured at or near Halley Bay since 1957. Values fluctuated between 250 and 350 DU for the first 20 years of the record, then showed a marked decline beginning in the late 1970s. Although most of the data record is from Dobson instruments, the low ozone values have been confirmed with other ground-based techniques,[88-90] with balloon-borne ozone sondes,[91] and by satellite measurements.[92,93] The reductions occur between early September and mid- or late November, and total ozone values as low as 108 DU had been reached in early October 1991.[1] Vertical soundings indicate that most of the depletion is occurring in the lower stratosphere, between 14 and 22 km,[91] where ozone is destroyed almost completely. Although several hypotheses have been proposed for this decline, the most widely accepted explanation is that reservoir chlorine species (HCl and $ClONO_2$) are converted into active species Cl_2 and ClO by reactions occurring on the surface of polar stratospheric clouds (PSCs) during the

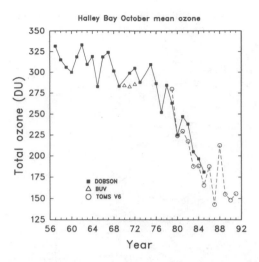

Figure 22 October ozone column measured over Antarctica. Squares are ground-based measurements from Halley Bay; triangles and circles are from satellite-borne instruments. (Reprinted from Reference 1.)

dark polar winter, followed by photochemical initiation of the ozone-destroying chlorine catalytic cycles when the sun rises in the early spring.[1]

Springtime UV radiation during the Antarctic ozone hole episodes may approach levels which are more typical for summer at those same locations.[94] These values are still smaller than the amounts received during summer at middle latitudes and through the year in the tropics (see for example Figure 7), but the effects on biota adapted to low UV levels are of obvious concern.

The austral spring ozone reductions are confined to the polar vortex, which covers an area roughly similar to that of the Antarctic continent. Upon spring warming, the breakup of the vortex allows mixing of air richer in ozone from lower latitudes, thus restoring the polar ozone levels to higher values. For the same reason, ozone-poor polar air may be transported to lower latitudes and has been observed (with concomitant UV increases) at mid-latitudes during late spring and early summer (e.g., Reference 95).

Global trends in ozone are more difficult to estimate because the changes to date have been much smaller than those observed in the Antarctic spring. Ground-based Dobson instruments have been used to measure the total ozone column at about 30 locations (mostly in the northern hemisphere) since 1958, and new monitoring sites have been added in recent years, bringing the total to about 70 stations. At some particularly polluted locations, ozone measurements using the Dobson technique may have been affected by high levels of atmospheric SO_2, which also

TOMS TOTAL OZONE TRENDS [%/YEAR]

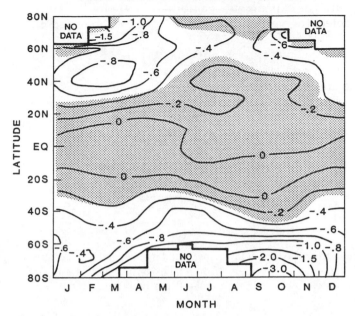

Figure 23   Ozone trends determined from the total ozone mapping spectrometer
(TOMS) over the years 1979–1989. Shading indicates regions where
trends are negligible within two standard deviations. (Reprinted from
Reference 102. Copyright by the American Geophysical Union.)

absorbs at UV-B wavelengths.[96] Trends derived from the Dobson instruments have been reviewed recently.[1,97,98]

Nearly complete global geographic coverage has been available only
since late 1978, from the satellite-borne TOMS instrument (see Figure
4). Preliminary analyses of the TOMS data gave erroneous trends (e.g.,
References 60, 99, 100) due to incomplete correction for the progressive
deterioration of some of the optical components of the TOMS instrument. More recent correction schemes appear to have solved this difficulty, and the newer data (version 6) have been validated against ground-
based Dobson instruments.[101] Bojkov et al.[97] and Stolarski et al.[98,102] have
used the Dobson and TOMS version 6 data to deduce ozone trends after
subtraction of variations due to natural cycles including the quasi-bien-
nial oscillation (QBO), the 11-year solar cycle, and autocorrelation effects.
The trends derived from the TOMS data are in good agreement with
those obtained from the Dobson network over the time and locations
where the data sets overlap. Trends are negligible in the tropics and
increase toward high latitudes in both hemispheres, as shown in Figure
23 for the TOMS data. Some longitudinal dependence is also found in
the northern hemisphere.[98]

Additional satellite measurements are available from the stratospheric aerosol and gas experiments I and II (SAGE I and II). The SAGE instruments detect the vertical distribution of ozone above about 17 km, and the long-term trends[103] suggest that most of the ozone reduction has occurred in the lower stratosphere (below about 25 km), consistent with the trends in total ozone.

In the absence of direct measurements of global UV trends, the best estimates are probably obtained by combining the measured ozone trends with radiative transfer calculations. Figure 24 shows the trends in DNA-damaging radiation, based on TOMS ozone measurements over one complete solar cycle (1979–1989). The increases due to the ozone hole are clearly visible on both percentage and energy increment bases. Mid-latitude increases occur at all times of the year and range over 5–20% per decade. The effect of the breakup of the polar vortex is evident from the increased levels at latitudes between 30 S and 60 S during December and January — that is, during the period of largest natural irradiation. No significant trends are seen in the tropics; however, it should be noted that tropical UV levels are naturally already high, so that even small percentage increases may be important in the future. Trends for annual doses, also based on TOMS data, are shown in Table 6. Dobson measurements from 26 locations in the northern hemisphere have been similarly analyzed by Frederick et al.[105] and are generally in agreement with the TOMS-derived trends. The UV trends derived from the Dobson data are not statistically significant over the entire data record (1957–1988), but become significant if only the more recent years 1970–1988 are considered, suggesting that the largest UV increases have occurred during the more recent years.

Tropospheric ozone has been increasing in the northern hemisphere since the preindustrial times, when levels appear to have been near 10 ppb.[106] This increase is likely related to anthropogenic emissions such as nitrogen oxides and hydrocarbons, which produce ozone in the troposphere through a complex but fairly well understood series of photochemical reactions (see, for example, Reference 107). Logan[108] has estimated that these reactions have raised the ozone levels by 6–22 ppb above preindustrial levels in rural regions of developed countries. Staehelin and Schmid[109] have measured an increase of ozone concentrations at the surface in Payerne (Switzerland) from 34 ppb in 1969 to 46 ppb in 1989, with different trends depending on season and altitude, as shown in Figure 25. In more pristine areas, tropospheric ozone trends are significantly smaller; e.g., surface ozone measurements through the 1970s and 1980s show increases of 0.79 ± 0.44% per year at Barrow, Alaska and 0.78 ± 0.42% per year at Mauna Loa, Hawaii, and decreases of 0.26 ± 0.65% per year at Samoa and 0.46 ± 0.37% per year at the South Pole.[110]

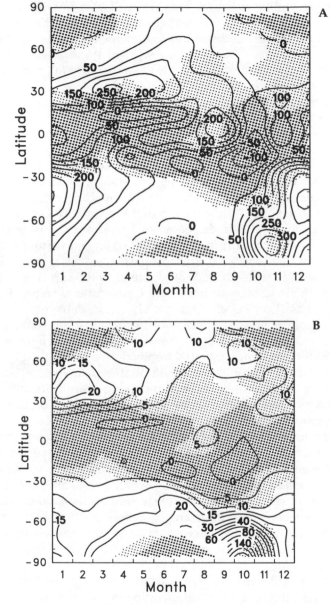

Figure 24   Trends in DNA-damaging daily doses during 1979–1989. Dark shading shows regions where trends differ from zero by less than one
standard deviation, light shading by less than two standard deviations. White areas denote regions with significant trends. Values are
in (A) absolute units, J m^{-2} per decade; (B) percent per decade.
(Reprinted from Reference 104. Copyright by the American Geophysical Union.)

Table 6 Trends in Annual Values, Percent per Decade, 1979–1989

Latitude	Total Ozone	RB Meter	Erythema Induction	Plant Damage	DNA Damage
85°N	−4.5 ± 3.0	5.1 ± 1.5	4.7 ± 1.4	14.8 ± 4.3	10.1 ± 3.2
75°N	−4.0 ± 2.7	3.9 ± 1.3	4.1 ± 1.4	10.8 ± 3.4	9.0 ± 2.9
65°N	−4.2 ± 1.7	3.4 ± 1.3	4.0 ± 1.5	8.9 ± 3.3	8.1 ± 3.0
55°N	−4.4 ± 1.2	3.3 ± 1.2	4.0 ± 1.5	8.1 ± 3.0	7.7 ± 2.9
45°N	−4.5 ± 1.0	3.1 ± 1.0	4.0 ± 1.4	7.2 ± 2.6	7.2 ± 2.7
35°N	−4.5 ± 1.3	3.0 ± 1.1	4.3 ± 1.6	7.0 ± 2.7	7.5 ± 3.0
25°N	−2.7 ± 1.6	1.8 ± 1.1	2.8 ± 1.9	4.2 ± 2.8	4.8 ± 3.3
15°N	−0.7 ± 1.2	0.5 ± 0.8	0.8 ± 1.4	1.1 ± 1.9	1.3 ± 2.3
5°N	−1.2 ± 1.4	0.8 ± 1.0	1.3 ± 1.6	1.8 ± 2.3	2.2 ± 2.7
5°S	−1.2 ± 1.3	0.8 ± 0.8	1.3 ± 1.4	1.8 ± 2.0	2.1 ± 2.4
15°S	−0.3 ± 1.2	0.2 ± 0.8	0.4 ± 1.3	0.6 ± 1.8	0.7 ± 2.2
25°S	−1.2 ± 1.7	1.0 ± 1.1	1.8 ± 1.7	2.7 ± 2.5	3.3 ± 2.8
35°S	−3.1 ± 1.7	2.3 ± 1.1	3.5 ± 1.6	5.6 ± 2.6	6.3 ± 2.9
45°S	−4.9 ± 1.5	3.7 ± 1.1	5.3 ± 1.6	9.3 ± 2.8	9.9 ± 3.0
55°S	−7.3 ± 1.7	6.0 ± 1.5	7.7 ± 1.9	15.4 ± 4.0	15.1 ± 3.9
65°S	−10.8 ± 2.2	9.5 ± 2.3	11.4 ± 2.8	25.4 ± 6.6	23.4 ± 6.1
75°S	−13.2 ± 2.8	12.8 ± 3.9	15.0 ± 4.8	39.0 ± 13.4	34.4 ± 11.9
85°S	−14.5 ± 3.4	15.6 ± 5.1	16.8 ± 5.7	53.9 ± 20.2	42.7 ± 15.8

Source: Reference 104. Copyright by the American Geophysical Union.

Note: Uncertainties are one standard deviation.

The tropospheric ozone increases add some complexity to the interpretation of the total ozone trends. First, they add a significant longitudinal variability to the ozone distribution, since continental industrialized regions have typically higher tropospheric ozone levels than more remote oceanic regions. Second, even at a constant ozone column, changes in tropospheric ozone may affect UV levels differently than changes in stratospheric ozone, as already discussed earlier. Third, there is uncertainty about how effectively tropospheric ozone is detected by the TOMS instrument,[102,111] a problem which, however, is not present with the ground-based Dobson instruments. Fortunately, the tropospheric vertical ozone column is still only about 1/10 of the total ozone column, so that the uncertainties in the calculation of UV radiation are reduced accordingly. Recent estimates[104] indicate that the long-term increase (i.e., since the preindustrial days) of tropospheric ozone may have decreased DNA-damaging UV levels by 3–10% in developed countries, and the current trends may be contributing a negative UV-B trend component, about −2% per decade, to the total UV trend. Table 7 illustrates the trends in biologically active UV corresponding to both the tropospheric and stratospheric trends of Figure 25. The UV trends over Payerne are thus estimated to be substantially lower than those for the zonally averaged northern hemisphere mid-latitudes shown in Table 6.

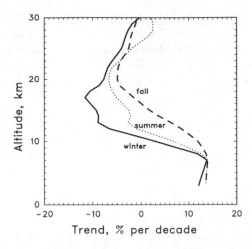

Figure 25   Ozone concentration trends at Payerne (Switzerland), over 1967–
1990. (Reprinted from Reference 1.)

**Table 7 Trends in Daily UV Doses at Payerne (Switzerland),
Percent per Decade**

Season	Total Ozone	RB Meter	Erythema Induction	Plant Damage	DNA Damage
Winter	−4.1	4.0	4.1	11.2	8.8
Summer	−1.4	0.9	1.4	2.2	2.4
Autumn	−0.4	0.4	0.4	1.0	0.8

Note: Based on U.S. Standard Atmosphere ozone profile perturbed by altitude-dependent trends shown in Figure 25.

Urban ozone levels typically range between 50 ppb and 200 ppb and
can reach values as high as 500 ppb.[107] The high values are confined
largely to the PBL, which, if taken to be of ca. 1 km height, contains 10
DU for each 100 ppb of ozone, or about 2–3% of the total column at
northern hemisphere mid-latitudes. Thus severe photochemical smog
episodes can reduce UV levels substantially. Urban ozone levels have
clearly increased since the preindustrial times (e.g., Reference 106), but
may have reached a plateau in recent years, at least in urban areas of
highly developed countries.

Clouds, Aerosols, and the Oxides of Sulfur and Nitrogen

Long-term trends in cloud cover are difficult to deduce because of the
inherent variability of cloudiness. Two important mechanisms have been
proposed which might result in a change in clouds due to human activities. Increased emissions of CO_2, CH_4, and other so-called greenhouse gases may affect the entire climate system including the hydrol-

ogical cycle and the general atmospheric patterns which result in cloud formation and dissipation.[112] Preliminary studies based on atmospheric general circulation models suggest UV changes of the order of 5–10%,[113,114] but both magnitude and direction of the change are sensitive to the choice of different climate models.

Increased emissions of SO_2 may result in the increase of atmospheric sulfate aerosols which are effective cloud condensation nuclei and may therefore increase the number of smaller particles in clouds, thus increasing their reflectivity. This effect, if already occurring, would be expected to be strongest in the northern hemisphere, where sulfur emissions are greatest. However, the data record is still too sparse to assess the possible contributions of this effect on UV radiation.

Sulfate aerosols also may have affected UV radiation directly. It is estimated that in rural regions of the United States the visible range has declined from a preindustrial value of about 95 km to a current value between 15 and 25 km. From Figure 21 it can be seen that this amounts to a reduction of DNA damaging dose between 5 and 18%.[83] Future trends in tropospheric aerosols may depend on industrialization trends and on local and regional efforts to improve air quality. Sulfate emissions have decreased in recent years at some locations in the U.S., while staying constant or increasing at others.[115]

Little historical data is available on SO_2 and NO_2 in the troposphere. However, it is clear that even today, atmospheric levels of these two gases in regions distant from emission sources are negligible with regard to their effect on UV. Thus, it appears reasonable to conclude that natural, or preindustrial, levels of SO_2 and NO_2 are of no consequence to UV transmission. A survey of NO_2 concentrations in the U.K. showed mean values ranging over 20–40 ppb in major urban areas, with occasional maximum hourly averages as high as 270 ppb.[116,117] Average urban NO_2 in the U.S. is about 35 ppb,[107,118] with values exceeding 450 ppb during severe pollution events (e.g., Reference 119). Average annual urban SO_2 levels fall between 10 and 100 ppb,[120] but occasional values exceeding 1 ppm have been reported.[107] Thus, under average urban conditions the effects of SO_2 and NO_2 on UV radiation are relatively minor, but specific pollution episodes may cause great reductions in the UV levels.

MEASUREMENTS OF UV TRENDS

Few direct UV measurements are available over Antarctica for pre-ozone hole years. Baker-Blocker et al.[121] reported measurements at the South Pole over 1979–1981, but because broad-band UV detectors were used, it is impossible to deduce ozone-related trends. Measurements of the ozone column by the Dobson technique, which have been available since 1957 and are based on the ratio of two UV-B wavelengths with

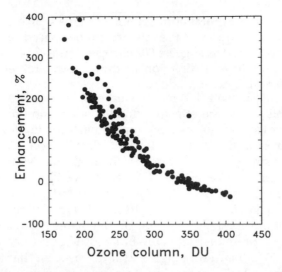

Figure 26 Measured enhancement of DNA dose rates, relative to 350 DU, at Palmer Station during the austral spring of 1988 and 1990. (Reprinted from Reference 123. Copyright by the American Geophysical Union.)

differential sensitivity to ozone, may be regarded as direct evidence for a change in the wavelength distribution of the UV radiation.

Following the detection of the ozone hole, several comprehensive Antarctic UV measurement programs have been initiated.[88-90,122-128] Although the absence of historical data precludes comparison with pre-ozone hole UV levels, significant information has been derived from these recent studies. The measurements confirm quantitatively the theoretical expectation that enhanced UV levels are associated with reduced ozone levels. Figure 26 shows the dependence of noon-time DNA damage dose enhancements as a function of the ozone column and may be compared to Figure 10. For cloudy skies, the comparison is less direct because the cloud optical properties are not well known for the specific measurement days. However, clouds are expected to have relatively small effects on the ratio of UV at different wavelengths, while ozone absorption increases rapidly with decreasing wavelength. Figure 27 shows that the measured ratio of UV spectral irradiance at 306.5 nm (which is very sensitive to ozone absorption) to that at 350 nm (insensitive to ozone) is significantly higher than that calculated for pre-ozone hole conditions. Several of these studies[88-90] have used spectral UV-B irradiance measurements in reverse, to deduce the amount of overhead ozone, obtaining results in good agreement with other ozone measuring techniques (satellite, Dobson instruments, and ozone sondes). Another study has taken advantage of the motion of the polar vortex boundary (which marks the transition from high to low ozone column amounts) to measure simultaneously ozone decreases, UV-B increases, and re-

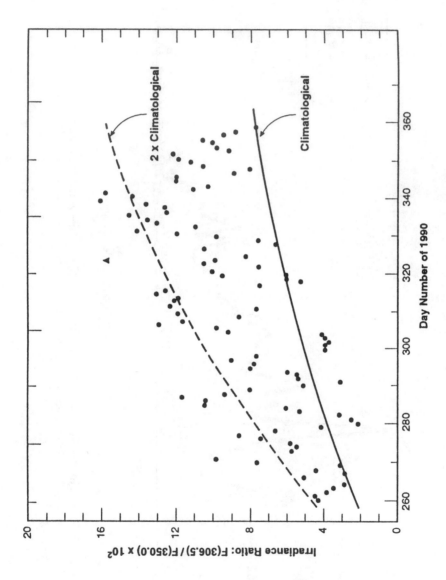

Figure 27 Ratio of UV spectral radiance at 306.5 nm to that at 350.0 nm at Palmer Station. (Reprinted from References 1 and 128. Copyright by the American Geophysical Union.)

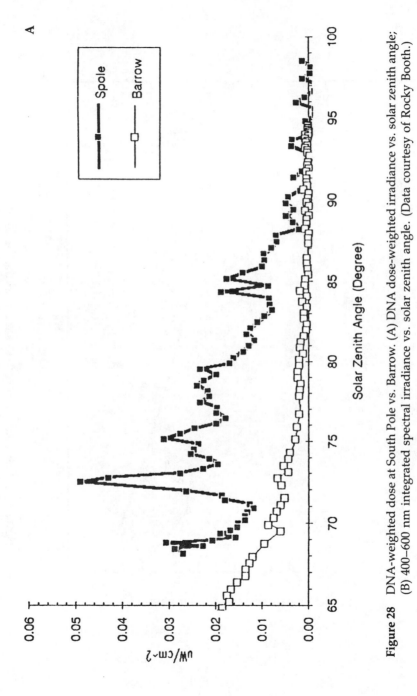

Figure 28 DNA-weighted dose at South Pole vs. Barrow. (A) DNA dose-weighted irradiance vs. solar zenith angle; (B) 400–600 nm integrated spectral irradiance vs. solar zenith angle. (Data courtesy of Rocky Booth.)

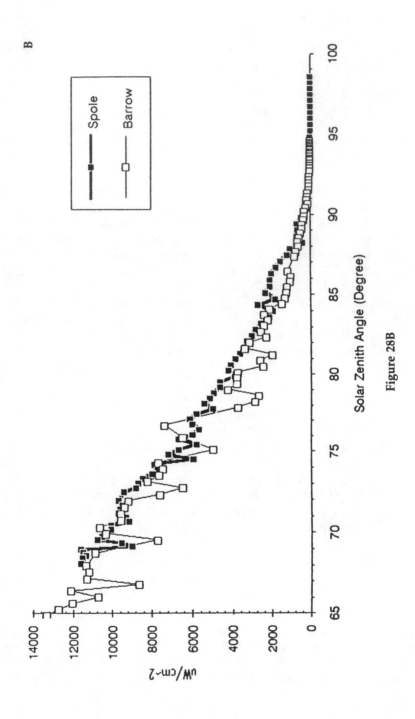

Figure 28B

ductions of phytoplankton growth in the Bellinhausen Sea.[127] Useful comparisons have also been made between UV measurements obtained during the Antarctic ozone hole and those obtained at comparable northern high latitudes during spring (i.e., offset by 6 months). These are shown in Figure 28 for DNA-damaging doses obtained by convoluting the measured spectral irradiances with the DNA actions spectrum of Setlow.[3] Thus, the evidence appears to be strong for large enhancements of UV-B radiation during the austral spring. A few measurements in Australia and New Zealand have also confirmed the higher UV levels expected at southern mid-latitudes following the breakup of the polar vortex.[59,95]

An adequate global UV measurement network does not exist at the present time. Some data have been obtained over the past two decades with a network of Robertson-Berger (RB) meters located at 25 U.S. sites and 11 non-U.S. sites,[129] but the trends reported from these measurements are largely inconclusive. For example, Scotto et al.[130] reported a UV decrease of 0.5% to 1.1% per year from 1974 to 1985, at mostly urban locations in the U.S., and Garadzha and Nezval[131] reported a 12% decrease in Moscow over 1968–1983, in apparent conflict with the expectation of increased UV levels due to stratospheric ozone depletion. It has been suggested that these decreases may have resulted from increased urban atmospheric turbidity[83,132] and tropospheric ozone,[61] as also indicated by a UV increase of $1.1 \pm 0.4\%$ per year between 1981 and 1989 measured above the polluted atmospheric boundary layer in the Swiss Alps.[133] Measurements by Correll et al.[134] obtained from 1975 through 1990 in Maryland suggest that the maximum monthly mean UV-B irradiance in 1983–1989 was substantially higher (by 13%) than the corresponding mean value for the entire data record. The interpretation of these conflicting measurements is complicated by the difficulty of maintaining calibrations of instruments over long periods of time, by the different sensitivity of various instruments to ozone depletion, and by the high variability and possible trends in clouds and aerosols, as well as tropospheric and stratospheric ozone.

SUMMARY

Much is known about UV radiation and the factors which affect it. Yet it should also be realized that many uncertainties remain, especially with regard to global trends. Strong UV changes associated with the Antarctic ozone hole have been predicted and detected, and they confirm our basic understanding of the relationships between atmospheric composition and UV levels at the surface. But the global-scale changes appear to be much smaller and therefore more subtle, leading to considerable theoretical and experimental equivocation about the opposing effects of stratospheric ozone depletion, increases in local and regional pollutants, and possible variations in cloud cover. Even relatively small global UV changes are potentially quite serious for the biosphere, not only due to ubiquity, but also because the natural UV levels are already high at mid-latitudes and in the tropics. Any real global trends should be detected at the earliest possible stage in order to provide a rational basis for social and policy planning.

No amount of words would be excessive in re-emphasizing the need for a reliable, global, long-term UV monitoring network. The urgency for such a network becomes all the more apparent when considering that human activities may already have altered the optical properties of the atmosphere, so that the opportunity for an accurate determination of the natural UV environment may already have been lost, and at best we can hope to establish a perturbed "baseline" in the near future, against which to judge any later trends. Probably several years, perhaps even a few decades, of monitoring will be required to establish a statistically valid baseline, given the natural cycles and fluctuations in environmental conditions which affect UV levels. Measurements will need to be supplemented by UV climatology modeling, for the dual purpose of interpolating between network stations and predicting future UV trends under different atmospheric compositions scenarios. Clearly the needed efforts are larger than have been undertaken to date.

REFERENCES

1. "Scientific Assessment of Ozone Depletion: 1991," Global Ozone Research and Monitoring Project Report 25, World Meteorological Organization (WMO), Geneva (1991).
2. Smith, R. C. and W. H. Wilson, Jr. "Photon Scalar Irradiance," *Appl. Opt.* 11:934–938 (1972).
3. Setlow, R. B. "The Wavelengths in Sunlight Effective in Producing Skin Cancer: A Theoretical Analysis," in *Proc. Natl. Acad. Sci. U.S.A.* 71:3363–3366 (1974).
4. Caldwell, M. M., L. B. Camp, C. W. Warner, and S. D. Flint. "Action Spectra and Their Key Role in Assessing Biological Consequences of Solar UV-B Radiation Change," in *Stratospheric Ozone Reduction, Solar Ultraviolet Radiation and Plant Life*, R. C. Worrest and M. M. Caldwell, Eds. (Berlin: Springer-Verlag, 1986), pp. 87–111.
5. McKinlay, A. F. and B. L. Diffey. "A Reference Action Spectrum for Ultraviolet-Induced Erythema in Human Skin," in *Human Exposure to Ultraviolet Radiation: Risks and Regulations*, W. R. Passchler and B. F. M. Bosnajokovic, Eds. (Amsterdam: Elsevier, 1987).

6. Urbach, F., D. Berger, and R. E. Davies. "Field Measurements of Biologically Effective UV Radiation and Its Relation to Skin Cancer in Man," in *Proceedings of the Third Conference on Climatic Impact Assessment Program,* A. J. Broderick and T. M. Hard, Eds. (U.S. Dept. of Transportation, Washington, D.C., 1974).

7. Smart, W. M. *Textbook on Spherical Astronomy* (Cambridge: Cambridge University Press, 1979).

8. Spencer, J. W. "Fourier Series Representation of the Position of the Sun," *Search* 2:172 (1971).

9. Madronich, S. and G. Weller. "Numerical Integration Errors in Calculated Tropospheric Photodissociation Rate Coefficients," *J. Atmos. Chem.* 10:289–300 (1990).

10. "Atmospheric Ozone 1985," Global Research and Monitoring Project Report 16, WMO, Geneva (1985).

11. Nicolet, M. "Solar Spectral Irradiances with Their Diversity Between 120 and 900 nm," *Planet. Space Sci.* 37:1249–1289 (1989).

12. Neckel, H. and D. Labs. "The Solar Radiation Between 3300 and 12500 A," *Solar Phys.* 90:205–258 (1984).

13. Aversen, J. C., R. N. Griffin, Jr., and B. D. Pearson, Jr. "Determination of Extraterrestrial Solar Spectral Irradiance from Research Aircraft," *Appl. Opt.* 8:2215–2232 (1969).

14. Mentall, J. E., J. E. Frederick, and J. R. Herman. "The Solar Irradiance from 200 to 33nm," *J. Geophys. Res.* 86:9881–9884 (1981).

15. Van Hoosier, M. E., J.-D. Bartoe, G. E. Brueckner, and D. K. Printz. "Solar Irradiance Measurements 120–400 nm from Space Lab-2," IUGG Assembly, Vancouver (1987).

16. Molina, L. T. and M. J. Molina. "Absolute Absorption Cross Sections of Ozone in the 185- to 350-Wavelength Range," *J. Geophys. Res.* 91:14,501–14,508 (1986).

17. Davidson, J. A., C. A. Cantrell, A. H. McDaniel, R. E. Shetter, S. Madronich, and J. G. Calvert, "Visible-Ultraviolet Absorption Cross Section for NO_2 as a Function of Temperature," *J. Geophys. Res.* 93:7105–7112 (1988).

18. Warneck, P., F. F. Marmo, and J. O. Sullivan. "Ultraviolet Absorption of SO_2: Dissociation Energies of SO_2 and SO," *J. Chem. Phys.* 40:1132–1132 (1964).

19. McGee, T. J. and J. Burris, Jr. "SO_2 Absorption Cross Section in the Near U.V.," *J. Quant. Spectrosc. Radiat. Transfer* 37:165–182 (1987).

20. Fröhlich, C. and G. E. Shaw. "New Determination of Rayleigh Scattering in the Terrestrial Atmosphere," *Appl. Opt.* 19:1773–1775 (1980).

21. Nicolet, M. "On the Molecular Scattering in the Terrestrial Atmosphere: An Empirical Formula for its Calculation in the Homosphere," *Planet. Space Sci.* 32:1467–1468 (1984).

22. Stephens, G. L. "Radiation Profiles in Extended Water Clouds. I. Theory," *J. Atmos. Sci.* 35:2111–2122 (1978).

23. Stephens, G. L. "Radiation Profiles in Extended Water Clouds. II. Paremeterization Schemes," *J. Atmos. Sci.* 35:2111–2122 (1978).

24. Stephens, G. L., G. W. Paltridge, and C. M. R. Platt. "Radiation Profiles in Extended Water Clouds. III. Observations," *J. Atmos. Sci.* 35:2111–2122 (1978).

25. Feigelson, E. M. *Radiation in a Cloudy Atmosphere* (Dordrecht: D. Reidel, 1984).
26. Elterman, L. "UV, Visible, and IR Attenuation for Altitudes to 50 km," Report 68-0153, Air Force Cambridge Research Laboratories (AFCRL), Cambridge, MA (1968).
27. Shettle, E. P. and R. W. Fenn. "Models for the Aerosols of the Lower Atmosphere and the Effects of Humidity Variations on Their Optical Properties," Report TR-79-0214, Air Force Geophysics Laboratory (AFGL), Cambridge, MA (1979).
28. "US Standard Atmosphere," National Oceanic and Atmospheric Administration (NOAA), National Aeronautics and Space Administration (NASA), United States Air Force, Washington, D.C. (1976).
29. Chandrasekhar, S. *Radiative Transfer* (New York: Dover, 1960).
30. Hansen, J. E. and L. D. Travis. "Light Scattering in Planetary Atmospheres," *Space Sci. Rev.* 16:527–610 (1974).
31. Goody, R. M. and Y. L. Yung. *Atmospheric Radiation* (New York: Oxford University Press, 1989).
32. Meador, W. E. and W. R. Weaver. "Two-Stream Approximations to Radiative Transfer in Planetary Atmospheres: A Unified Description of Existing Methods and a New Improvement," *J. Atmos. Sci.* 37:630–643 (1980).
33. Toon, O. B., C. P. McKay, T. P. Ackerman, and K. Santhanam. "Rapid Calculation of Radiative Heating Rates and Photodissociation Rates in Inhomogeneous Multiple Scattering Atmospheres," *J. Geophys. Res.* 94:16,287–16,301 (1989).
34. Joseph, J. H., W. J. Wiscombe, and J. A. Weinman. "The Delta-Eddington Approximation for Radiative Flux Transfer," *J. Atmos. Sci.* 33:2452–2459 (1976).
35. Madronich, S. "The Natural Ultraviolet Radiation Environment," paper presented at the 20th Annual Meeting of the American Society for Photobiology, Marco Island, Florida, June 20–24, 1992.
36. McKenzie, R. L. and J. M. Elwood. "Intensity of Solar Ultraviolet Radiation and its Implications for Skin Cancer," *New Zealand Med. J.* 103:152–154 (1990).
37. Frederick, J. E. and D. Lubin. "Possible Long-Term Changes in Biologically Active Ultraviolet Radiation Reaching the Ground," *Photochem. Photobiol.* 47:571–578 (1988).
38. van der Leun, J. C., M. Tevini, and R. C. Worrest, Eds. *Environmental Effects of Ozone Depletion: 1991 Update.* (Nairobi, Kenya: United Nations Environmental Program [UNEP], 1991).
39. Zölzer, F. and J. Kiefer. "Wavelength Dependence of Inactivation and Mutation Induction to 6-Thioguanine Resistance in V79 Chinese Hamster Fibroblasts," *Photochem. Photobiol.* 40:49–53 (1984).
40. Peak, M. J., J. G. Peak, M. P. Mohering, and R. B. Webb. "Ultraviolet Action Spectra for DNA Dimer Induction, Lethality and Mutagenesis in *Escherichia coli* with Emphasis on the UVB Region," *Photochem. Photobiol.* 40:613–620 (1984).
41. Keyse, S. M., S. H. Moses, and D. J. G. Davies. "Action Spectra for Inactivation of Normal and Xeroderma Pigmentosum Human Skin Fibroblasts by Ultraviolet Radiation," *Photochem. Photobiol.* 37:307–312 (1983).

42. Chan, G. L., M. J. Peak, J. G. Peak, and W. A. Haseltine. "Action Spectrum for the Formation of Endonuclease-Sensitive Sites and (6-4) Photoproducts Induced in a DNA Fragment by Ultraviolet Radiation," *Int. J. Radiat. Biol.* 50:641–648 (1986).

43. Stein, B., H. J. Rahmsdorf, A. Steffen, M. Litfin, and P. Herrlich. "UV-Induced DNA Damage is an Intermediate Step in UV-Induced Expression of Human Immunodeficiency Virus Type 1, Collagenase, C-fos, and Metallothionein," *Mol. Cell. Biol.* 9:5169–5181 (1989).

44. Steinmetz, V. and E. Wellman. "The Role of Solar UV-B in Growth Regulation of Cress (*Lepidium sativum* L.) Seedlings," *Photochem. Photobiol.* 43:189–193 (1986).

45. Wellman, E. "UV-B-Signal/Response-Beziehungen unter Natürlichen und Artifiziellen Lichtbedingungen," *Ber. Deutsch. Bot. Ges.* 98:99–104 (1985).

46. Beggs, C. J. and E. Wellmann. "Analysis of Light-Controlled Anthocyanin Formation in Coleoptiles of *Zea mays*. 1. The Role of UV-B, Blue, Red and Far-Red Light," *Photochem. Photobiol.* 41:481–486 (1985).

47. Yatsuhashi, H., T. Hashimoto, and S. Shimizu. "Ultraviolet Action Spectrum for Anthocyanin Formation in Broom Sorghum First Internodes," *Plant Physiol.* 70:735–741 (1982).

48. Bornman, J. F., L. O. Björn, and H.-E. Akerlund. "Action Spectrum for Inhibition by Ultraviolet Radiation of Photosystem II Activity in Spinach Thylakoids," *Photobiochem. Photobiophys.* 8:305–313 (1984).

49. Rundel, R. D. "Action Spectra and the Estimation of Biologically Effective UV Radiation," *Physiol. Plant.* 58:360–366 (1983).

50. Sharma, R. C. and J. Jagger. "Ultraviolet (254–405 nm) Action Spectrum and Kinetic Studies of Analine Uptake in *Escherichia coli* B/R," *Photochem. Photobiol.* 30:661–666 (1979).

51. Imbrie, C. W. and T. M. Murphy. "UV-Action Spectrum (254–405 nm) for Inhibition of a K$^+$-stimulated Adenosine Triphosphatase from a Plasma Membrane of *Rosa damascena*," *Photochem. Photobiol.* 36:537–542 (1982).

52. Kligman, L. H. and R. M. Sayre. "An Action Spectrum for Ultraviolet-Induced Elastosis in Hairless Mice: Quantification of Elastosis by Image Analysis," *Photochem. Photobiol.* 53:237–242 (1991).

53. Cole, C. A., D. Forbes, and R. E. Davies. "An Action Spectrum for UV Photocarcinogenesis," *Photochem. Photobiol.* 43:275–284 (1986).

54. de Gruijl, F. R. and J. C. van der Leun. "Action Spectra for Carcinogenesis Contribution," Symposium on the Biologic Effects of UV-A Radiation, San Antonio, TX (1991).

55. Longstreth, J. D., F. R. de Gruijl, Y. Takizawa, and J. C. van der Leun. "Health Effects," in *Environmental Effects of Ozone Depletion: 1991 Update*, J. C. van der Leun, M. Tevini, and R. C. Worrest, Eds. (Nairobi, Kenya: UNEP, 1991).

56. Pitts, D. G., A. P. Cullen, and P. D. Hacker. "Ocular Effects of Ultraviolet Radiation from 295 to 365 nm," *Invest. Ophthalmol. Visual Sci.* 16:932–939 (1977).

57. Häder, D.-P. and R. C. Worrest. "Effects of Enhanced Solar Ultraviolet Radiation on Aquatic Ecosystems," *Photochem. Photobiol.* 53:717–725 (1991).

58. De Fabo, E. C. and F. P. Noonan. "Mechanism of Immune Suppression by Ultraviolet Radiation In Vivo. I. Evidence for the Existence of a Unique Photoreceptor in Skin and its Role in Photoimmunology," *J. Exp. Med.* 158:84–98 (1983).

59. McKenzie, R. L., W. A. Matthews, and P. V. Johnston. "The Relationship Between Erythemal UV and Ozone, Derived from Spectral Irradiance Measurements," *Geophys. Res. Lett.* 18:2269–2272 (1991).

60. "Scientific Assessment of Stratospheric Ozone: 1989, Volume I," Global Ozone Research and Monitoring Project Report 20, WMO, Geneva (1989).

61. Brühl, C. and P. J. Crutzen. "On the Disproportionate Role of Tropospheric Ozone as a Filter Against Solar UV-B Radiation," *Geophys. Res. Lett.* 16:703–706 (1989).

62. Madronich, S., L. O. Björn, M. Ilyas, and M. M. Caldwell. "Changes in Biologically Active Ultraviolet Radiation Reaching the Earth's Surface," in *Environmental Effects of Ozone Depletion: 1991 Update*, J. C. van der Leun, M. Tevini, and R. C. Worrest, Eds. (Nairobi, Kenya: UNEP, 1991).

63. Tsay, S.-C. and K. Stamnes. "Ultraviolet Radition in the Arctic: The Impact of Potential Ozone Depletions and Cloud Effects," *J. Geophys. Res.* 97:7829–7840 (1992).

64. Kondratyev, K. Y. *Radiation in the Atmosphere* (New York: Academic Press, 1969).

65. Blumthaler, M. and W. Ambach. "Solar UV-B albedo of Various Surfaces," *Photochem. Photobiol.* 48:85–88 (1988).

66. Doda, D. D. and A. E. S. Green. "Surface Reflectance Measurements in the UV from an Airborne Platform. Part 1," *Appl. Opt.* 19:2140–2145 (1980).

67. Dickerson, R. R., D. H. Stedman, and A. C. Delany. "Direct Measurements of Ozone and Nitrogen Dioxide Photolysis Rates in the Troposphere," *J. Geophys. Res.* 87:45,933–45,946 (1982).

68. Coulson, K. L. and D. W. Reynolds. "The Spectral Reflectance of Natural Surfaces," *J. Appl. Meterol.* 10:1285–1295 (1971).

69. Shetter, R. E., A. H. McDaniel, C. A. Cantrell, S. Madronich, and J. G. Calvert. "Actinometer and Eppley Radiometer Measurements of the NO_2 Photolysis Rate Coefficient During MLOPEX," *J. Geophys. Res.* 97:10,349–10,359 (1992).

70. Doda, D. D. and A. E. S. Green. "Surface Reflectance Measurements in the UV from an Airborne Platform. Part 2," *Appl. Opt.* 20:636–642 (1981).

71. Madronich, S. "Photodissociation in the Atmosphere. 1. Actinic Flux and the Effects of Ground Reflections and Clouds," *J. Geophys. Res.* 92:9740–9752 (1987).

72. Haurwitz, B. "Insolation in Relation to Cloud Type," *J. Meteorol.* 5:110–113 (1948).

73. "Meteorological Aspects of the Utilization of Solar Radiation as an Energy Source," Technical Note 172, WMO, Geneva (1981).

74. Frederick, J. E. and D. Lubin. "The Budget of Biologically Active Ultraviolet Radiation in the Earth-Atmosphere System," *J. Geophys. Res.* 93:3825–3832 (1988).

75. Webb, A. R. "Solar Ultraviolet Radiation in Southeast England: The Case for Spectral Measurements," *Photochem. Photobiol.* 54:789–794 (1991).

76. Rossow, W. B., L. C. Gardner, P.-J. Lu, and A. Walker. "Documentation of Cloud Data," Report WMO/T International Satellite Cloud Climatology Project (ISCCP), (1991).
77. Frederick, J. E. and H. E. Snell. "Tropospheric Influence on Solar Ultraviolet Radiation: the Role of Clouds," *J. Climate* 3:373–381 (1990).
78. Ilyas, M. "Effect of Cloudiness on Solar Ultraviolet Radiation Reaching the Surface," *Atmos. Environ.* 21:1483–1484 (1987).
79. Cutchis, P. "A Formula for Comparing Annual Damaging Ultraviolet (DUV) Radiation Doses at Tropical and Mid-Latitude Sites," Federal Aviation Administration Report FAA-EE 80-21, U.S. Department of Transportation, Washington, D.C. (1980).
80. Josefsson, W. "Solar Ultraviolet Radiation in Sweden," SMHI Report 53, National Institute of Radiation Protection in Stockholm, Norrköping, Sweden, (1986).
81. Paltridge, G. W. and I. J. Barton. "Erythemal Ultraviolet Radiation Distribution over Australia — The Calculations, Detailed Results and Input Data Including Frequency Analysis of Observed Australian Cloud Cover," Division of Atmospheric Physics Technical Paper 33, Commonwealth Scientific and Industrial Research Organization, Australia (1978).
82. Irving, P. M., Ed. *Acid Deposition: State of Science and Technology, Summary Report of the U.S. National Acid Deposition Program.* (Washington, D.C.: National Acid Precipitation Assessment Program [NAPAP] 1991).
83. Liu, S. C., S. A. McKeen, and S. Madronich. "Effects of Anthropogenic Aerosols on Biologically Active Ultraviolet Radiation," *Geophys. Res. Lett.* 18:2265–2268 (1991).
84. Michelangeli, D. V., M. Allen, Y. L. Yung, R.-L. Shia, D. Crisp, and J. Eluszkiewicz. "Enhancement of Atmospheric Radiation by an Aerosol Layer," *J. Geophys. Res.* 97:865–874 (1991).
85. Hoffman, D. J. and S. Solomon. "Ozone Destruction Through Heterogeneous Chemistry Following the Eruption of El Chichon," *J. Geophys. Res.* 94:5029–5041 (1989).
86. Brasseur, G. P., C. Granier, and S. Walters. "Future Changes in Stratospheric Ozone and the Role of Heterogeneous Chemistry," *Nature* 348:626–628 (1990).
87. Farman, J. C., B. G. Gardiner, and J. D. Shanklin. "Large Losses of Total Ozone in Antarctica Reveal Seasonal ClO_x/NO_x Interaction," *Nature* 315:207–210 (1985).
88. Lubin, D. and J. E. Frederick. "Column Ozone Measurements from Palmer Station, Antarctica: Variations During the Austral Springs of 1988 and 1989," *J. Geophys. Res.* 95:13,883–13,889 (1990).
89. Stamnes, K., J. Slusser, M. Bowen, C. Booth, and T. Lucas. "Biologically Effective Ultraviolet Radiation, Total Ozone Abundance, and Cloud Optical Depth at McMurdo Station, Antarctica September 15 1988–April 15 1989," *Geophys. Res. Lett.* 17:2181–2184 (1990).
90. Stamnes, K., Z. Jin, J. Slusser, C. Booth, and T. Lucas. "Several-fold Enhancement of Biologically Effective Ultraviolet Radiation Levels at McMurdo Station Antarctica During the 1990 Ozone 'Hole'," *Geophys. Res. Lett.* 19:1013–1016 (1992).

91. Deshler, T. and D. J. Hofmann. "Ozone Profiles at McMurdo Station, Antarctica, the Austral Spring of 1990," *Geophys. Res. Lett.* 18:657–660 (1991).

92. Stolarski, R. S., M. R. Schoeberl, P. A. Newman, R. D. McPeters, and A. J. Kruger. "The 1989 Antarctic Ozone Hole as Observed by TOMS," *Geophys. Res. Lett.* 17:1267–1270 (1990).

93. Newman, P., R. Stolarski, M. Schoeberl, R. McPeters, and A. Kruger. "The 1990 Antarctic Ozone Hole as Observed from TOMS," *Geophys. Res. Lett.* 18:661–664 (1991).

94. Frederick, J. E. and H. E. Snell. "Ultraviolet Radiation Levels During the Antarctic Spring," *Science* 241:438–440 (1988).

95. Roy, C. T., H. P. Gies, and E. Graeme. "Ozone Depletion," *Science* 347:235–236 (1990).

96. De Muer, D. and H. De Backer. "Revision of 20 Years of Dobson Total Ozone Data at Uccle (Belgium): Fictitious Dobson Total Ozone Trends Induced by Sulfur Dioxide Trends," *J. Geophys. Res.* 97:5921–5937 (1992).

97. Bojkov, R., L. Bishop, W. J. Hill, G. C. Reinsel, and G. C. Tiao. "A Statistical Trend Analysis of Revised Dobson Total Ozone Data over the Northern Hemisphere," *J. Geophys. Res.* 95:9785–9807 (1990).

98. Stolarski, R., R. Bojkov, L. Bishop, C. Zerefos, J. Staehelin, and J. Zawodny. "Measured Trends in Stratospheric Ozone," *Science* 256:342–349 (1992).

99. "Present State of Knowledge of the Upper Atmosphere 1988: An Assessment Report," NASA Reference Publication 1208, Washington, D.C. (1988).

100. van der Leun, J. C., M. Tevini, and R. C. Worrest, Eds. "Environmental Effects Panel Report," UNEP, Nairobi, Kenya (1989).

101. Herman, J. R., R. Hudson, R. McPeters, R. Stolarski, Z. Ahmad, X.-Y. Gu, S. Taylor, and C. Wellemeyer. "A New Self-Calibration Method Applied to TOMS and SBUV Backscattered Ultraviolet Data to Determine Long-Term Global Ozone Change," *J. Geophys. Res.* 96:7531–7545 (1991).

102. Stolarski, R. S., P. Bloomfield, R. D. McPeters, and J. R. Herman. "Total Ozone Trends Deduced from Nimbus 7 TOMS Data," *Geophys. Res. Lett.* 18:1015–1018 (1991).

103. McCormick, M. P., R. E. Veiga, and W. Chu. "Stratospheric Ozone Profile and Total Ozone Trends Derived from the SAGE I and SAGE II Data," *Geophys. Res. Lett.* 19:269–272 (1992).

104. Madronich, S. "Implications of Recent Total Atmospheric Ozone Measurements for Biologically Active Ultraviolet Radiation Reaching the Earth's Surface," *Geophys. Res. Lett.* 19:37–40 (1992).

105. Frederick, J. E., E. C. Weatherhead, and E. K. Haywood, "Long-Term Variations in Ultraviolet Sunlight Reaching the Biosphere: Calculations for the Past Three Decades," *Photochem. Photobiol.* 54:781–788 (1991).

106. Volz, A. and D. Kley. "Evaluation of the Montsouris Series of Ozone Measurements Made in the Nineteenth Century," *Nature* 332:240–242 (1988).

107. Finlayson-Pitts, B. J. and J. N. Pitts. *Atmospheric Chemistry* (New York: Wiley-Interscience, 1986).

108. Logan, J. A. "Tropospheric Ozone: Seasonal Behavior, Trends, and Anthropogenic Influence," *J. Geophys. Res.* 90:10,463–10,482 (1985).

109. Staehelin, J. and W. Schmid. "Trend Analysis of Tropospheric Ozone Concentrations Utilizing The 20-Year Data Set of Ozone Balloon Soundings over Payerne (Switzerland)," *Atmos. Environ.* 25A:1739–1749 (1991).

110. Oltmans, S. J., W. D. Komhyr, P. R. Franchois, and W. A. Matthews. "Tropospheric Ozone: Variations from Surface and ECC Ozonesonde Observations," in *Ozone in the Atmosphere, Proceedings of the Quadrennial Ozone Symposium 1988 and Tropospheric Ozone Workshop,* Hampton, VA, 1988, R. Bojkov and P. Fabian, Eds. (Göttingen, Germany: Deepak Publishing, 1989).

111. Klenk, K. F., P. K. Bhartia, A. J. Fleig, V. G. Kaveeshwar, R. D. McPeters, and P. M. Smith. "Total Ozone Determination from the Backscattered Ultraviolet (BUV) Experiment," *J. Appl. Meteorol.* 21:1672–1684 (1982).

112. Cess, R. D., G. L. Potter, J. P. Blanchet, G. J. Boer, S. J. Ghan, J. T. Kiehl, H. Le Treut, Z.-X. Li, X.-Z. Liang, J. F. B. Mitchel, J.-J. Morcrette, D. A. Randall, M. R. Riches, E. Roeckner, U. Shlese, A. Slingo, K. E. Taylor, W. M. Washington, R. T. Wetherald, and I. Yagai. "Interpretation of Cloud-Climate Feedback as Produced by 14 Atmospheric General Circulation Models," *Science* 245:513–516 (1989).

113. Madronich, S., "Changes in Biologically Damaging Ultraviolet (UV) Radiation: Effect of Overhead Ozone and Cloud Amount," in *Effects of Solar Ultraviolet Radiation on Biogeochemical Dynamics on Aquatic Environments,* Report of a Workshop held in Woods Hole, October 23–26, 1989 N. V. Blough and R. G. Zepp, Eds. (Woods Hole, MA: Woods Hole Oceanographic Institution, 1990), pp. 30–31.

114. Bachelet, D., P. W. Barnes, D. Brown, and M. Brown. "Latitudinal and Seasonal Variation in Calculated Ultraviolet-B Irradiance for Rice-Growing Regions of Asia," *Photochem. Photobiol.* 54:411–422 (1991).

115. *Acid Deposition Long Term Trends* (Washington, D.C.: National Academy Press, 1986).

116. Bower, J. S., G. F. J. Broughton, M. T. Dando, A. J. Lees, K. J. Stevenson, J. E. Lampert, B. P. Sweeney, V. J. Parker, G. S. Driver, C. J. Waddon, and A. J. Wood. "Urban NO_2 Concentrations in the U.K. in 1987," *Atmos. Environ.* 25B:267–283 (1991).

117. Bower, J. S., J. E. Lampert, K. J. Stevenson, D. H. F. Atkins, and D. V. Law. "A Diffusion Tube Survey of NO_2 Levels in Urban Areas of the U.K.," *Atmos. Environ.* 25B:255–265 (1991).

118. Logan, J. A. "Nitrogen Oxides in the Troposphere: Global and Regional Budgets," *J. Geophys. Res.* 88:10,785–10,807 (1983).

119. Ferman, M. A., G. T. Wolff, and N. A. Kelly. "An Assessment of the Gaseous Pollutants and Meteorological Conditions Associated with Denver's Brown Cloud," *J. Environ. Sci. Health* A16:315–339 (1981).

120. Bennet, B. G., J. G. Kretzschmar, G. G. Akland, and H. W. de Koning. "Urban Air Pollution Worldwide," *Environ. Sci. Technol.* 19:298–304 (1985).

121. Baker-Blocker, A., J. F. DeLuisi, and E. Dutton. "Received Ultraviolet Radiation at the South Pole," *Sol. Energy* 32:659–662 (1984).

122. Lubin, D., J. E. Frederick, and A. J. Krueger. "The Ultraviolet Radiation Environment of Antarctica: McMurdo Station During September–October 1987," *J. Geophys. Res.* 94:8491–8496 (1989).

123. Lubin, D., B. G. Mitchell, J. E. Frederick, A. D. Roberts, C. R. Booth, T. Lucas, and D. Neuschuler. "A Contribution Toward Understanding the Biospherical Significance of Antarctic Ozone Depletion," *J. Geophys. Res.* 97:7817–7828 (1992).

124. Lubin, D. and J. E. Frederick. "Measurements of Enhanced Springtime Ultraviolet Radiation at Palmer Station, Antarctica," *Geophys. Res. Lett.* 16:783–785 (1989).

125. Beaglehole, D. and G. G. Carter. "Antarctic Skies. 1. Diurnal Variations of the Sky Irradiance, and UV Effects of the Ozone Hole, Spring 1990," *J. Geophys. Res.* 97:2589–2596 (1992).

126. Beaglehole, D. and G. G. Carter. "Antarctic Skies. 2. Characterization of the Intensity and Polarization of Skylight in a High Albedo Environment," *J. Geophys. Res.* 97:2597–2600 (1992).

127. Smith, R. C., B. B. Prezelin, K. S. Baker, R. R. Bidigare, N. P. Boucher, T. Coley, D. Karentz, S. MacIntyre, H. A. Matlick, D. Menzies, M. Ondrusek, Z. Wan, and K. J. Waters. "Ozone Depletion: Ultraviolet Radiation and Phytoplankton Biology in Antarctic Waters," *Science* 255:952–959 (1992).

128. Frederick, J. E. and A. D. Alberts. "Prolonged Enhancement in Surface Ultraviolet Radiation During the Antarctic Spring of 1990," *Geophys. Res. Lett.* 18:1869–1871 (1991).

129. Cotton, G. F. "Robertson-Berger UVB Meter," in *Summary Report 1989,* Climate Monitoring and Diagnostics Laboratory Report 18, NOAA, Boulder, CO (December 1990).

130. Scotto, J., G. Cotton, F. Urbach, D. Berger, and T. Fears. "Biologically Effective Ultraviolet Radiation: Surface Measurements in The United States, 1974 to 1985," *Science* 239:762–764 (1988).

131. Garadzha, M. P. and Y. I. Nezval. "Ultraviolet Radiation in Large Cities and Possible Ecological Consequences of its Changing Flux Due to Anthropogenic Impact," in *Proceedings of Symposium on Climate and Human Health,* WCPA Report 2 (Leningrad: World Climate Programme Applications, 1987), pp. 64–68.

132. Grant, W. B. "Global Stratospheric Ozone and UVB Radiation," *Science* 242:1111 (1988).

133. Blumthaler, M. and W. Ambach. "Indication of Increasing Solar Ultraviolet-B Radiation Flux in Alpine Regions," *Science* 248:206–208 (1990).

134. Correll, D. L., C. O. Clark, B. Goldberg, V. R. Goodrich, D. R. Hayes, Jr., W. H. Klein, and W. D. Schecher. "Spectral Ultraviolet-B Radiation Fluxes at the Earth's Surface: Long-Term Variations at 39°N, 77°W," *J. Geophys. Res.* 97:7579–7591 (1992).

3

Solar UV Measurements

Mario Blumthaler

INTRODUCTION

Within the solar spectrum the shortest wavelengths reaching the earth's surface are in the UV-B range (280–320 nm). At the top of the atmosphere this range of wavelengths contributes up to 1.5% of total solar irradiance, while at the earth's surface they constitute no more than 0.5%. Thus, the UV-B range of the solar spectrum is energetically of minor importance; however, it is highly important for the earth's biosphere. Besides the absolute intensity, the variations of solar UV-B radiation flux play a significant role for organisms. These variations are at most a consequence of naturally varying atmospheric and environmental conditions; however, the recent development of air pollution begins to play another significant role. Generally, the attenuation of solar radiation within the earth's atmosphere can be calculated with parameterized models[1-4] or with sophisticated radiation transfer models.[5-7] But these calculations suffer from insufficient knowledge of all related parameters; therefore, real measurements of solar radiation under different conditions are highly appreciated.

In this chapter the high varability of solar UV-B radiation flux is discussed based upon 12 years of measurements with different detectors in the European Alps. The measurements were carried out at the High Alpine Research Station Jungfraujoch in the Swiss Alps (3576 m above sea level, 7.98° east, 46.55° north) and in Innsbruck, Austria (577 m above sea level, 11.38° east, 47.31° north). The high mountain station was

0-87371-911-5/93/$0.00 + $.50
© 1993 by Lewis Publishers

selected to study the influence of various parameters without distur-
bances by air pollution from great cities or from industrial regions, whereas
the Innsbruck station represents an urban area in an Alpine valley which
sometimes has high air pollution.

From the extensive data base obtained by these measurements it is
possible to deduce the relation between global and diffuse radiation flux
under cloudless sky and the influences of solar elevation, total ozone
content, albedo, turbidity and altitude on the UV-B radiation flux. Furthermore, the influence of cloudiness can be analyzed.

Besides these systematic variations of solar UV-B radiation flux, a trend
analysis for 11 years of measurements at the high mountain station is
given. For this time period a slight but highly significant increase of UV-
B radiation flux is determined which is attributed to the slight total ozone
depletion over mid-latitudes during the last decade.

These results validate the usefulness of long-term measurements with
broadband detectors. However, measurements with high spectral resolution are necessary to study in detail the individual physical processes
of absorption and scattering of solar radiation in the atmosphere. Also,
the validation of model calculations under specific conditions can be
done only by comparison with high-quality spectral measurements.
Therefore, principle features of those spectral measurements also are
discussed in a separate section.

Throughout this chapter, a few standardized terms are used to dis-
criminate characteristics of solar radiation fluxes:

- *global* radiation: radiation from the upper hemisphere upon a horizontal detector surface, with no specification for wavelength regions
- *total* radiation: solar radiation flux measured with a pyranometer,
  which is sensitive to wavelengths between 300 nm and 3000 nm
- *erythemal* UV-B radiation: solar UV-B radiation flux measured with a
  Robertson-Berger Sunburn Meter, which has a spectral sensitivity
  close to the human skin erythema

METHODS OF MEASUREMENTS

Measuring solar radiation flux in the UV-B wavelength range is more
difficult than in the UV-A or visible wavelength ranges, because in the
UV-B very low intensities are to be measured, whereas the intensities
at wavelengths nearby are more than 1000-fold higher. That means that
a very high stray light suppression is essential; otherwise radiation from
the higher wavelengths dominates the measurements.

In principal, two types of detectors can be used for UV-B measurements: broadband detectors and spectroradiometers. Broadband detectors are made sensitive to a certain wavelength range in the UV-B by
combinations of special filters. One of the most popular broadband detectors for UV-B radiation, the Robertson-Berger sunburn meter (RB-
meter),[8] which is also used in the study presented here, uses an addi-

tional fluorescence layer to convert UV-B radiation into radiation of longer wavelengths. However, no broadband detector has an ideal wavelength-independent sensitivity over the UV-B range. While the maximum sensitivity lies within this range, they have a more or less steep decrease of sensitivity at longer wavelengths. Therefore, results of different broadband detectors with different spectral sensitivities cannot be simply compared one against the other. Some types of broadband detectors, such as the RB-meter, have a spectral sensitivity adapted to the action spectrum of a biological reaction like the human skin erythema.[9] This adaptation is never complete; therefore, the calibration of these detectors in biologically weighted units is only valid for one distinct spectrum of a radiation source, as can be seen from the dependance of the calibration factor of the RB-meter on solar elevation.[10] This is of some importance if the results are to be interpreted as biologically relevant doses, but it is neglectable if the results are only taken as a measure of solar UV-B radiation flux.

Spectroradiometers measure the radiation flux at individual wavelengths with a relative narrow spectral bandwidth. One detector of this type is the Eppley filter spectroradiometer,[11,12] which is also used in this study. It has eight interference filters with maximal transmissions between 290 and 325 nm and with a half-bandwidth of about ± 3 nm. The filters are mounted on a wheel, which rotates once a second while a photomultiplier measures the intensity of the radiation in each channel. For wavelengths above 305 nm this detector was found to be very useful, but with the filter channels below 300 nm mainly stray light is detected. The main advantage of this detector is the nearly simultaneous measurement at all filter channels and the weatherproof design of the detector.

The most precise spectral measurements are made with double monochromator spectroradiometers. They have two gratings for high straylight suppression and operate at wavelengths between about 250 and 500 nm. The half-bandwidth can be as low as about ± 0.2 nm and the wavelength step sizes are usually between 0.1 and 1 nm. This allows high-quality measurements even at the shortest wavelengths of solar radiation reaching the earth's surface. However, these systems are expensive, not so easy to operate and sensitive to environmental factors such as temperature variations. Therefore, they are not used for routine measurements generally, but for specific studies with high quality requirements.

The absolute calibration of UV-B detectors is no simple task, and an uncertainty of 3–5% is a good result. However, reproducibility is quite good, whereas long-term stability is difficult to control at a high level. For spectroradiometers, generally tungsten halogen lamps of 1000 W are used as calibration sources. These lamps are calibrated by national institutes such as the National Institute of Standards and Technology (NIST) in the U.S.A., the National Physical Laboratory (NPL) in the U.K. or Physikalisch Technische Bundesanstalt (PTB) in Germany. If the relative spectral sensitivity of a broadband detector is known, absolute calibration can be performed by comparison with a calibration source. A recent study showed that for RB-meters the relative spectral sensitivity is quite stable after long-term usage,[13] whereas the absolute calibration showed some fluctuations, especially in the first years of operation.[14] To control this absolute calibration, a carefully maintained detector of the same type was sent routinely by the manufacturer to each site of measurements for intercomparisons. For the broadband UV-B measurements presented here an additional control was performed by comparing four detectors of the same type regularly in the field. Therefore, no long-term trends of the calibration factors of the RB-meters used are to be expected.

The measurements at Jungfraujoch presented here were carried out since 1980 during intensive field campaigns with a duration of about 8 weeks each, one or two times a year. From one year to another the time within the year for these campaigns is varied; therefore, the whole seasonal course has been covered more than twice. The detectors mainly used are an Eppley pyranometer for total global radiation (wavelengths between 300 and 3000 nm), an Eppley UV-A radiometer, a RB-meter for erythemal UV-B radiation and an Eppley filter spectroradiometer. All these detectors were installed twice, once for global radiation fluxes (radiation on a horizontal surface from the upper hemisphere, from both the sun itself and the sky) and once for diffuse radiation fluxes (radiation from the sky only) by shielding direct sun with a shadow band or a rotating shadow disk. Measurements were stored every minute and the respective weather conditions were observed carefully. In order to eliminate the influence of temperature variations on the results of the RB-meter, the temperature coefficient was determined for temperature variations between 0°C and 30°C. A positive temperature coefficient of 8% per 10° was found for solar radiation,[15] which is in good agreement with other studies.[16] Therefore, for all RB measurements the temperature of the RB-meter was measured and the temperature correction was made using a reference temperature of 20°C. As the spectral sensitivity of the RB-meter is close to the human skin erythema, the "sunburn unit" (SU) is used as a biologically weighted unit which is correlated to the minimal erythema dose (MED).

VARIABILITY OF SOLAR UV-B

Overview

The radiation of the sun reaching the top of the earth's atmosphere decreases with decreasing wavelengths, whereby the intensity at 280 nm is about one third of that at 320 nm. Furthermore, the intensity is modulated by the varying earth-sun distance by about ±3.3% within a year, with maximal values in early January. Also, the 11-year variations of solar activity have an influence on the radiation flux from the sun; however, the related fluctuations are more pronounced in the UV-C range, whereas at wavelengths greater than 300 nm the effect is less than 1%.[17]

On its way through the atmosphere solar radiation is absorbed and scattered by molecules, aerosols and clouds. The resulting attenuation depends on the absolute amount of the respective absorber, expressed by the vertical thickness of the absorbing layer, and on the respective attenuation coefficient. The attenuation coefficients strongly depend on wavelength, in a different way for each absorber. The coefficient for molecular scattering increases with the fourth power of decreasing wavelength (Rayleigh scattering), whereas the coefficient for attenuation by aerosols increases only slightly with decreasing wavelength (Mie scattering). For clouds the absorption coefficient decreases slightly with decreasing wavelength.

In the UV-B range, the most effective molecule for absorption is ozone. Its absorption coefficient is very high in the UV-C range and decreases by more than two orders of magnitude between 280 and 320 nm. As a consequence, no UV-C radiation flux can reach the earth's surface, and in the UV-B range the radiation flux increases by several orders of magnitude. Absorption and scattering by aerosols are of minor importance in the UV-B range compared with absorption by ozone and molecular scattering. Attenuation by clouds is also strongly pronounced in the UV-B range; however, it strongly varies with type and spatial distribution of the clouds.

The attenuation of sunrays in the atmosphere is furthermore increased by the length of their pathway through the atmosphere in relation to a vertical path through. This effect is especially important for UV-B radiation flux, as their attenuation by the ozone layer is strongly increased with increasing pathlengths. Therefore, the actual solar elevation, which determines the pathlength of the solar beam through the atmosphere, is the most important parameter for temporal and geographical variations of solar UV-B radiation flux.

Besides attenuation of sun rays in the atmosphere, two geographical parameters are significant for the intensity of solar radiation at the earth's surface. On the one hand is the altitude above sea level, because it reduces the relevant air mass for molecular and aerosol absorption. On the other hand the reflectivity of the surface, the albedo, influences the diffuse radiation flux due to multiple reflections between the earth's surface and the atmosphere.

In the following sections the variation of UV-B radiation is analyzed based on measurements for cloudless sky as well as for sky covered with clouds. First, the relations between global, direct and diffuse radiation fluxes are discussed. Then, the influence of solar elevation, ozone, albedo, turbidity and altitude above sea level on the UV-B radiation flux

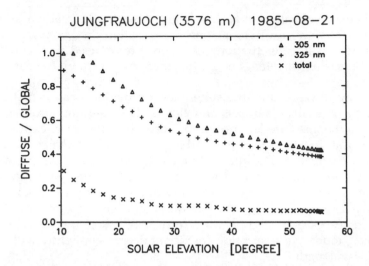

Figure 1 Ratio of diffuse radiation to global radiation versus solar elevation on a cloudless day for filter channels 305 nm and 325 nm, and for total radiation. (Reprinted from Blumthaler, M. and W. Ambach, *Photochem. Photobiol.* 54:429, 1991.)

is demonstrated. The sequence of the influencing parameters is roughly a ranking of their importance to the variations of UV-B radiation flux.

Variability of Solar UV-B Under Cloudless Sky

Global, Direct and Diffuse UV-B Radiation

Radiation from the upper hemisphere upon a horizontal detector surface is called global radiation. Generally, global radiation consists of a contribution from the sun itself, the direct radiation, and of a contribution from the sky, the diffuse radiation. Diffuse radiation is measured using a properly mounted shadow band or a rotating shadow disk, shielding the detector from direct sunlight.

If the sky is completely overcast, all radiation is diffuse. Under cloudless sky the ratio of diffuse radiation to global radiation varies both with wavelength and solar elevation. Figure 1 shows this variation for two wavelength bands in the UV range (305 and 325 nm) and for total radiation (integral over wavelengths between 300 and 3000 nm), measured on a cloudless day at Jungfraujoch.[12] Due to stronger molecular scattering at shorter wavelengths, the diffuse share in global radiation increases with shorter wavelengths. Furthermore, the diffuse share in global radiation increases with lower solar elevations due to longer path lengths. From Figure 1 one can see that at 305 nm and solar elevations below 15° all radiation is diffuse radiation, whereas for total radiation only 20% is diffuse. Even at high solar elevations (50°) about 50% of UV-B radiation is diffuse, but only 10% of total radiation. These figures hold for the measurements at the mountain station; however, at lower altitudes the diffuse share in global radiation increases for all wavelengths due to longer path lengths.

A consequence of the large share of diffuse UV-B radiation compared with total radiation is that in the shadow of the sun relatively large UV-B doses are also to be expected, larger doses than estimated from a pure visual impression. This visual impression is close to the results given here for total radiation.

Influence of Solar Elevation

The influence of varying solar elevation on UV-B radiation flux can be seen in some different results. It is relevant for the diurnal and seasonal variation as well as for the variation with latitude. In all cases, UV-B radiation flux is more effectively attenuated with decreasing solar elevations than are radiation fluxes of greater wavelengths. Therefore, diurnal, annual, and latitudinal variations are most significant for UV-B radiation flux.

The diurnal variation of radiation fluxes with different wavelengths is demonstrated in Figure 2 for a cloudless day at the high mountain station.[12] Measurements were carried out with an Eppley filter spectrometer for narrow wavelength bands between 305 and 325 nm. Besides the differences in absolute intensities (Figure 2a), normalization of noon values (Figure 2b) shows that shorter wavelengths register a steeper increase in the diurnal course than longer wavelengths. Consequently, highest doses are concentrated around noon all the more as wavelengths decrease.

Daily totals of radiation fluxes show annual courses, which are a consequence of the annual variation of solar declination. Again, the annual course is steeper for shorter wavelengths, which is demonstrated in Figure 3, where results of measurements at the high mountain station with broadband detectors for total solar radiation (G) and for erythema UV-B (G_{ER}) are shown.[18] The measurements originate from days with varying weather conditions; however, days in which measurement conditions were impaired by precipitation were not taken into account. The maximal daily totals that are possible in the seasonal course can be obtained from envelopes drawn in the seasonal course of the measured daily totals. From these data one can calculate the increase of intensities in spring and summer relative to intensities in winter for both radiation fluxes (Table 1). Seasonal variations represented by these ratios are much higher for UV-B radiation flux than for total radiation. Furthermore, a much greater variation occurs between winter and spring than between spring and summer, especially for the UV-B range.

A consequence of the different seasonal variation for radiation fluxes of different wavelengths is that the ratio of UV-B radiation flux to total

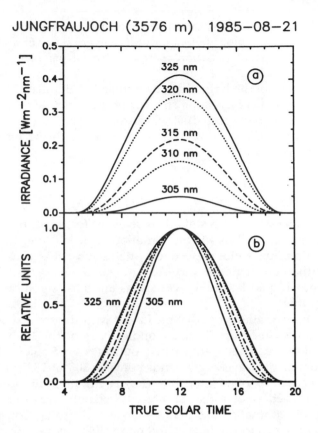

Figure 2   Daily course of spectral intensity in filter channels from 305 nm to 325 nm on a cloudless day; (a) in absolute units, (b) in relative units normalized to noon values. (Reprinted from Blumthaler, M. and W. Ambach, *Photochem. Photobiol.* 54:429, 1991.)

radiation also varies throughout the year. In Figure 4 this ratio is plotted for cloudless days to show the influence of varying solar elevation without disturbance of varying cloud cover. But these results are also influenced by varying ozone content, which causes on the one hand scattering of individual measurement points relative to the average seasonal variation (solid line in Figure 4). On the other hand, the average seasonal variation is not symmetrical to the summer solstice, but is slightly shifted towards autumn. This is a consequence of the typical annual variation of the ozone content at the respective latitude, which shows maximal values in spring and minimal values in autumn, and therefore UV-B radiation flux is higher in autumn compared with spring at the same solar elevations.

A variation of the latitude of the measurement site can be interpreted as a variation of solar elevation both within the day and within the year. For example, moving 10° toward the equator will increase noon values

JUNGFRAUJOCH (3576 m)

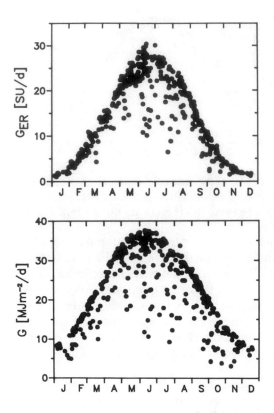

Figure 3 Seasonal course of daily totals of total global radiation (G) and erythemal UV-B radiation (G_{ER}).

Table 1 Seasonal Variation of
Erythemal UV-B Radiation
(G_{ER}) and Total Radiation (G)

	G_{ER}	G
Ratio spring/winter	9:1	3:1
Ratio summer/winter	18:1	5:1

of radiation fluxes by the same amount as the seasonal increase within the month of April.

Influence of Total Atmospheric Ozone

The influence of atmospheric ozone on solar UV-B radiation flux is increasing with decreasing wavelengths, because the ozone absorption coefficient increases strongly with decreasing wavelengths. There is almost no influence of ozone at wavelengths greater than 330 nm. The

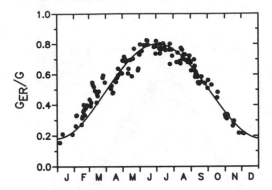

Figure 4 Seasonal course of the ratio of daily totals of erythemal UV-B radiation
(G_{ER}) to total global radiation (G) for cloudless days at Jungfraujoch
(3576 m). The solid line represents the average annual course.

quantitative influence of ozone can be calculated using a radiation model,
and the result can be expressed as the so-called "radiation amplification
factor" (RAF). The RAF defines the percentage increase of radiation flux
if ozone decreases by 1%. It can be calculated for single wavelengths or
for a broadband range, and it is slightly dependent on solar elevation
and on total ozone content. For example, the RAF amounts to 2.6 at 310
nm and to 10 at 300 nm, calculated for 30° solar elevation.[19] This means
that at 300 nm the radiation flux is increased by 10% if ozone is depleted
by 1%.

If the RAF is calculated for broadband ranges of a radiation flux, the
result strongly depends on the detailed spectral definition of the wavelength band. If not only UV-B but also UV-A is included in the spectral
weighting function, then the RAF is smaller compared to the same spectral function in the UV-B range only. A detailed summary of RAFs
calculated for various biological reactions in the UV range is given by
Madronich et al.[20] From there, for example, the RAF for the generalized
DNA damage is 1.9 and that of the reference erythema action spectrum
is 1.1.

Besides the application of model calculations, the RAF can also be
deduced from extensive measurements of solar UV radiation flux, either
spectrally or broadband, together with nearby ozone total column measurements. McKenzie et al.[21] found a RAF of 1.25 ± 0.2 using spectral
measurements of solar UV radiation flux in New Zealand, valid for the
reference erythema action spectrum, which is in good agreement with
model calculations.

A further experimental evaluation of the RAF with a broadband detector could be done based on the long-term measurements at the high
mountain station Jungfraujoch with the RB-meter. For this analysis the
residuals (deviations) of the measurements from the average seasonal

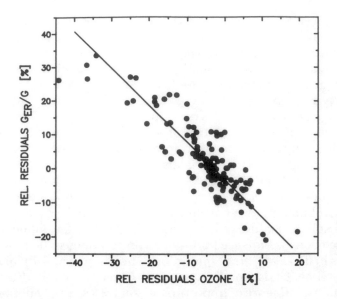

Figure 5   Relation between relative residuals of ozone, measured in Arosa, and the relative residuals of the ratio of erythemal UV-B radiation (G_{ER}) to total global radiation (G) for cloudless days at Jungfraujoch (3576 m). The residuals are the respective deviations of the average annual courses. The solid line represents the regression line.

course of the ratio of UV-B radiation over total radiation (Figure 4) were calculated. Relative residuals were obtained by dividing each residual by the respective value of that ratio. In the same way the relative residuals of total ozone content were calculated for the days of UV-B measurements at Jungfraujoch using ozone data from Arosa, which is about 100 km from Jungfraujoch. Monthly means for the last 10 years were used as the average ozone values in the seasonal course. In Figure 5 the relative residuals of ozone are plotted against the relative residuals of the ratio of UV-B to total radiation flux, both variables expressed as percentages. There is a strong correlation between these two variables, and the slope of the regression line represents the RAF. From this analysis, calculated under the assumption that both variables were varying, the RAF for the RB-meter was found to be 1.1 ± 0.2, as an average over all seasons and valid for daily totals. This is in good agreement with model calculations using Green's radiation model together with the spectral sensitivity of the RB-meter, which was provided by the manufacturer. From these calculations the RAF for the RB-meter varies between 1.0 in winter and 1.2 in summer. These results demonstrate that the RB-meter is really sensitive to ozone variations and that the calibration factor was quite stable over the 12 years of measurements, because no long-term variation of the RAF was found.

Based on the RAF one can discuss actual variations of solar UV-B radiation flux as a consequence of ozone variation. For example, total ozone content in early spring varies over ±30% within a few days in mid-northern latitudes. Consequently, solar UV-B radiation flux varies correspondingly. In addition, day-to-day variation of solar elevation is also relatively high in spring, when it increases by about 4° within 10 days, which gives about a 10% increase in UV-B. Therefore, these combinations of large natural variations of solar UV-B radiation flux even under cloudless sky should be taken into accout if the influence of anthropogenic factors on solar UV-B is discussed.

The influence of ozone discussed so far refers to total column amount, which is the integral over the vertical distribution. Atmospheric ozone is mainly distributed in the stratosphere (91%), and only 9% is present in the troposphere. Model calculations indicate that the influence of tropospheric ozone is enhanced under certain conditions due to longer path lengths in denser layers of the atmosphere.[22] Up to now there have been no experimental data on the quantitative amount of this effect. An overproportional influence of tropospheric ozone is especially important for ozone trend analyses, because the ozone content decreases in the stratosphere and increases in the troposphere.[23] The quantitative influence of these two contrary variations in solar UV-B radiation flux is difficult to calculate, and generally the superposition of both trends is effective for measurements.

Influence of Albedo

The albedo of a horizontal terrain is defined as the amount of reflected radiation in relation to incoming radiation. It influences the diffuse part of global radiation flux due to multiple reflections between surface and atmosphere. Because of the especially high share of diffuse radiation in the UV-B range, there the influence of varying albedo is also more pronounced. In addition, the albedo of different types of surfaces depends in a different way on wavelength. Comparative measurements of the albedo for total radiation and for erythemal UV-B radiation, measured with the RB-meter, were carried out for different types of surfaces.[24] They show a different result for snow-free and for snow-covered surfaces (Figure 6). For all snow-free surfaces the albedo for erythemal UV-B radiation is less than the albedo for total radiation. This difference is particularly great for grassland, where the average albedo for total radiation is 20.7%, but only 1.3% for erythemal UV-B radiation. For snow-covered surfaces the albedo in both wavelength ranges is comparable. The highest values were found for new dry snow, when the albedo for erythemal UV-B radiation reaches nearly 100% and is even greater than the albedo for total radiation.

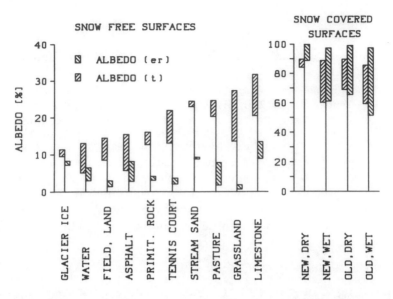

Figure 6   Albedo for erythemal UV-B radiation (er) and total radiation (t) for
snow-free and snow-covered surfaces. Hatched columns mark the
variation between minimum and maximum values measured. (Reprinted from Blumthaler, M. and W. Ambach, *Photochem. Photobiol.*
48:85, 1988.)

The albedo of the terrain is of special importance for ocular radiant
exposure, because it can be assumed that the eyes are mainly directed
toward the ground. Therefore, UV-B exposure of the eye increases about
16 fold if one changes from snow-free terrain (albedo about 5%) to snow-
covered terrain (albedo about 90%). This enormous difference is the
reason that keratitis photoelectrica (snow blindness) results only from
exposure in snow-covered terrain. Clinical studies in the Alpine region
showed that keratitis occurs only from about mid-February onward,
when the intensity of solar UV-B radiation is sufficiently high.[25]

Influence of Turbidity

Atmospheric turbidity is a consequence of scattering and absorption
of solar radiation by aerosols. The amount of aerosols in the vertical
profile and their size distribution are of significance. The influence of
aerosols only slightly depends on wavelength, with a greater effect at
lower wavelengths. Therefore, the UV-B range is seriously affected by
aerosols; however, ozone absorption and molecular scattering are much
more important. This makes it difficult to isolate the influence of aerosols
on UV-B radiation flux, especially at the high mountain station, where
the amount of aerosols is very small.

**Table 2 Altitude Effect (Percentage Increase per
1000 m) of Erythemal UV-B Radiation (G_{ER})
and Total Radiation (G) in Different Seasons**

	G_{ER}	G
Summer	18 ± 5%/1000 m	9 ± 2%/1000 m
Winter	23 ± 6%/1000 m	15 ± 3%/1000 m

A very special influence of aerosols on solar UV-B radiation flux is
found for a stratospheric haze layer resulting from the injection of aer-
osol-forming material into the stratosphere by volcanic eruptions.[26] From
model calculations it is apparent that solar radiation flux at the earth's
surface may increase under this condition by as much as 45% at 290 nm,
while at 300 nm a decrease of 5% would be expected. These results also
demonstrate the strong wavelength dependency of the effects in the UV-
B range.

Influence of Altitude

The increase of solar radiation flux with altitude above sea level is
called the altitude effect, and it is given as the percentage increase over
1000 m relative to the lower station. It is above all a consequence of the
smaller irradiated air mass at higher altitudes. Therefore, the altitude
effect depends on solar elevation due to the varying amount of irradiated
air mass and on wavelength due to stronger scattering at shorter wavelengths. Consequently, the altitude effect is higher at lower solar elevations and at shorter wavelengths.

An additional contribution to the increase of solar radiation flux, especially in the high mountains, results from the higher albedo, which
is present in snow-covered mountains. Furthermore, the altitude effect
is increased due to the generally lower turbidity in the high mountains
compared with valley stations.

The altitude effect can be determined from measurements of total and
UV-B radiation fluxes at the high mountain station Jungfraujoch and the
valley station Innsbruck.[27] The two stations have a difference in altitude
of 2999 m. To calculate the altitude effect, the respective envelopes of
the seasonal courses of daily totals of total and UV-B radiation flux are
compared (Table 2). One can see that in summer the increase of solar
radiation flux with altitude is about two times greater for the UV-B range
compared with the total range. The indicated standard deviations are
an estimate of the uncertainties made by drawing the envelopes of the
seasonal courses. However, due to the dependence of the altitude effect
on various parameters, a range of variation results from model calculations too.

Variability of Solar UV-B Under Cloud Cover

The reduction of solar radiation fluxes at the earth's surface due to
cloudiness can vary within a broad range. It depends on the optical

depths of the clouds and on their distribution over the sky, especially if clouds occult the sun itself. Therefore, a large number of measurements under different situations of cloudiness are necessary to determine the influence of cloudiness on solar radiation fluxes. Such an analysis could be carried out from long-term measurements at Jungfraujoch.[18] Daily sums of total, UV-A and UV-B radiation fluxes were used as the basis of the evaluation. Cloudiness was calculated as a daily average, derived upon half-hourly observations of the amount of clouds, expressed as tenths of the sky covered by clouds. In order to separate the influence of cloudiness from other parameters, daily totals on individual days in the seasonal course were related to the maximal daily totals possible on the respective days. The maximal daily totals were obtained from the envelope of the measured daily totals in the seasonal course. Therefore, this normalization takes into account the seasonal course of the daily totals and the results are related to the cloudless situation.

The dependence of the radiation fluxes in different wavelength regions on the amount of cloudiness is shown in Figure 7a. Normalized daily totals for total (G_0^*), UV-A (G_{UVA}^*) and erythemal UV-B radiation fluxes (G_{ER}^*) were averaged for each tenth of cloudiness. The increase of the standard deviation with increasing cloudiness is a consequence of the natural differences in cloud density at one and the same amount of cloudiness. The larger standard deviation for the UV-B range even with low cloudiness results from the additional influence of varying ozone content.

In order to examine the influence of cloudiness on different wavelength ranges, normalized daily totals in the UV-A and UV-B range were related to that of the total range by calculating the ratios G_{UVA}^*/G_0^* and G_{ER}^*/G_0^* (Figure 7b). Therefore, values greater than 1 for these ratios indicate that cloudiness reduces total radiation more strongly than UV-A and UV-B radiation fluxes. The higher range of variation for the UV-B ratio is again a consequence of varying ozone content. The observed less marked weakening of UV-A and UV-B radiation fluxes through cloudiness as compared with total global radiation is in agreement with results reported by Robinson[28] and Reiter et al.[29] However, the absolute reduction of the radiation fluxes through cloudiness measured at Jungfraujoch is considerably lower compared with observations cited above because of lesser opacity of clouds at high altitudes.

UV-B TREND

A slight depletion of total column amount of ozone over mid-latitudes of the northern hemisphere during the last decades is now well established. Since 1978 a downward trend of about 4% per decade has been found over Europe and North America, based on both ground-based and satellite measurements.[30] Therefore, it should be expected that with

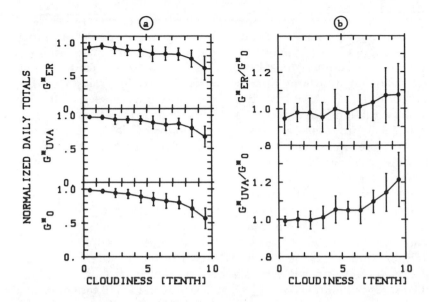

Figure 7   (a) Daily totals normalized to a cloudless sky for global erythemal
UV-B radiation (G^*_{ER}), UV-A radiation (G^*_{UVA}) and total radiation (G^*_0) versus cloudiness at Jungfraujoch (3576 m). Mean
values and standard deviations for intervals of $^1/_{10}$ cloudiness.
(b) Ratios of the normalized daily totals G^*_{ER}/G^*_0 and G^*_{UVA}/G^*_0
versus cloudiness at Jungfraujoch (3576 m). Mean values and
standard deviations for intervals of $^1/_{10}$ cloudiness. (Reprinted
from Blumthaler, M. and W. Ambach, *Atmos. Environ.* 22:749,
1988.)

this depletion of ozone an increase of solar UV-B radiation flux at the
earth's surface is correlated. But as a consequence of the large natural
variability of solar UV-B radiation flux, as discussed in the previous
paragraphs, it is very difficult to deduce a small trend from measurements of solar UV-B, and a long time series of observations is necessary.

The first attempt to find a trend in UV-B radiation flux was made by
Scotto et al. Measurements between 1974 and 1985 from the network of
Robertson-Berger meters in the United States were analyzed.[31] No significant increase of solar UV-B radiation flux was found; there was even
a slight decrease at some stations. The main reason for this surprising
result might be meteorological and environmental factors at the sites of
measurements, which were mainly located in highly polluted areas of
large cities.[32] Furthermore, the effects of cloudiness were included in
the analysis, which produces large additional fluctuations.

From long-term measurements of solar UV-B radiation flux at the high
mountain station Jungfraujoch a trend analysis could be carried out.[33,34]
The advantages of this station are the small influence of air pollution,

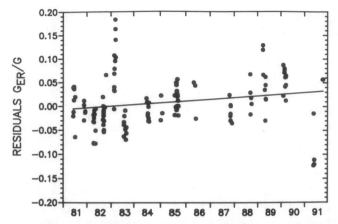

Figure 8 Long-term tendency of the residuals G_{ER}/G from 1981 to 1991 at Jungfraujoch (3576 m). The residuals are the deviations of the average annual course (Figure 4). The solid line represents the regression line.

the possibility to restrict the evaluation on complete cloudless days and the opportunity to relate the UV-B radiation flux to total global radiation, which was measured simultaneously. The natural annual variation of the ratio of UV-B radiation flux to total radiation was taken into account by looking only at the deviations (residuals) of the individual measurements from the average seasonal course (Figure 4). These residuals are then plotted against the dates of measurements between 1981 and 1991 (Figure 8). Besides the statistical fluctuations within each period of measurement there is a statistically highly significant trend of increase ($p <$ 0.02) which gives an increase of 7 $\pm$ 3% per decade for the UV-B radiation flux. The relatively large standard deviation indicates that the time period of measurement is still rather short. The restriction of the measurements to certain periods each year can induce an additional uncertainty. Nevertheless, the trend is in good agreement with the observed ozone depletion in Arosa of between 3% and 6% per decade over time since 1978.[28] This calculated ozone trend must be further multiplied with the RAF of 1.1 to give the expected increase in UV-B radiation flux.

From the trend analyses of the measurements at the high mountain station Jungfraujoch it is documented that there is really a slight increase of solar UV-B radiation flux associated with the slight depletion of total column ozone, but at the moment the absolute amount of this variation is so small that it is usually masked by large natural variations of solar UV-B radiation flux, especially in highly polluted urban areas.

SPECTRAL MEASUREMENTS OF SOLAR UV-B

The best data about solar UV-B radiation flux are gained by spectral measurements. As a number of technical and operational problems must be solved to get serious data, such measurements have been carried out exactly enough only in the past few years. Some of the associated problems are very high stray light suppression, which generally can only be achieved by use of a double monochromator, control of wavelength accuracy, control of the calibration function in the field, wavelength dependence of the cosine error and temperature dependence of the wavelength setting and of the calibration function.

The advantages of spectral measurements are twofold. On the one hand, the physical properties of the atmosphere can be studied in detail by determination of the respective parameters and radiation transfer models can be checked exactly. On the other hand, biologically relevant doses can be determined without any restrictions on the action spectrum of the biological reaction simply by multiplying the measured spectrum with the desired action spectrum and integrating over the respective wavelengths. This is especially important for biological studies, because by selecting a special broadband detector the choice of an appropriate action spectrum need not be made in advance of the study.

A typical example of solar UV spectra under different conditions is given in Figure 9.[35] Global measurements with a double monochromator spectral radiometer taken at the high mountain station Jungfraujoch and in Innsbruck are compared at solar elevations of 20° and 40°. The slit width for all spectra was ±0.5 nm and the wavelength step size was 0.5 nm. The dates of measurements at Jungfraujoch and in Innsbruck were chosen to ensure similar total ozone contents of about 300 Dobson units. Besides the measurements (crosses), the results of a fit with Green's radiation model are also plotted (solid line), and the agreement is quite good for the whole spectral region. The increase of solar radiation due to increasing solar elevation and due to increasing altitude above sea level is significant. In Figure 9a the Fraunhofer structure of the extraterrestrial solar spectrum is clearly seen; it is all the more marked as the slit width of spectral measurements is reduced. As intensities below about 310 nm are very small, a logarithmic scale is favorable there (Figure 9b). The steep increase of solar radiation flux by more than four orders of magnitude within the UV-B range is clearly seen. The shortest wavelength detectable at a level of intensity of about $0.005 \text{ mWm}^{-2}\text{nm}^{-1}$ is shifted from 293 nm to 297.5 nm at Jungfraujoch if solar elevation is reduced from 40° to 20°; the respective values for Innsbruck are about 1 nm greater. This clearly demonstrates the strong influence of solar elevation on the intensity of solar UV-B radiation flux.

The application of complex radiation models allows one to determine the total ozone content of the atmosphere from global solar UV spectra.[36,37] These models have their largest range of deviations in the cal-

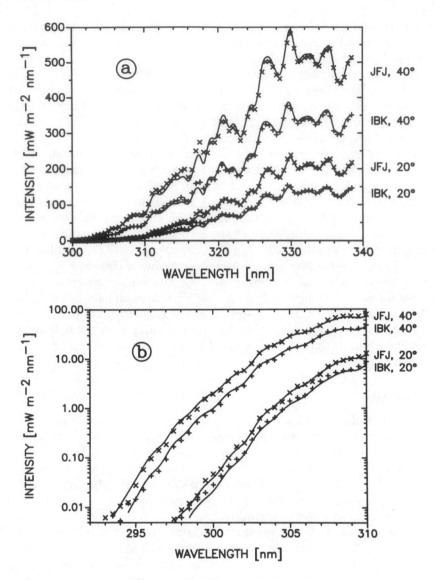

Figure 9   Spectral intensity of solar UV radiation flux at Jungfraujoch (JFJ, 3576 m, March 19, 1990) and in Innsbruck (IBK, 577 m, April 4, 1990) for 20° and 40° solar elevation (x, +) and results of a fit with Green's radiation model (solid line). See text for details. (Reprinted from Blumthaler, M. et al., Proceedings of the 21st International Meeting on Alpine Meteorology, Engelberg, Switzerland, September 17–21, 1990, p. 291.)

culation of diffuse radiation, especially at low solar elevations. This limits the accuracy of the resulting value of the ozone content. An alternative method is to measure the direct spectrum of the sun. Then, the ozone content can be calculated using the relatively simple equations for attenuation of the direct beam. This method gives very good agreement, also in the diurnal course, between the ozone values calculated from UV spectra and those determined at a nearby standard ozone station with a Dobson or a Brewer instrument.[38]

Spectral measurements of solar UV radiation flux in England,[39] New Zealand,[40] Australia[41] and Antarctica[42] demonstrate the worldwide effort to obtain more information about the physical variations of solar UV under different conditions. However, all these studies were carried out with different types of spectrometers, each calibrated independently. Because of the great sensitivity of spectrometers to systematic errors, it is important to get information on the comparability of the results. This can only be achieved by a field intercomparison of different spectrometers, where the actual conditions of solar measurements are equal for all instruments. Until now, only a few intercomparisons have been made.[43] The measurements showed an agreement of generally about 10%. However, at wavelengths below about 300 nm the differences became greater and, therefore, interpretation of results in this range should be carried out very carefully.

SUMMARY

The variability of solar UV-B radiation flux is evaluated from data of long-term measurements at Jungfraujoch, Switzerland (3576 m) and in Innsbruck, Austria (577 m). The main parameters influencing solar UV-B radiation flux are cloudiness, solar elevation, atmospheric ozone content, albedo, turbidity and altitude. UV-B radiation on a horizontal plane is mainly diffuse radiation from the sky, namely at the shortest wavelengths and at low solar elevations.

Under cloudless sky the most important parameter is solar elevation, dominating the diurnal, seasonal and latitudinal variation of UV radiation flux. Different solar elevations cause different path lengths through the ozone layer, where UV-B radiation is strongly absorbed. Consequently, the diurnal and seasonal variation becomes more pronounced at shorter wavelengths, and daily totals of UV-B radiation flux increase from winter to summer about 18-fold, while daily totals of total global radiation increase only 5-fold. Therefore, the share of UV-B radiation flux in total global radiation is smaller in winter than in summer.

At the same solar elevations, solar UV-B radiation fluxes are mainly determined by atmospheric ozone content. A 1% decrease of ozone causes about a 1.1% increase of UV-B, measured with a Robertson-Berger Sunburn meter, and a 1.25% increase for the reference erythema action spectrum.

The albedo of the terrain influences diffuse radiation flux via multiple reflections between surface and atmosphere. Over snow-free surfaces, the albedo for UV-B radiation is smaller than for total global radiation. Over new, dry snow the albedo is slightly higher for UV-B radiation and even reaches 100%. Therefore, UV-B radiation is especially increased over snow-covered terrain. Turbidity, which is a consequence of the aerosol content of the atmosphere, weakens UV radiation slightly more than radiation of greater wavelengths. However, ozone absorption and molecular scattering are far more effective than attenuation by aerosols. The increase of radiation fluxes with altitude is stronger for shorter wavelengths and for lower solar elevations. For UV-B radiation flux it amounts to about 18% per 1000 m in summer, while for total global radiation it is only about 9% per 1000 m.

Attenuation of solar radiation fluxes by clouds can vary within a broad range due to varying amount and optical thickness of the clouds. Moreover, cloudiness affects UV-B and UV-A radiation fluxes less than it does total global radiation.

A slight increase of solar UV-B radiation flux of 7 ± 3% per decade was derived from measurements between 1981 and 1991 at the high mountain station Jungfraujoch. This increase is related to the slight decrease in total ozone of 3 to 6 % per decade, measured in Arosa (Switzerland).

More detailed information about solar UV-B radiation flux can be gained by high-resolution spectral measurements. Such measurements have been carried out all over the world the past few years. From these spectra total ozone content can be determined, as well as erythemal or DNA-weighted doses, but no trend analyses are possible so far. However, the high sensitivity of spectroradiometers makes it necessary to improve the quality control by intercomparison of different systems in use, especially for measurements at the shortest wavelengths reaching the earth's surface.

REFERENCES

1. Green, A. E. S., K. R. Cross, and L. A. Smith. "Improved Analytic Characterization of Ultraviolet Skylight," *Photochem. Photobiol.* 31:59–65 (1980).
2. Green, A. E. S., T. Sawada, and E. P. Shettle. "The Middle Ultraviolet Reaching the Ground," *Photochem. Photobiol.* 19:251–259 (1974).
3. Schippnik, P. F. and A. E. S. Green. "Analytical Characterization of Spectral Actinic Flux and Spectral Irradiance in the Middle Ultraviolet," *Photochem. Photobiol.* 35:89–101 (1982).

4. Rundel, R. "Computation of Spectral Distribution and Intensity of Solar UV-B Radiation," in *Stratospheric Ozone Reduction, Solar Ultraviolet Radiation and Plant Life*, NATO ASI Series G, Vol. 8, R. C. Worrest and M. M. Caldwell, Eds. (Berlin: Springer-Verlag, 1986), pp. 49–62.

5. Frederick, J. and D. Lubin. "The Budget of Biologically Active Ultraviolet Radiation in the Earth-Atmosphere System," *J. Geophys. Res.* 93(D4):3825–3832 (1988).

6. Stamnes, K., S. Tsay, W. Wiscombe, and K. Jayaweera. "Numerically Stable Algorithm for Discrete-Ordinate-Method Radiative Transfer in Multiple Scattering and Emitting Layered Media," *Appl. Opt.* 27:2502–2509 (1988).

7. Lenoble, J., Ed. *Radiative Transfer in Scattering and Absorbing Atmospheres: Standard Computational Procedures* (Deepak Publishing, 1985).

8. Berger, D. S. "The Sunburning Ultraviolet Meter — Design and Performance," *Photochem. Photobiol.* 24:587–593 (1976).

9. McKinlay, A. F. and B. L. Diffey. "A Reference Spectrum for Ultraviolet Induced Erythema in Human Skin," *CIE J.* 6:17–22 (1987).

10. DeLuisi, J. and M. Harris. "A Determination of the Absolute Radiant Energy of a Robertson-Berger Meter Sunburn Unit," *Atmos. Environ.* 17:751–758 (1983).

11. Goldberg, B. and W. H. Klein. "Radiometer to Monitor Low Levels of Ultraviolet Irradiance," *Appl. Opt.* 13:493–496 (1974).

12. Blumthaler, M. and W. Ambach. "Spectral Measurements of Global and Diffuse Solar Ultraviolet-B Radiant Exposure and Ozone Variations," *Photochem. Photobiol.* 54:429–432 (1991).

13. DeLuisi, J., J. Wendell, and F. Kreiner. "An Examination of the Spectral Response Characteristics of Seven Robertson-Berger Meters after Long-Term Field Use," *Photochem. Photobiol.*, 56:115–122 (1992).

14. Kennedy, B. C. and W. E. Sharp. "A Validation Study of the Robertson-Berger Meter," *Photochem. Photobiol.*, 56:133–141 (1992).

15. Blumthaler, M. and W. Ambach. "Messungen der Temperaturkoeffizienten des Robertson-Berger Sunburn Meters und des Eppley UV-radiometers," *Arch. Met. Geoph. Biokl. Ser. B* 36:357–363 (1986).

16. Johnsen, B. and J. Moan. "The Temperature Sensitivity of the Robertson-Berger Sunburn Meter, Model 500," *J. Photochem. Photobiol. B: Biol.* 11:277–284 (1991).

17. Lean, J. "Solar Ultraviolet Irradiance Variations: A Review," *J. Geophys. Res.* 92(D1):839–868 (1987).

18. Blumthaler, M. and W. Ambach. "Human Solar Ultraviolet Radiant Exposure in High Mountains," *Atmos. Environ.* 22:749–753 (1988).

19. Frederick, J. E., H. E. Snell, and E. K. Haywood. "Solar Ultraviolet Radiation at the Earth's Surface," *Photochem. Photobiol.* 50:443–450 (1989).

20. Madronich, S., L. O. Björn, M. Ilyas, and M. M. Caldwell. "Changes in Biologically Active Ultraviolet Radiation Reaching the Earth's Surface," in *Environmental Effects of Ozone Depletion: 1991 Update* (Nairobi: United Nations Environmental Program, 1991), pp. 1–14.

21. McKenzie, R. L., W. A. Matthews, and P. V. Johnston. "The Relationship Between Erythemal UV and Ozone, Derived from Spectral Irradiance Measurements," *Geophys. Res. Lett.* 18:2269–2272 (1991).

22. Brühl, C. and P. J. Crutzen. "On the Disproportionate Role of Tropospheric Ozone as a Filter Against Solar UV-B Radiation," *Geophys. Res. Lett.* 16:703–706 (1989).

23. Staehelin, J. and W. Schmidt. "Trend Analysis of Tropospheric Ozone Concentrations Utilizing the 20 Year Data Set of Ozone Balloon Soundings over Payerne (Switzerland)," *Atmos. Environ.* 25A:1739 (1991).

24. Blumthaler, M. and W. Ambach. "Solar UV-B Albedo of Various Surfaces," *Photochem. Photobiol.* 48:85–88 (1988).

25. Blumthaler, M., W. Ambach, and F. Daxecker. "On the Threshold Radiant Exposure for Keratitis Solaris," *Invest. Ophthalmol. Vis. Sci.* 28:1713–1716 (1987).

26. Michelangeli, D. V., M. Allen, Y. L. Yung, R. Shia, D. Crisp, and J. Eluszkiewicz. "Enhancement of Atmospheric Radiation by an Aerosol Layer," *J. Geophys. Res.* 97(D1):865–874 (1992).

27. Blumthaler, M., W. Ambach, and W. Rehwald. "Solar UV-A and UV-B Radiation Fluxes at Two Alpine Stations at Different Altitudes," *Theor. Appl. Climatol.* 46:39–44 (1992).

28. Robinson, N. *Solar Radiation* (Amsterdam: Elsevier, 1966).

29. Reiter, R., K. Munzert, and R. Sladkovic. "Results of 5-Year Concurrent Recordings of Global, Diffuse and UV-Radiation at Three Levels (700, 1800, and 3000 m a.s.l.) in the Northern Alps," *Arch. Met. Geoph. Biokl. Ser. B* 30:1–28 (1982).

30. Stolarski, R., R. Bojkov, L. Bishop, C. Zerefos, J. Staehelin, and J. Zawodny. "Measured Trends in Stratospheric Ozone," *Science* 256:342–349 (1992).

31. Scotto, J., G. Cotton, F. Urbach, D. Berger, and T. Fears. "Biologically Effective Ultraviolet Radiation: Surface Measurements in the United States, 1974 to 1985," *Science* 239:762–764 (1988).

32. Grant, W. B. "Global Stratospheric Ozone and UV-B Radiation," *Science* 242:1111–1112 (1988).

33. Blumthaler, M. and W. Ambach. "Indication of Increasing Solar Ultraviolet-B Radiation Flux in Alpine Regions," *Science* 248:206–208 (1990).

34. Staehelin, J., M. Blumthaler, W. Ambach, and J. Torhorst. "Skin Cancer and the Ozone Shield," *Lancet* 336:502 (1990).

35. Huber, M., M. Blumthaler, and W. Ambach. "Solar UV-Spectra in Various Environmental Conditions" in *Proceedings of the 22nd International Conference on Alpine Meteorology*, Toulouse, France (1992), p. 413–415.

36. Stamnes, K., J. Slusser, and M. Bowen. "Derivation of Total Ozone Abundance and Cloud Effects from Spectral Irradiance Measurements," *Appl. Opt.* 30:4418–4426 (1991).

37. Lubin, D. and J. E. Frederick. "Column Ozone Measurements from Palmer Station, Antarctica: Variations During the Austral Springs of 1988 and 1989," *J. Geophys. Res.* 95:13,883–13,889 (1990).

38. Blumthaler, M., W. Ambach, and M. Huber. "Höheneffekt der solaren UV-Strahlung," in *Proceedings of the 21st International Meeting on Alpine Meteorology*, Engelberg, Switzerland (1990), p. 291–294.

39. Webb, A. R. "Solar Ultraviolet Radiation in Southeast England: The Case of Spectral Measurements," *Photochem. Photobiol.* 54:789–794 (1991).

40. Bittar, A. and R. L. McKenzie. "Spectral Ultraviolet Intensity Measurements at 45°S: 1980 and 1988," *J. Geophys. Res.* 95(D5):5597–5603 (1990).
41. Roy, C. R., H. P. Gies, and G. Elliott. "Ozone Depletion," *Nature* 347:235–236 (1990).
42. Lubin, D. and J. E. Frederick. "The Ultraviolet Radiation Environment of the Antarctic Peninsula: The Roles of Ozone and Cloud Cover," *J. Appl. Meteorol.* 30:478–493 (1991).
43. Gardiner, B. G. and P. J. Kirsch, Eds. "European Intercomparison of Ultraviolet Spectrometers," Air Pollution Research Report 38, STEP Project 76, CEC, (1992).

4

Influences of Ozone Depletion on Human and Animal Health

Jan C. van der Leun and Frank R. de Gruijl

INTRODUCTION

The consequences of increased exposure of the human body to UV-B radiation will in the first instance be characterized by the physical properties of this type of radiation. UV-B radiation does not penetrate far into the body; most of it is absorbed in the superficial tissue layers of 0.1 mm depth. This limits the primary effects to the skin and the eyes. There are, however, also systemic effects; these start with a primary reaction in the superficial layers, but have consequences throughout the body.

The sunlight reaching us consists of only approximately 0.5% UV-B radiation, in terms of radiant energy. Yet this small fraction is responsible for most of the effects of sunlight on the body. It is the main cause of sunburn and tanning, as well as the formation of vitamin D_3 in the skin, and it has influences on the immune system. UV-B radiation is also the main cause of snowblindness and an important factor in the induction of cataracts. UV-B radiation contributes significantly to the aging of the skin and eyes, and it is the UV-B range that is the most effective in causing skin cancer.

Will all these effects increase with an increase of UV-B irradiance? That is the first impression. Closer study indicates that this is not necessarily so. The effects we observe, such as sunburn or skin cancer, are the end points of complicated chains of events. The chain begins with a primary reaction, a photochemical reaction in the skin. This primary reaction will usually increase with increased UV-B exposure. If the primary reaction leads to damage, repair processes may come into play. For damage to the DNA molecule, several repair systems have been demonstrated to be active in living cells. These may mend the damage, or part of the damage. The repair systems may, however, themselves be damaged by increased UV-B exposure. Even at this early stage in the chain of events it is difficult to predict the outcome. Cells or tissue components which are altered by the radiation may be recognized as foreign by the immune system and removed. Certain functions of the immune system are, however, suppressed by exposure to UV-B radiation. When skin is exposed to more UV-B radiation than it is accustomed to, it has the ability to adapt. The epidermal layers become thicker, and melanin pigment is formed and dispersed throughout the epidermis. These reactions limit the effects of subsequent exposures to UV-B radiation. With such a complicated sequence of events, it is difficult to answer the question of whether or not the final effects on the skin will increase. This is especially so for effects resulting from repeated exposures.

We will see that the outcome is not always an increase of the grossly observable effect. Some effects of UV-B radiation on health will indeed increase, some will not be influenced appreciably and some will even decrease in the case of increased UV-B irradiance.

METHODS OF PREDICTION

There appear to be three methods to predict the ultimate health effects of increased UV-B exposure.

Direct Calculation

The most direct way is to investigate a particular health effect of UV-B radiation, with the mechanism, including the entire chain of intermediate steps in quantitative terms. On this basis it should be possible, at least in principle, to make a calculation through the entire system, resulting in a quantitative prediction.

This method is not yet feasible for any effect of increased UV-B radiation on human health. It may be a long time before this goal is achieved. The direct method will always remain vulnerable; every new discovery of an intermediate step in the mechanism may change the prediction.

The Black Box

The other extreme is not to include any mechanistic study, but to consider an entire health effect as a black box. It is known what goes in, the UV-B radiation, and one may observe what comes out, e.g., sunburn. Information on how the effect reacts to increased ambient UV-B irradiance may be acquired by making observations at different geographical locations; do people living closer to the equator have more sunburn? If not, no increase in sunburn is to be expected when the ambient UV-B irradiance increases. Do people living closer to the equator have more skin cancer? If so, more skin cancer is to be expected in case of increased ambient UV-B irradiance.

This method may be used as a first approximation, but it oversimplifies the problem. Going closer to the equator is not a fully realistic simulation of ozone depletion. Places closer to the equator have more light of all wavelengths; ozone depletion increases only the UV-B irradiance. Moreover, places closer to the equator have a different length of the day, higher temperatures and different weather. People living at different latitudes may not be comparable because of different genetic constitutions. Also, if that factor is eliminated by limiting the investigation to people of similar genetic background, they may still have different behavior at different latitudes. Without information on the influence of these complicating factors, this black box method yields very uncertain predictions.

An Intermediate Solution

A third method uses basically the same information as the black box method does — for instance, a latitudinal gradient of the skin cancer incidence. Now the reasoning is guided, however, by as much additional knowledge as possible.

In order to expect any influence of ozone depletion on a particular health effect, the effect in question should be a result of exposure to UV-B radiation. The "action spectrum" shows how a particular effect depends on the wavelength of the radiation; the concept was discussed in earlier chapters. In the first instance this gives a yes-or-no answer: if the action spectrum does not show any influence of UV-B radiation, no change is to be expected in the case of ozone depletion. If UV-B radiation is important in causing the effect, there may be an influence of ozone depletion. The action spectrum may also give quantitative information. Ozone depletion results in an increase of UV-B radiation, but the shorter the wavelength, the stronger the increase, even within the UV-B range. A health effect caused predominantly by the shorter UV-B wavelengths is likely to be influenced more than an effect mainly caused by the longer wavelengths in the UV-B range. This is technically accounted for in the "radiation amplification factor" (RAF, Chapter 2).

Another important piece of information is the dose-effect relationship: it shows how the health effect under consideration depends on the dose of UV radiation received (in technical terms: the radiant exposure). This dose-effect relationship is a dominant factor in determining how much the health effect studied will be influenced by increased UV-B radiation. In the case of a steep dose-effect relationship, the influence may be strong. In the case of a shallow dose-effect relationship or a "saturation", where the effect is the same for different doses, there may be hardly any influence or no influence at all, even if the health effect is caused by short-wavelength UV-B radiation.

Studies on the influence of ozone depletion on human health effects have yielded predictions for effects that increase steeply with increasing UV-B irradiance, for other effects that are not or not appreciably influenced, and even for one set of diseases where increased UV-B irradiance leads to a decreased effect. The reasoning leading to these three different predictions will be explained here, with an example for each of the possibilities mentioned. This will make it easier to explore the influence of increased UV-B irradiance in many other health effects later on.

SUNBURN WILL NOT APPRECIABLY BE INFLUENCED BY OZONE DEPLETION

If human skin is exposed to too much sunlight, it may develop a "sunburn": the skin reddens, becomes tender, and in severe cases blistering may occur. Finally the superficial skin layers slough off and the skin looks normal again. The term sunburn suggests that people first have ascribed the effect to the heat of the sun's rays, but investigations have shown that mainly the UV-B radiation in sunlight is responsible (Figure 1). This is precisely the wavelength range that will increase in the case of ozone depletion. It is not surprising that one of the first expectations was that with ozone depletion there would be more sunburn. The same idea is coming up again and again.

On closer examination, that expectation is not well founded. In the first instance, we may gain some insight by looking at what happens in sunnier areas. People living in northwestern Europe develop sunburns now and then, especially while they are on a vacation in a sunnier region, e.g., in the Mediterranean area. People originating in northwestern Europe who settled in a Mediterranean country, however, do not have more sunburn than those who stayed in northwestern Europe. The skin of the emigrant apparently adapts to the higher UV-B exposures in his new environment. This suggests that the same will happen in northwestern Europe when the UV-B irradiance there gradually increases.

The reasoning is basically correct, but it has weak spots. The UV-B irradiance is not the only difference between northern and more southern regions. Temperatures, for instance, are also different. The cold northern winter requires more clothing, and covered skin will not adapt to UV radiation. It is not impossible to devise a situation where a sunburn becomes more likely under increased UV-B irradiance. In general, how-

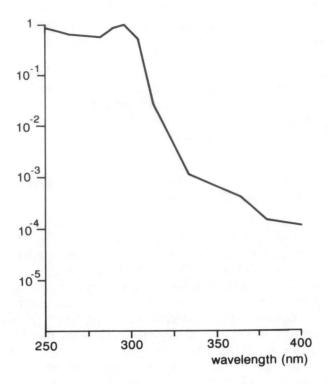

Figure 1   An action spectrum for UV erythema. The curve shows the effectiveness of UV radiation for reddening of caucasian skin as a function
of wavelength. (Based on data from Parrish et al.[1])

ever, the avoidance of sunburn depends largely on behavior. In countries
with dark winters, such as in northwestern Europe, the irradiance of
sunburning UV-B in summer is typically 10 or 20 times higher than in
winter. Bridging of that difference requires a lot of adaptation. The
adaptation of the skin to UV-B radiation is effected mainly by hyper-
plasia, a thickening of the most superficial layer of the skin, the epidermis. In a series of repeated exposures, as given in UV-B phototherapy, adaptation typically proceeds by steps of about 20%.[3] This means
that with the next exposure the UV dose required for eliciting an observable reddening of the skin, the "minimal erythema dose" (MED),
is increased by about 20%. A calculation shows that about 15 of such
exposures are necessary to adapt the skin from its winter condition to
the increased UV-B irradiance in summer. The avoidance of sunburn
depends on going through this process carefully. This becomes not appreciably more difficult at a level of UV-B irradiance increased by, say,
20 or 30%, such as might occur with a gradual ozone depletion. This is
a small change for sunburn, approximately equivalent to one of the 15
steps in the adaptation process. If anything, the adaptation will become

even a bit easier, as ozone depletion will increase the UV-B irradiance in winter more than in summer. The factor to be bridged by adaptation then becomes slightly smaller.

The conclusion is that in general sunburn, although being a typical UV-B effect, will not become more of a problem under a decreased ozone layer. Some knowledge of the adaptation of the skin to UV radiation was helpful, but basically the conclusion could be reached without detailed knowledge of the mechanisms leading to sunburn.

PATIENTS HAVING PHOTODERMATOSES WILL GENERALLY BENEFIT FROM OZONE DEPLETION

Photodermatoses are skin diseases where the skin lesions are caused by light. Such lesions may be itching papules, whealing of the skin, fierce reddening and peeling, etc. The more sensitive patients cannot even stand one minute of outdoor daylight. In several of these diseases the UV-B radiation in sunlight is the predominant causative agent. It is understandable that many patients, and their doctors, expect an aggravation of these diseases under a decreasing ozone layer.

There are reasons to question this expectation. In the first place, if we make a comparison with a sunnier area, closer to the equator, we do not observe an increase of these diseases, either in incidence or severity. On the contrary, photodermatoses are more common and more severe in countries with dark winters. Loss of adaptation of the skin to light appears to be a predominant factor in these diseases. Such loss occurs more readily in an area with dark winters than in an always sunny climate. Many patients with photodermatoses may be treated effectively by regular exposures to low-dose UV-B radiation, especially during winter.[2,3] Depletion of the ozone layer will increase the UV-B irradiance, especially in winter. This will, to some extent, improve the patients' condition, in the same way as the exposures given by their doctors.

SKIN CANCER WILL INCREASE

There are various types of skin cancer. One main class is formed by the cutaneous melanomas, the cancers of the pigment cells. The other main types are basal cell carcinomas and squamous cell carcinomas, cancers of the epithelial cells. These carcinomas of the skin are sometimes, collectively, called "non-melanoma skin cancers". For the present example we will deal with these non-melanoma skin cancers. In white caucasians, the incidence of these cancers ranks high among the various types of cancer; in some populations it is in fact the highest of all. The incidence is lower in more pigmented populations, typically by a factor of 10 or even 100. The mortality rate is low in comparison with that for other types of cancer: approximately 1% in areas with good medical care.

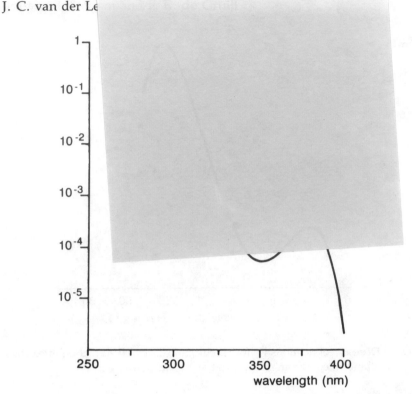

Figure 2 An action spectrum for UV carcinogenesis. The curve shows the effectiveness of UV radiation for the induction of squamous cell carcinoma in hairless albino mice, as a function of wavelength. (From de Gruijl and van der Leun.[6] With permission.)

The non-melanoma skin cancers are clearly correlated to sunlight.[4] They occur mostly in light-skinned people, and then predominantly on skin areas most exposed to sunlight, such as the face. In people of comparable genetic background, the incidences are higher in the sunnier geographical areas. Such observations strongly suggest the involvement of sunlight, but do not point to any particular wavelength range in sunlight. Determination of the wavelengths responsible for carcinogenesis requires experimental observations.

Early experiments showed that white rats exposed to sunlight developed skin cancers, but similar rats exposed to sunlight filtered through window glass did not.[5] As the window glass absorbed mainly UV-B radiation, this result indicated that the carcinogenic effect was to a large extent due to the UV-B radiation in sunlight. This was later confirmed in many experiments, mainly with mice. The present state of knowledge on the wavelength dependence is shown in the action spectrum depicted in Figure 2. It gives the carcinogenic effectiveness of UV radiation as a function of wavelength. This action spectrum was determined in ex-

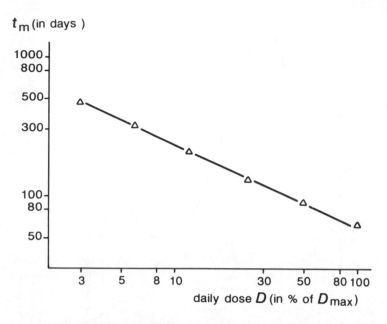

Figure 3   Dose-effect relationship for carcinogenesis by UV radiation in hairless albino mice. (From de Gruijl et al.[7] With permission.)

periments where hairless albino mice SKH-HRI were exposed every day to doses of UV radiation in a realistic range for human exposures. In technical terms, carcinogenic effectiveness was defined as the reciprocal value of the daily dose of radiation at a certain wavelength required for the induction of tumors of 1 mm diameter in 50% of a group of mice in 300 days. The tumors in these mice were predominantly squamous cell carcinomas.

The action spectrum confirms that the carcinogenic effectiveness of UV radiation is maximal in the UV-B range, near the 300-nm wavelength. This makes skin cancer another candidate to increase as a result of depletion of the ozone layer.

The dose-effect relationship for carcinogenesis by UV radiation may be investigated in similar experiments. Groups of mice are given daily exposures to UV radiation; the various groups receive different UV doses. In this way the carcinogenic effect may be examined as a function of the daily dose. Experiments with mice receiving daily UV doses which are realistic for human populations lead to tumors in practically all of the animals. Under such conditions, a suitable measure for the carcinogenic effect is t_m, the time in which 50% of the mice bear tumors. The dose-effect relationship then gives t_m as a function of the daily dose D. Such a relationship is shown in Figure 3. It was determined for tumors of 1 mm diameter in hairless albino mice SKH-HRI.[7] The relationship covers a wide range of daily doses. The highest daily dose was slightly below the dose required for acute reactions in the mouse skin, such as edema or erythema; the lowest was smaller by a factor of 33. This dose range roughly corresponds with the doses received by human populations, with outdoor workers on the high-dose end and people staying indoors and receiving their UV radiation from the lamps used for indoor lighting on the low-dose end.

The relationship depicted in Figure 3 may be expressed mathematically in the form

$$t_m = k_1 D^{-0.6} \tag{1}$$

where   D is the daily dose of ultraviolet radiation
k_1 is a proportionality constant

Equation 1 is a power relationship; it is basically in agreement with relationships for similar tumors over a smaller dose range and for larger tumors in the ears of haired mice.[8,9]

In most human populations only a minority of the people develop skin cancers. In such a situation a more suitable measure for the carcinogenic effect is the incidence, the number of new patients with skin carcinomas per 100,000 of the population per year. A directly related quantity in the mouse experiments is the yield, the average number of tumors per mouse. The yield may be related to powers of the daily dose D and the age of the mice, t:

$$Y = k_2 D^c t^d \tag{2}$$

where   Y is the yield
D is the daily dose uf UV radiation
t is the number of days of exposure (which is approximately equal to the age of the mice
k_2 is a proportionality constant
c and d are numerical exponents

This description of the mouse observations offers the possibility of comparison with human epidemiological data. Human populations are also regularly exposed to ultraviolet radiation, mainly in sunlight. There is, however, more spread in the human data. Human populations have more genetic variability than one strain of hairless albino mice. Moreover, individuals in a human population have different behavior; this includes different exposures to sunlight, even in the same location. Human populations are, however, far greater in size than groups of experimental animals, and this makes it possible to make up meaningful averages. In the Third National Skin Cancer Survey in the United States, the genetic variability was limited by including only the "white" populations in eight cities in the U.S. The incidence was correlated with the UV dose available outdoors.[10]

The relationship between incidence and the ambient UV dose could be described in a way similar to our Equation 2 for mouse data; the values of the exponents c and d were, however, smaller than in the mouse data. Because of the large spread, the human data also allowed different mathematical descriptions.[11] It appears preferable, however, to use an equation which describes experimental as well as epidemiological data.

With the help of the data summarized here, it is possible to make a prediction of the influence of ozone depletion on the incidence of skin cancer in human populations. We make the following assumptions:

1. The action spectrum for carcinogenesis in humans is the same as that in mice.
2. Population exposure behavior and susceptibility do not vary with latitude or UV exposure.
3. The exposure habits in human populations will not change after ozone levels decrease.

From assumption 1 we can calculate a radiation amplification factor of 1.4. This means that a 1% decrease of total-column ozone will cause an increase of the carcinogenically effective dose by 1.4%; this is for the yearly dose available outdoors.[12] The RAF does not vary appreciably with latitude between 60°S and 60°N; for higher latitudes it is smaller.[13] Assumption 3 allows a calculation of the consequences for the incidence of skin cancer. That is the long-term consequence, because skin cancer is a long-term reaction of the skin, typically taking at least several decades. The power relationship in Equation 2 implies that the incidence will not increase in direct proportionality to the doses available. Differentiation of Equation 2 with respect to D gives as a result

$$\frac{\Delta I}{I} = c \frac{\Delta D}{D} \tag{3}$$

which means that the percentage change of the incidence is c times the percentage change of the dose; c is called the "biological amplification factor", abbreviated BAF.[14] This amplification factor originates from the dose-effect relationship. In principle the biological amplification factor is independent of the action spectrum; in the mouse experiments, Equation 2 holds also for practically monochromatic exposures.

Because of a complication, the derivation of the BAF for human populations comes to depend on the action spectrum chosen. For human populations exposed to sunlight, the D in Equation 2 is the carcinogenically effective dose — that is, the dose of sunlight spectrally weighted with the action spectrum for UV carcinogenesis. When the correlation between skin cancer incidence and UV dose was made, the action spectrum for UV carcinogenesis was not yet known.[10] The carcinogenic dose was approximated by "sunburn units" as measured with a Robertson-Berger meter. In this way, the sensitivity curve of this meter was used as an approximation of the action spectrum for photocarcinogenesis. Now that we have an action spectrum for photocarcinogenesis, the correlation of incidence and effective UV dose has to be corrected; this correction depends on the action spectrum. Doing this, the biological amplification factor for squamous cell carcinoma in white populations in the U.S. becomes 2.5, while that for basal cell carcinoma is 1.4.[68]

If the findings about the RAF and BAF are now combined, it can be concluded that a 1% decrease of total-column ozone leads to a 1.4% increase in the carcinogenically effective irradiance. That in turn leads to an increase of the incidence of squamous cell carcinoma by 1.4 × 2.5 = 3.5% and to an increase of the incidence of basal cell carcinoma by 1.4 × 1.4 = 2.0%. These percentage increases of incidence for a 1% decrease in ozone are sometimes referred to as the overall amplification factors (AF). In many cancer registries, squamous cell carcinomas and basal cell carcinomas are lumped together as non-melanoma skin cancers. With a 4:1 ratio of the incidences of basal cell carcinoma and squamous cell carcinoma, the overall amplification factor for non-melanoma skin cancer becomes (4 × 2 + 1 × 3.5)/5 = 2.3. That means a 1% decrease of total ozone will lead to a 2.3% increase of non-melanoma skin cancer.

The expression of these numbers as a consequence of a 1% ozone decrease is given in order to provide the data for calculating the consequences of stronger ozone decreases. It is done in this way because the prediction of ozone depletion has varied markedly with time, reflecting improvements in the atmospheric models. Now that ozone decrease can be measured, the measurements also show variations with place and time. For ozone depletions larger than 1% the fractional increase in the incidence of non-melanoma skin cancer may be calculated with the help of the equation

$$\frac{\Delta I}{I} = \left(1 - \frac{p}{100}\right)^{-2.3} - 1 \qquad (4)$$

where p is the percentage of ozone depletion. Some numerical results are shown in Table 1. For the radiation amplification, this equation gives a fair approximation for ozone decreases smaller than 30%.[69] For the biological amplification the equation is the best representation of present knowledge. For depletions p greater than 30% it is better to derive the radiation amplification from the full atmospheric model computations.

Table 1   Percentage Increase Calculated for the
          Incidence of Basal Cell Carcinomas,
          Squamous Cell Carcinomas and the
          Total of Non-Melanoma Skin Cancers
          as a Result of a Decrease of Total-
          Column Ozone by p Percent

p	BCC	SCC	NMSC
1	2.0	3.5	2.3
5	11	20	13
10	23	45	27
20	56	118	67
30	104	248	127

Note: BCC = basal cell carcinoma; SCC = squa-
      mous cell carcinoma; NMSC = non-mela-
      noma skin cancer.

This section on non-melanoma skin cancer differs from most other sections in that numbers are calculated. Some comments should, however, be made. The numbers are not as accurate as the decimals given suggest. There are uncertainties which are difficult to quantify. The uncertainties are not primarily of a statistical nature. The main uncertainty results from the fact that the numbers were calculated on the basis of only partially available knowledge. Some indication of what this means for the result may be given by the history of these predictions (see Table 2). The changes are due to improving knowledge. Between McDonald's pioneering work and the value given by the UNEP Coordinating Committee on the Ozone Layer in 1980, the available data and the theory were improved.[15,16] The changes since 1980 were primarily caused by the new finding of a contribution of UV-A radiation (315–400 nm) to carcinogenesis in sunlight. The action spectrum is shown in Figure 2. This contribution to the effect is insensitive to ozone change; that leads to lower predictions.[13] No one could have known this before the carcinogenic contribution of UV-A radiation was observed in experimental work. That means that an uncertainty analysis in 1980 would not have included this uncertainty. In a similar way, the numbers given now may still contain such uncertainties.

An example of a piece of knowledge still lacking is an action spectrum for the induction of basal cell carcinoma. The experimental mice used until now do not react to UV-B radiation by forming basal cell carcinomas. For lack of knowledge it was assumed that basal cell carcinomas would follow the same action spectrum as squamous cell carcinomas. Some support for this assumption came from a limited number of clinical accidents where basal cell carcinomas arose in human skin after exposure to large doses of UV-B radiation.[17]

If new information becomes available, it may be used to improve the predictions given. At the same time, the uncertainty in the predictions

Table 2 Estimates of the Overall
Amplification Factor for the
Incidence of Non-Melanoma
Skin Cancer (NMSC)

Year	AF (NMSC)
1971	6
1980	4
1989	3
1991	2.3

Sources: McDonald,[15] UNEP.[16,39,40]

will be reduced. There are also pieces of new information that do not change the quantitative predictions. An example is the discovery that UV-B radiation also influences the immune system (see section on infectious diseases). This work was published while the predictions listed in Table 2 were well under way.[18] The influences of UV-B radiation on the immune system were shown to be of quantitative importance in the process of UV carcinogenesis.[19] Yet, because the method of prediction still had the black-box aspect, these unknown influences had already been taken into account implicitly. The observational data used, from mouse experiments as well as human epidemiology, were all obtained in situations where the influences of UV-B radiation on the immune system were already present. That is the reason why the predictions about the influence of ozone depletion on the incidence of non-melanoma skin cancer did not show any discontinuity at the time of this new discovery. There is little doubt that non-melanoma skin cancer will prove to be an example where the incidence will indeed increase with increasing UV-B irradiance.

CUTANEOUS MELANOMA

Cutaneous melanomas are cancers of the pigment cells in the skin. Their incidence is much lower than that of non-melanoma skin cancers, typically by a factor of 10. The mortality rate is, however, much higher; in countries with good medical care the mortality rate has been brought down to 25%, mainly by early diagnosis.

The question of whether or not the incidence of cutaneous melanoma will increase as a result of ozone depletion is complicated. Much of the knowledge relevant in this connection has been reviewed.[20-22] This knowledge is summarized in the present section.

For a long time the clinical impression was that cutaneous melanomas had nothing to do with sunlight. A primary melanoma could occur in a skin region seldom receiving any sunlight. Moreover, statistics in several countries showed indoor workers to have a higher risk of melanoma than outdoor workers, in contrast to the experience with non-melanoma skin cancer.

Newer investigations have not contradicted these observations, but have added data giving the opposite suggestion, that sunlight does play a role. In several countries the incidence is highest in the sunniest areas. The increase in incidence with decreasing latitude is less steep than for non-melanoma skin cancer, but is significant. People who emigrated from northwestern Europe to sunnier countries, such as Israel or Australia, had a higher risk of melanoma than those who stayed in northwestern Europe.[23,24] This was especially true for those who were at childhood age at the time of emigration. Emigrants' children who were born after the move had a risk comparable to that in their new country.

Confronted with these seemingly conflicting indications, most researchers tend to accept the mounting evidence that sunlight appears to play some role. It is difficult, however, to come to a coherent conception. Interpretation of the observations is usually attempted along the following lines. The fact that outdoor workers have a lower risk than indoor workers is ascribed to adaptation due to the regular exposures. Indoor workers are exposed very little during their work. When they go on a weekend or holiday trip they may suddenly receive a high dose of UV radiation to which the skin is not adapted. The emigration studies suggest that the exposures in childhood are decisive. The combination would suggest sudden exposure to high doses during childhood to be the important factor. Some epidemiological case-control studies have indeed found that melanoma patients reported more sunburn experiences than control persons; such studies draw heavily on the memories of the people questioned and on the absence of bias. An unsatisfactory element in these explanations is that office workers are not at childhood age. The interpretation is not made any easier by the trend analyses. Cutaneous melanoma has for decades shown one of the fastest-rising incidences among all types of cancer. The increase was steepest in the cohorts born between 1875 and 1925.[25] Recent trend analyses show a reversal of this tendency. Younger age groups in the U.S.A. have a markedly lower risk of dying from cutaneous melanoma than their parents' age groups had. The reversal occurred in males for those born after 1950 and in females born after 1930.[26] The overall mortality in populations is still rising, but if the reversal persists, the overall mortality will peak in about 20 years and then go down. As long as only the increases were known, the usual explanation was in terms of increased exposure to sunlight. People had more leisure time than earlier generations and more means to go on vacation to sunny areas; moreover, they covered less of the skin with clothing. This explanation may have had some plausibility, but the reversal is difficult to interpret in these terms. Most of the factors increasing the exposure, particularly the travel to sunnier areas, occurred after 1930–1950. Whatever the explanation, the data obtained in trend analysis make it clear that any prediction of an influence of ozone depletion on cutaneous melanoma will be one made against a baseline that is changing, so far for unknown reasons.

As long as it is not really known that UV-B radiation is involved, a prediction of an influence of ozone depletion on the incidence of cutaneous melanomas cannot even begin to be made. Most of the epidemiological observations suggesting a causative role for sunlight in cutaneous melanoma do not point to any particular wavelength range in sunlight. One possible exception is the role of episodes of severe sunburn; sunburn is mainly an effect of UV-B radiation. But the role of sunburn episodes rests on a shaky base, the memories of people. A role of UV-B radiation in melanoma can also be hypothesized on the assumption of analogy with non-melanoma skin cancer.

Knowledge of the wavelengths involved in the production of cutaneous melanoma has been lacking for so long because it has proved difficult to find an animal model for doing the necessary experiments. Whereas non-melanoma skin cancers have been related to sunlight in cattle, goats, sheep, cats and dogs, no such observations are available for cutaneous melanoma. Experimental induction of non-melanoma skin cancer by UV-B radiation has succeeded in mice, rats, hamsters and guinea pigs, starting from 1928.[27] It was only recently, however, that researchers found two animal models for the induction of melanomas by ultraviolet radiation alone: a marsupial, the South American opossum *Monodelphis domestica*, and a fish, the platyfish-swordtail hybrid.[28,29] Both of these animals were shown to develop melanomas after exposure to UV-B radiation. From the viewpoint of the problem of melanoma in humans, these are more far-removed models than those available for non-melanoma skin cancer. Yet the new models give support to the idea that solar UV-B radiation may play a role in the formation of cutaneous melanoma.

Because the animal models for UV-induced cutaneous melanoma were found only recently, data such as an action spectrum or a dose-effect relationship are not yet available. As was explained in the section on non-melanoma skin cancer, these data are essential for a good quantitative prediction.

In the present situation the only possible way to make any prediction about the influence of ozone depletion on the incidence of cutaneous melanoma is the black-box method. One such prediction was made by the U.S. Environmental Protection Agency on the basis of the correlation of the incidence with geographic latitude in the U.S.A.[30] The latitudinal gradient was significant, but not as steep as for non-melanoma skin cancer. The conclusion was that a 1% decrease of total-column ozone would, other things being equal, lead to a 2% increase of the incidence of cutaneous melanoma. Such a prediction implies the assumption that (a) the latitudinal gradient of the incidence was due to the latitudinal gradient of UV-B radiation and (b) a change in UV-B load by ozone decrease would have a similar effect. Because of the many unknowns involved, the validity of these assumptions appears questionable. Real improvement will have to wait for an action spectrum and, even more important, for a dose-effect relationship.

SNOWBLINDNESS

The eye is also directly accessible to solar UV radiation. It is protected to some extent by its shaded position in the eye socket and under the eyebrow. The shielding is especially effective with a high sun, when there is a great amount of UV-B radiation in sunlight.

One of the adverse effects caused by UV radiation in the eyes is "snowblindness". It occurs typically when the eyes are exposed to UV radiation coming from unusual directions, such as in snow-covered mountains. Snowblindness is very painful, sometimes described as the feeling of having sandpaper in the eyes. It usually starts several hours after exposure and gives the victim a very uncomfortable night; the pain may even last several days, depending on the severity. The eyes usually heal spontaneously.

The medical name for the condition is photokeratitis. It is an acute inflammation of the superficial layers of the eye, the cornea and conjunctiva. The effect is dose related. In severe cases there may be lasting damage. The eye has no adaptation against this effect; the eye even tends to become more sensitive to the next exposure. The action spectrum was determined experimentally in rabbits.[31] Within the solar spectrum, the most effective wavelengths are in the UV-B range. The radiation amplification factor was calculated to have a value of 1.1 or 1.2.[32]

The eyes may be protected by UV-absorbing sunglasses. In spite of this possibility, snowblindness is a frequently occurring problem. There is little doubt that increased solar UV-B irradiance, with unchanged behavior, will lead to increased incidence and severity of snowblindness.

CATARACTS AND BLINDNESS

Cataracts are opacities in the lens of the eye which impair vision. Cataracts occur mainly in elderly people and may ultimately lead to blindness. In countries with good medical facilities, surgery can prevent most cataracts from causing blindness. Even so, the cataract is one of the main causes of blindness in a country such as the U.S. In developing countries, cataracts result in a much higher incidence of blindness. It was estimated in 1985 that cataracts were responsible for 17 million cases of blindness, accounting for more than 50% of the blindness in the world.[33] The problem is increasing with increasing life expectancy, especially in the developing countries.

It is becoming increasingly clear that sunlight, among other factors, plays a role in the formation of cataracts. Ophthalmologists distinguish three main types of cataract: nuclear cataract, which occurs in the nucleus of the lens; cortical cataract, which occurs in the surrounding cortex; and posterior subcapsular cataract, which occurs beneath the posterior capsule of the lens.[34] An association with sunlight was reported for cortical cataracts by Taylor et al.,[34] for posterior subcapsular cataract by Bochow et al.[35] and for nuclear cataract by Mohan et al.[36]

In some of the epidemiological studies, the UV radiation in sunlight is stated to be responsible.[35] It is questionable whether the methods followed in epidemiological studies have the resolving power to reach such a conclusion. Taylor et al., in a study on Maryland "watermen", even singled out UV-B radiation as the causative agent, in distinction from UV-A radiation.[34] All exposures of the watermen were to full sunlight, and the individual exposures had to be reconstructed years afterward. Moreover, the exposures to solar UV-B radiation and UV-A radiation were highly correlated. This again raises the question about resolving power. A predominant role of UV-B radiation is, however, supported by data from animal experiments. Pitts et al. determined an action spectrum for the induction of cataracts in rabbits; the action spectrum peaked in the UV-B range.[31] For this action spectrum, the radiation amplification factor was calculated:[32]

$$RAF_{cataract} = 0.7 \qquad (5)$$

With this experimental result, the interpretation of epidemiological findings in terms of UV-B exposures appears to be supported.

That renders it possible to make a prediction on the influence of ozone depletion on the incidence of cataracts.[38,39] Taylor et al. concluded from their observations in watermen that a doubling of the cumulative UV-B exposure corresponded to a 1.6-fold increase in the incidence of cortical cataracts.[34] If this is interpreted, by analogy with non-melanoma skin cancer, as a dose-effect relationship according to a power law, that would read

$$I = k_3 D^{0.7} \qquad (6)$$

where I is the incidence
       D is the UV-B exposure
       k_3 a proportionality constant

Differentiation of this equation with respect to D shows that

$$\frac{\Delta I}{I} = 0.7 \frac{\Delta D}{D} \tag{7}$$

which implies that the biological amplification factor becomes

$$BAF = 0.7 \tag{8}$$

If it is assumed that the RAF and BAF found (Equations 5 and 8) apply to all forms of cataract, a 10% loss of total-column ozone would lead to a 7% increase in the cataract-effective UV-B doses, and that in turn would lead to a $0.7 \times 7 = 5\%$ increase in the incidence of cataracts. It would take several decades for this increase to come to full effect, because the formation of a cataract is a slow process, typically taking at least several decades.

This prediction may be made more explicit by taking into account the estimate that there are 17 million blind people in the world as a consequence of cataracts.[33] The calculation given shows that if during the past decades there would have been a sustained worldwide reduction of total-column ozone by 10%, the number of blind people would be higher by $0.05 \times 17,000,000 = 850,000$. Taking into account that cataract-induced blindness mostly occurs in the latter decades of life, the number of additional blind people per year would have been roughly 850,000/ $25 = 34,000$. Recognizing the large uncertainties in this reasoning, it appears that it is better to give the estimate as a round number, 30,000 additional blind people per year.

A similar conclusion applies with respect to reductions of stratospheric ozone in the future. Such a conclusion will have to be qualified, however, by the additional condition that all other influences would remain equal. Under that condition, a sustained 10% loss of ozone worldwide would, in the long term, lead to 30,000 additional blind people per year. Important "other influences" include the size of the world population, the life expectancy and the availability of medical care. There are good reasons to expect that these factors will not remain equal, but by themselves will produce a tendency of increasing incidence of cataracts and cataract-related blindness. The increase calculated for ozone depletion will be superimposed on any increase caused by the other factors.

WILL INFECTIOUS DISEASES INCREASE?

There is concern that one consequence of increased UV-B irradiance might be an increase of certain infectious diseases.[39,40] The concern arose from an increasing number of observations showing influences of UV-B radiation on the immune system. This has led to an entire new discipline called photoimmunology, a merger of photobiology and immunology.

Many influences of UV-B radiation on the immune system are suppressive. UV-B exposures can, for instance, suppress the resistance of the mouse immune system against UV-B-induced tumors.[41,42] Furthermore, the induction of hypersensitivity to contact allergens may be suppressed by prior exposure of the skin to UV-B radiation, both in mice and in humans; this may even lead to tolerance of the host to the allergen.[43-45] After sensitization to a contact allergen, the reaction of the skin to a challenge with the allergen may be suppressed by prior UV-B irradiation.[46] These observations raise the question of such suppressions also weakening the body's defense against infections. Might increased UV-B irradiance lead to an increase in the incidence or severity of infectious diseases? The answer is by no means obvious. The suppressions summarized are not signs of a general immunosuppression. They are quite specific. Many immune responses are not affected by UV irradiation. The same UV-B exposures that suppress the resistance of the mouse immune system against UV-B-induced tumors do not change the reaction of the animal to chemically induced tumors.[47] The changes caused by UV-B radiation are mediated through the skin. Infections that have a phase in the skin are, therefore, the most likely ones to be influenced. Malaria is such a candidate, as the mosquito brings the infection into the skin. The possibility that other infections, not contracted through the skin, are influenced cannot be ruled out, however, because the immune changes also lead to systemic effects.

It will be very difficult to make predictions on what effects are to be expected of ozone depletion in this context. In this case, that is not primarily due to the lack of photobiological data. The UV-B doses needed for the various influences on the immune system are fairly well known. One action spectrum is already available, for systemic suppression of contact sensitization in mice.[48] As far as the wavelengths available in sunlight are concerned, this suppression is clearly an effect of UV-B radiation. The radiation amplification factor was calculated to be about 0.9.[32] From these viewpoints, this influence on the immune system could well be increased in the case of increased UV-B irradiance. The real difficulty is in lack of knowledge on how to proceed with the prediction on infectious diseases.

The immune system itself is very complex, with several subsystems helping or suppressing each other. What UV-B irradiation does to some of the subsystems is known for certain experimental conditions, but this knowledge is far from sufficient to predict the overall outcome for the entire system. Moreover, the infectious agents themselves may be influenced by the UV-B radiation. It has long been known that bacteria and viruses may be inactivated by UV-B radiation; it has to be added now that the same type of radiation may activate viruses in the living cell.[49] The question of whether or not infectious diseases will be influenced by increased UV-B irradiation will be very difficult to answer along general lines.

Special investigations have been made in experiments with a few infections. Leishmaniasis is a tropical infectious disease. The parasite is brought into the skin by the sandfly. In experiments, the infection was brought into the skin of UV-B exposed and unexposed animals. In the UV-B exposed animals, the skin showed less initial reaction to the infection, but later the disease spread more fiercely through the body.[50]

In experiments with herpes simplex infections, the UV-B exposed animals were also affected more than the unexposed controls.[51] This appears to correlate with human experience; a latent herpes infection may exacerbate on exposure to sunlight.[52] Activation of the herpes virus may play a role here, besides the influence of UV-B irradiation on the immune system.

Activation of viruses by UV-B radiation was demonstrated in experiments with papilloma viruses and with HIV-1, the human immunodeficiency virus.[53,54] Such observations give, of course, reason for concern.

Activation of viruses by increased UV-B radiation would not lead to an increased rate of infection, but it might result in a more rapid course of the infection or an increased severity of the disease. Any prediction on the practical consequences would, however, carry a large uncertainty, in view of the differences between the conditions in the experiments and in real life.

For the time being it may be best to look for direct indications of any influences of UV-B radiation on infectious diseases in humans. One method to do this is, again, to look at what happens with respect to infectious diseases at the various geographical latitudes. It is obvious that infectious diseases are a much greater problem in tropical and subtropical areas than at higher latitudes. This roughly correlates with the UV-B irradiances at these latitudes. There are, however, many more differences — for instance, temperature, humidity, environmental conditions for vectors such as insects, living conditions for humans, including hygienic conditions, preventive medicine and medical care. It would not be justified to single out UV-B irradiance from such a list of possible causes, especially not if we also take into consideration areas like Australia and the southern U.S. In those areas infectious diseases are no great problem, in spite of a comparatively high UV-B irradiance. Infectious diseases form a problem field which is apparently too complex to be handled by a simple black box method.

Clinical evidence may also be considered. Dermatology has a long-standing interest in the influence of UV-B radiation on skin diseases. Apart from the photodermatoses, where the skin lesions are caused by sunlight, there are diseases that are aggravated by sun exposure, e.g., lupus erythematosus, an autoimmune disease.[55] There are, however, also skin diseases where sunlight improves the condition of the skin. Psoriasis, for example, is a widespread noninfectious skin disease; exposures to UV-B radiation form an effective medical treatment.[56]

The fact that UV radiation may act in both ways, aggravating or improving the condition of the skin, also applies to infectious skin diseases. Almost 100 years ago, Finsen dealt with the influence of light on two skin infections.[57] He found that patients having smallpox reacted unfavorably to sunlight. Exposure to sunlight aggravated the disease. The lesions became more virulent and left deeper scars; the patients had higher fever and a greater probability of dying. The practical solution was that patients with smallpox were kept out of the light; even the indoor daylight was excluded. This observation was later extended to vaccinia lesions; van't Riet and van der Leun found that scarring by cowpox vaccination could be prevented by keeping the lesions covered with a black cloth during the active stage.[58] A seemingly opposite observation was made by Finsen for another serious infectious disease, lupus vulgaris (skin tuberculosis).[57] He found that the lesions could be healed by repeated local exposures to UV radiation. It was the first effective treatment for this disfiguring disease, and Finsen was awarded the Nobel prize (1903). Later, heliotherapy was given to many patients with tuberculosis, not only of the skin, but also of the lungs. In several cases, the exposures to sunlight severely aggravated the condition of the lungs.[59]

Many of these early observations were made with regard to full sunlight, and it cannot be established afterwards what wavelength range was responsible. At least in the case of skin tuberculosis it was clearly UV radiation that was effective. The observations show that infectious diseases of the skin may react to light in opposite ways, and that even with the same infectious agent the skin and the lungs could show opposite reactions.

The question of what depletion of the ozone layer will do to infectious diseases is still open. The pieces of knowledge available give good reasons for concern, but more investigations are clearly needed. One part of the answer is likely to be that the consequences will be different for different infectious diseases.

VACCINATION PROGRAMS

Increased UV-B irradiance might also have consequences for the effectiveness of vaccination programs. Even less can be stated here with certainty than was concluded with regard to the direct influences on infectious diseases. There are, however, observations showing that immunization through UV-treated skin may render the individual more susceptible to the administered antigen, rather than less susceptible.[50] The concern is that increased UV-B irradiance might interfere with the effectiveness of vaccinations, which especially in poor countries are the main way of controlling infectious disease. More research in this area is urgently needed.

VITAMIN D$_3$

UV-B irradiation leads to the formation of vitamin D$_3$ in the skin. This vitamin is necessary for the formation and maintenance of our bone system and for several other health effects. The vitamin may also be supplied via the diet, but the formation in the skin by solar UV-B radiation usually forms an important part of the supply.

The metabolism of vitamin D and its medical consequences were investigated extensively in recent years.[60] Two results of these studies are of direct relevance with respect to the consequences of depletion of the ozone layer:

1. The formation of vitamin D$_3$ in the skin by UV-B radiation is self-limiting. This implies that exposure of the skin to too much UV-B radiation does not lead to the formation of too much vitamin D$_3$.
2. Deficiencies of vitamin D$_3$ occur in several groups of the population, such as dark-skinned children living in northern cities and elderly people who stay indoors practically all of the time.

These results make it relatively easy to predict the consequences of ozone depletion. Because the formation of vitamin D$_3$ in the skin by UV-B radiation is self-limiting, it is not to be expected that increased UV-B irradiance will lead to intoxication by vitamin D$_3$. Some of the deficiencies may be relieved by increased UV-B irradiance. The formation of vitamin D$_3$ in the skin of darkly pigmented children in northern cities may be expected to increase. Such an improvement is not to be expected for people whose shortage of vitamin D$_3$ is due to being indoors all the time. Solar UV-B radiation hardly comes indoors, due to the strong absorption of this type of radiation by window glass. This situation will not change appreciably in case of ozone depletion.

In short, depletion of the ozone layer is not expected to lead to intoxication by too much vitamin D$_3$, and some of the deficiencies may be relieved.

ANIMAL HEALTH

Much of what was set out in this chapter on the consequences of ozone depletion for human health applies in principle also to the health of animals. In fact, several conclusions on human health effects were partly based on observations in experimental animals, e.g., the action spectra for UV-induced skin cancer and cataract. Many animals have skins and eyes just as vulnerable to ultraviolet radiation as the human equivalents. This is not limited to mammals; even trout can develop sunburn.

There are, of course, also differences. Many animals have their skins protected by dense fur. Nocturnal animals will not be bothered too much by what happens to the sunlight at daytime. The immune systems of humans and animals are not identical.

The problem of possible consequences of ozone depletion for animal health is much broader than that for human health because of the numerous different species. Yet, there are even fewer data available for animals. Very little appears to be known about UV effects in wild animals. Most information relates to experimental animals; it is good to keep in mind that these animals are highly selected, usually for investigating problems of human health. Some more independent information is available on domestic animals from veterinary medicine.

A first general impression from comparison of animal and human data is that the effects are rather similar; this holds at least for the effects that are recognized. Animals of several species develop skin cancer in sparsely haired, light-colored parts of the skin. This applies to cows, goats, sheep, cats and dogs.[61-63] The cancers found were mainly squamous cell carcinomas. The observations strongly suggest sunlight as the cause; as these animals received full-spectrum sunlight, the wavelengths responsible cannot be specified. Similar tumors can, however, be induced experimentally in mice, rats and hamsters; in such experiments, the most effective wavelengths are in the UV-B range.[64]

Cancers of the eye also occur in many animal species, including horses, sheep, swine, cats and dogs, and are particularly frequent in cattle.[65] In several experiments designed to investigate the induction of skin cancer by ultraviolet radiation, a fraction of the animals also developed eye cancers. This occurred in mice, rats and hamsters and in the (nocturnal) South American opossum *Monodelphis domestica*.[28,66,67] In all of these experiments the irradiation had a strong UV-B component. Photokeratitis (snow blindness) and cataract were induced experimentally in rabbits; the action spectra showed a high effectiveness of UV-B radiation.[31]

In the species where these effects occur, an increased UV-B irradiance may be expected to lead to increased incidence of skin cancer, cancer of the eye, photokeratitis and cataract. It is hard to imagine that such effects would not also occur in some wild animals. The problems may, of course, be strongly modified by circumstances. A mole, living mainly underground, will have little problems with increased solar UV-B irradiance. A short lifespan, as may be usual for many animals in the wild, may also markedly influence the consequences of increased UV-B irradiance; it may limit the possibilities for chronic damage to develop. A short life is very likely to prevent a cataract from proceeding to blindness. But that does not necessarily mean that the consequence is less serious. A gazelle grazing in the steppe is exposed to sunlight practically all day. All that time it has to be on the watch for approaching predators. When solar UV-B radiation begins to impair its vision, its chances to escape will decrease. For this animal, the slight UV-B damage may be the very reason why its life is so short. If so, increasing UV-B radiation may make it even shorter.

QUANTITATIVE INVESTIGATIONS

In the present chapter an attempt was made to estimate the health effects of ozone depletion in quantitative terms as much as possible. In the area of animal health that was not possible at all, and with respect to human health it was possible only for two effects, skin cancer and cataract. For some potentially important effects, such as a possible influence on infectious diseases, even the direction is not clear. In our assessment, the state of knowledge on effects in areas other than health is certainly not better.

Fragmentary as the knowledge available may be, it has been sufficient in a first decisive phase: it has convinced the major nations that action is necessary to protect the ozone layer. The present knowledge is unlikely to be sufficient in the next phase. Even with the most drastic protective action, the ozone layer will be damaged for the century to come. Policymakers will have to know the effects to be expected and the possibilities for developing response strategies. Questions likely to come up are: What are the most important effects, and where should the response effort go? That takes more than expressions of concern. It requires quantitative knowledge, if possible for all potentially important effects. The same type of knowledge will be needed when the cost of further protective actions will have to be weighed against the damage to be prevented.

This means that many scientific investigations have to be developed well beyond the present orienting stage. Key elements needed for quantitative estimations are the action spectra and dose-effect relationships for all effects of concern. This is a great challenge to photobiologists.

ACKNOWLEDGMENTS

The authors wish to thank Sharon A. Miller for many improvements in the manuscript. Much of our work reflected in this chapter was supported by the Dutch Ministry of Housing, Physical Planning and the Environment, and by the Royal Dutch Academy of Sciences.

REFERENCES

1. Parrish, J. A., K. R. Jaenicke, and R. R. Anderson. "Erythema and Me-lanogenesis Action Spectra of Normal Human Skin," *Photochem. Photobiol.* 36:187–191 (1982).
2. Van Weelden, H. and J. C. van der Leun. "Lichtinduzierte Lichttoleranz bei Photodermatosen; ein Fortschrittsbericht," *Z. Hautkr.* 58:57–59 (1983).
3. Van der Leun, J. C., and H. van Weelden. "UVB Phototherapy: Principles, Radiation Sources, Regimens," *Curr. Probl. Dermatol.* 15:39–51 (1986).
4. Urbach, F. "Geographic Pathology of Skin Cancer," in *The Biologic Effects of Ultraviolet Radiation, with Emphasis on the Skin*, F. Urbach, Ed. (Oxford: Pergamon Press, 1969), pp. 635–650.
5. Roffo, A. H. "Ueber die physikalisch-chemische Aetiologie der Krebskrank-heit," *Strahlentherapie* 66:328–350 (1939).
6. De Gruijl, F. R., and J. C. van der Leun. "Action Spectra for Carcinogen-esis," in *The Biologic Effects of UVA Radiation*, F. Urbach, Ed. (Overland Park, Kansas, Valdenmar Publ., 1992), pp. 91–97.
7. De Gruijl, F. R., J. B. van der Meer, and J. C. van der Leun. "Dose-Time Dependency of Tumor Formation by Chronic UV Exposure," *Photochem. Photobiol.* 37:53–62 (1983).
8. Forbes, P. D., H. F. Blum, and R. E. Davies. "Photocarcinogenesis in Hairless Mice: Dose-Response and the Influence of Dose Delivery," *Pho-tochem. Photobiol.* 34:361–365 (1981).
9. Blum, H. F. *Carcinogenesis by Ultraviolet Light* (Princeton, N. J.: Princeton University Press, 1959).
10. Scotto, J., T. R. Fears, and F. Fraumeni. "Incidence of Nonmelanoma Skin Cancer in the United States," Publ. no. NIH 82-2433, U.S. Department of Health and Human Services (1981).
11. Fears, T. R. and J. Scotto. "Estimating Increases in Skin Cancer Morbidity due to Increases in Ultraviolet Radiation Exposure," *Cancer Invest.* 1:119–126 (1983).
12. Longstreth, J. D., F. R. de Gruijl, Y. Takizawa, and J. C. van der Leun. "Human Health," in *Environmental Effects of Ozone Depletion: 1991 Update*, J. C. van der Leun and M. Tevini, Eds. (Nairobi: United Nations Envi-ronment Programme, 1991), pp. 15–24.
13. Kelfkens, G., F. R. de Gruijl, and J. C. van der Leun. "Ozone Depletion and Increase in Annual Carcinogenic Ultraviolet Dose," *Photochem. Pho-tobiol.* 52:819–823 (1990).
14. Van der Leun, J. C. and F. Daniels, Jr. "Biologic Effects of Stratospheric Ozone Decrease: A Critical Review of Assessments," in *Impacts of Climatic Change on the Biosphere*, CIAP Monograph 5, Part 1 — Ultraviolet Radiation Effects, D. S. Nachtwey, Ed. (U.S. Dept. of Transportation, Climatic Impact Assessment Program, Washington, D.C., 1975), pp. 7–107 to 7–124.
15. McDonald, J. E. "Relationship of Skin Cancer Incidence to Thickness of Ozone Layer," statement submitted to hearings before the House Sub-committee on Transportation Appropriations, March 2, 1971. *Congr. Rec.* 117(39):3493 (1971).
16. United Nations Environment Programme, Co-ordinating Committee on the Ozone Layer, Report of the Fourth Session, Bilthoven (1980).

17. Schuppenhausen, E. and H. Ippen. "Lichtschaden durch Lichtabusus," in *Photodermatosen und Porphyrien*, H. Ippen and G. Goerz, Eds. (Düsseldorf: Publ. H. Ippen, 1974), pp. 8–9.
18. Kripke, M. L. and M. S. Fisher. "Immunologic Parameters of Ultraviolet Carcinogenesis," *J. Natl. Cancer Inst.* 57:211–215 (1976).
19. De Gruijl, F. R. and J. C. van der Leun. "Systemic Influence of Preirradiation of a Limited Skin Area on UV-Tumorigenesis," *Photochem. Photobiol.* 35:379–383 (1982).
20. Lee, J. A. H. "Melanoma and Exposure to Sunlight," *Epidemiol. Rev.* 4:110–136 (1982).
21. Elwood, J. M., R. P. Gallagher, G. B. Hill, and J. C. G. Pearson. "Cutaneous Melanoma in Relation to Intermittent and Constant Sun Exposure — The Western Canada Melanoma Study," *Int. J. Cancer* 35:427–433 (1985).
22. De Gruijl, F. R. "Ozone Change and Melanoma," in *Atmospheric Ozone Research and its Policy Implications*, T. Schneider et al., Eds. (Amsterdam: Elsevier Science Publishers, 1989), pp. 813–821.
23. Katz, L., S. Ben-Tuvia, and R. Steinitz. "Malignant Melanoma of the Skin in Israel: Effect of Migration," in *Trends in Cancer Incidence: Causes and Practical Implications*, K. Magnus, Ed. (New York: Hemisphere Publishers, 1982), pp. 419–426.
24. Holman, C. D. J. and B. K. Armstrong. "Cutaneous Malignant Melanoma and Indicators of Total Accumulated Exposure to the Sun: An Analysis Separating Histogenic Types," *J. Natl. Cancer Inst.* 73:75–82 (1984).
25. Stevens, R. G. and S. H. Moolgavkar. "Malignant Melanoma: Dependence of Site-Specific Risk on Age," *Am. J. Epidemiol.* 119:890–895 (1984).
26. Scotto, J., H. Pitcher, and J. A. H. Lee. "Indications of Future Decreasing Trends in Skin-Melanoma Mortality Among Whites in the United States," *Int. J. Cancer* 49:490–497 (1991).
27. Findlay, G. M. "Ultraviolet Light and Skin Cancer," *Lancet* 2:1070–1073 (1928).
28. Ley, R. D., L. A. Applegate, R. S. Padilla, and T. D. Stuart. "Ultraviolet Radiation-Induced Malignant Melanoma," *Photochem. Photobiol.* 50:1–5 (1989).
29. Setlow, R. B., A. D. Woodhead, and E. Grist. "Animal Model for Ultraviolet Radiation-Induced Melanoma: Platyfish-Swordtail Hybrid," *Proc. Natl. Acad. Sci. U.S.A.* 86:8922–8926 (1989).
30. Longstreth, J. D., Ed. *Ultraviolet Radiation and Melanoma — With a Special Focus on Assessing the Risks of Ozone Depletion, Vol. IV* (Washington, D.C.: U.S. Environmental Protection Agency, 1987).
31. Pitts, D. G., A. P. Cullen, and P. D. Hacker. "Ocular Effects of Ultraviolet Radiation from 295 to 365 nm," *Invest. Ophthalmol. Vis. Sci.* 16:932–939 (1977).
32. Madronich, S., L. O. Björn, M. Ilyas, and M. M. Caldwell. "Changes in Biologically Effective Ultraviolet Radiation Reaching the Earth's Surface," in *Environmental Effects of Ozone Depletion: 1991 Update*, J. C. van der Leun and M. Tevini, Eds. (Nairobi: United Nations Environment Programme, 1991), pp. 1–13.

33. Maitchouk, I. F. "Trachoma and Cataract: Two WHO Targets," *Int. Nurs. Rev.* 32:23–25 (1985).

34. Taylor, H. R., S. K. West, F. S. Rosenthal, B. Munoz, H. S. Newland, H. Abbey, and E. A. Emmett. "Effect of Ultraviolet Radiation on Cataract Formation," *New England J. Med.* 319:1429–1433 (1988).

35. Bochow, T. W., S. K. West, A. Azar, B. Munoz, A. Sommes, and H. R. Taylor. "Ultraviolet Light Exposure and the Risk of Posterior Subcapsular Cataract," *Arch. Ophthalmol.* 107:369–372 (1989).

36. Mohan, M., R D. Sperduto, S. K. Angra, R. C. Milton, R. L. Mathur, B. A. Underwood, N. Jaffery, C. B. Pandya, V. K. Chhabra, R. B. Vajpayee, V. K. Kalra, and Y. R. Sharma, The India-U.S. case-control study group. "India-U.S. Case-Control Study of Age Related Cataracts," *Arch. Ophthalmol.* 107:670–676 (1991).

37. Hollows, F. and D. Moran. "Cataract-The Ultraviolet Risk Factor," *Lancet* 2:1249–1250 (1981).

38. U.S. EPA, *Assessing the Risks of Trace Gases that Can Modify the Stratosphere, Vol. III* (Washington, D.C.: U.S. Environmental Protection Agency, 1987).

39. Van der Leun, J. C. and M. Tevini, Eds. *Environmental Effects Panel Report: Pursuant to Article 6 of the Montreal Protocol on Substances that Deplete the Ozone Layer* (Nairobi: United Nations Environment Programme, 1989).

40. Van der Leun, J. C. and M. Tevini, Eds. *Environmental Effects of Ozone Depletion: 1991 Update. Panel Report Pursuant to Article 6 of the Montreal Protocol on Substances that Deplete the Ozone Layer* (Nairobi: United Nations Environment Programme, 1991).

41. Fisher, M. S. and M. L. Kripke. "Systemic Alteration Induced in Mice by Ultraviolet Light Irradiation and its Relationship to Ultraviolet Carcinogenesis," *Proc. Natl. Acad. Sci. U.S.A.* 74:1688–1692 (1977).

42. Daynes, R. A., C. W. Spellman, J. G. Woodward, and D. A. Stewart. "Studies into the Transplantation Biology of Ultraviolet-Induced Tumors," *Transplantation* 23:343–348 (1977).

43. Kripke, M. L. "Immunological Unresponsiveness Induced by Ultraviolet Radiation," *Immunol. Rev.* 80:87–102 (1984).

44. Yoshikawa, T., V. Rae, W. Bruins-Slot, J. W. van den Berg, J. R. Taylor, and J. W. Streilein. "Susceptibility to Effects of UV-B Radiation on Induction of Contact Hypersensitivity as a Risk Factor for Skin Cancer in Humans," *J. Invest. Dermatol.* 95:530–536 (1990).

45. Toews, G. B., P. R. Bergstresser, and J. W. Streilein. "Epidermal Langerhans Cell Density Determines Whether Contact Hypersensitivity or Unresponsiveness Follows Skin Painting with DNFB," *J. Immunol.* 124:445–453 (1980).

46. Noonan, F. P., E. C. DeFabo, and M. L. Kripke. "Suppression of Contact Hypersensitivity by UV Radiation and its Relationship to UV-Induced Suppression of Tumor Immunity," *Photochem. Photobiol.* 34:683–689 (1981).

47. Kripke, M. L., R. M. Thorn, P. H. Lill, C. I. Civin, M. S. Fisher, and N. H. Pazmino. "Further Characterization of Immunologic Unresponsiveness Induced in Mice by UV Radiation: Growth and Induction of Non-UV Induced Tumors in UV-Irradiated Mice," *Transplantation* 28:212–217 (1979).

48. DeFabo, E. C. and F. P. Noonan. "Mechanism of Immune Suppression by Ultraviolet Irradiation In Vivo. I. Evidence for the Existence of a Unique Photoreceptor in Skin and Its Role in Photoimmunology," *J. Exp. Med.* 157:84–98 (1983).

49. Zmudzka, B. Z. and J. Z. Beer. "Yearly Review: Activation of Human Immunodeficiency Virus by Ultraviolet Radiation," *Photochem. Photobiol.* 52:1153–1162 (1990).

50. Giannini, M. S. H. and E. C. DeFabo. "Abrogation of Skin Lesions in Cutaneous Leishmaniasis," in *Leishmaniasis: The First Centenary (1885–1985) — New Strategies for Control,* D. T. Hart, Ed. (London: Plenum Press, 1987).

51. Spruance, S. L. "Pathogenesis of Herpes Simplex Labialis: Experimental Induction of Lesions with UV Light," *J. Clin. Microbiol.* 22:366–368 (1985).

52. Perna, J. J., J. E. Mannix, J. E. Rooney, A. L. Notkins, and S. E. Straus. "Reactivation of Latent Herpes Simplex Virus Infection by Ultraviolet Radiation: A Human Model," *J. Am. Acad. Dermatol.* 17:197–212 (1987).

53. Schmitt, J., J. R. Schlehofer, K. Mergener, L. Gissmann, and H. zur Hausen. "Amplification of Bovine Papillomarvirus DNA by N-Methyl-N'-nitro-N-nitrosoguanidine, Ultraviolet Irradiation, or Infection with Herpes Simplex Virus," *Virology,* 172:73–81 (1989).

54. Valerie, K., A. Delers, C. Bruck, C. Thiriart, H. Rosenberg, C. Debouck, and M. Rosenberg. "Activation of Human Immunodeficiency Virus Type 1 by DNA Damage in Human Cells, *Nature* 333:78–81 (1988).

55. Cripps, D. J. and J. Rankin. "Action Spectra of Lupus Erythematosus and Experimental Immunofluorescence," *Arch. Dermatol.* 107:563–567 (1973).

56. Van Weelden, H., H. Baart de la Faille, E. Young, and J. C. van der Leun. "A New Development in UVB Phototherapy of Psoriasis," *Brit. J. Dermatol.* 119:11–19 (1988).

57. Finsen, N. R. *Ueber die Bedeutung der chemischen Strahlen des Lichtes für Medicin und Biologie* (Leipzig: Vogel, 1899).

58. van der Leun, J. C. "Ultraviolet Erythema: a Study on Diffusion Processes in Human Skin," Ph.D. Thesis, University of Utrecht, Utrecht, The Netherlands, (1966), statement 5.

59. Sorgo, J. "Die Lichtbehandlung der Lungentuberkulose," in *Handbuch der Lichttherapie,* W. Hausmann and R. Volk, Eds. (Wien: Julius Springer, 1927), pp. 284–301.

60. Holick, M. F. "Photosynthesis of Vitamin D in the Skin: Effect of Environment and Lifestyle Variables," *Fed. Proc.* 46:1876–1882 (1987).

61. Emmett, E. A. "Ultraviolet Radiation as a Cause of Skin Tumors," *Crit. Rev. Toxicol.* 2:211–255 (1973).

62. Dorn, C. R., D. O. N. Taylor, and R. Schneider. "Sunlight Exposure and Risk of Developing Cutaneous and Oral Squamous Cell Carcinomas in White Cats," *J. Natl. Cancer Inst.* 46:1073–1078 (1971).

63. Nikula, K. J., S. A. Benjamin, G. M. Angleton, W. J. Saunders, and A. C. Lee. "Ultraviolet Radiation, Solar Dermatosis, and Cutaneous Neoplasia in Beagle Dogs," *Radiat. Res.* 129:11–18 (1992).

64. Stenbäck, F. "Species-Specific Neoplastic Progression by Ultraviolet Light," *Oncology* 31:209–225 (1975).

65. Russell, W. O., E. S. Wynne, G. S. Loquvam, and D. A. Mehl. "Studies on Bovine Ocular Squamous Carcinoma ("Cancer Eye"). I. Pathological Anatomy and Historical Review," *Cancer* 9:1–52 (1956).

66. Lippincott, S. W. and H. F. Blum. "Neoplasms and Other Lesions of the Eye Induced by Ultraviolet Radiation in Strain A Mice," *J. Natl. Cancer Inst.* 3:545–554 (1943).

67. Freeman, R. G. and J. M. Knox. "Ultraviolet-Induced Corneal Tumors in Different Species and Strains of Animals," *J. Invest. Dermatol.* 43:431–436 (1964).

68. De Gruijl, F. R. and J. C. van der Leun. "Influence of Ozone Depletion on the Incidence of Skin Cancer: Quantitative Prediction," in *Environmental UV Photobiology,* L. O. Björn, J. Moan, and A. R. Young, Eds. (Overland Park, Kansas, Valdenmar Publ., 1993), in press.

69. Madronich, S. Personal communication.

5

Effects of Enhanced UV-B Radiation on Terrestrial Plants

Manfred Tevini

SUMMARY

The effects of increased levels of UV-B radiation on plant growth and physiology have been investigated by subjecting plants to artificial UV-B radiation in greenhouses, growth chambers, or in the field. Since these artificial light sources differ from the solar spectrum and as photobiological processes are wavelength dependent, weighting functions had to be developed. They are based on action spectra for specific responses and serve to assess the biological effectiveness of the light sources and of simulated ozone depletion. In addition, ozone cuvettes have been used to filter the solar radiation in order to simulate conditions of reduced UV-B for comparative reasons.

Among species and cultivars the degree of the effectiveness of UV-B varies. Sensitive plants often exhibit a reduction in height, dry weight, leaf area, photosynthetic activity, and flowering. These growth responses might also influence competitive interactions. Photosynthetic enzymes, metabolic pathways, photosynthetic pigments, and stomatal function might be affected directly or indirectly by UV-B radiation; as a result, photosynthetic activity decreases.

UV-B-absorbing compounds located in the outer tissue layer of plant leaves or shoots presumably protect sensitive targets and might accu-

0-87371-911-5/93/$0.00 + $.50
© 1993 by Lewis Publishers

mulate in response to UV-B irradiation. It has been shown that UV-B radiation induces some key enzymes in the biosynthetic pathways.

A 6-year study on the effects of UV-B radiation on soybean showed yield reductions under a simulated ozone depletion of 25%. Through microclimate conditions these effects can be altered further, and it has been demonstrated that the sensitivity of plants to UV-B radiation increases with low levels of white light. A decrease of sensitivity could be observed in plants subjected to water stress or mineral deficiency. Possible changes of our environment and present stress conditions, both in interaction with UV-B effects, are mechanisms which need to be understood. Furthermore, it is anticipated that due to the greenhouse effect temperature will increase. Experiments on sunflower, maize, rye, and oat have shown that some plant species can compensate for the growth reductions induced by UV-B under conditions of increased temperature. It is also expected that CO_2 levels might double by the middle of the 21st century. These levels of CO_2 would substantially alter growth and photosynthesis of many plant species as investigations have demonstrated. In a factorial greenhouse experiment different CO_2 concentrations and different levels of UV-B radiation were combined, and results indicated that wheat, rice, and soybean responded with an increase in biomass to elevated CO_2. However, concurrent elevations of UV-B demonstrated that CO_2-induced increases in photosynthesis and yield are modified by UV-B. Only in soybean did the growth response not seem to be altered after UV-B levels had been increased as well.

INTRODUCTION

Terrestrial plants as sessile organisms have to cope with UV-B radiation, unlike aquatic organisms which are capable of movement. The protection against UV-B radiation during the plant history (evolution) was not perfect through the plant kingdom, resulting in UV-B sensitive, tolerant, and resistant plant species. Damaging effects of enhanced UV-B radiation equivalent to relatively high ozone depletion rates have been demonstrated by many research groups. Typically, reductions in leaf area, stem length, fresh and dry weight, and photosynthetic activity were found in UV-B-sensitive plant species and cultivars. Additionally, alterations of leaf surface structure, epicuticular waxes, UV-absorbing pigments, and stomatal responses have been reported.

There are previous comprehensive publications for further information.[1-13] The United Nations Environmental Program (UNEP) reports from 1989 and 1991 summarize the most important results in respect to ozone depletion and also contributed to the following overview.[14,15]

Table 1 Stem Length and Leaf Area in Cucumber Seedlings (*Cucumis sativus* cv. Delikatess Robusta) after 18 Days Growth under Artificial Light Using Selected Cutoff Filters[31]

Filters Used	Daily Dose (J m^{-2})	Simulated Location[a]	Stem Length (cm)	Leaf Area (cm^2)
WG 295/2 mm	14,087	0°N[1]	4.41	5.28
WG 305/2 mm	9,532	30°N[2]	5.74	6.27
WG 305/3 mm	5,231	49°N[3]	6.74	7.45
WG 305/4 mm	3,695	69°N[4]	6.97	9.04
WG 305/5 mm	2,275	65°N[5]	7.66	9.06
WG 320/2 mm	1,016	70°N[6]	7.28	9.59

Note: Artificial light via 6000 W xenon lamp + two UV-B fluorescent tubes. Daily doses weighted according to the generalized plant weighting function normalized at 300 nm.[1] Locations calculated for day 127 of the year, according to equivalent daily doses.[118]

[a] Location (ozone layer thickness): [1]220 D, [2]280 D, [3]320 D, [4]300 D, [5]300 D, [6]>300 D.

ARTIFICIAL AND SOLAR RADIATION

The effects of UV-B radiation were mainly investigated by using artificial light sources, either supplementing white light (PAR = photosynthetic active radiation between 400 and 700 nm) in growth chambers or solar radiation in greenhouses or in the field. It has been demonstrated that UV-B damage is more pronounced under low levels of white light (<200 μmol m^{-2} s^{-1} between 400 and 700 nm).[16-18] Photorepair mechanisms and amelioration of UV-B damage could be induced by high levels of PAR as well as UV-A/blue light.[19,20] Xenon lamps up to 6000 W can provide more than 1000 μmol m^{-2} s^{-1} and, together with stable and selective cutoff filters of the Schott WG series, simulate the best approximation of natural radiation conditions (Table 1).

Cellulose acetate films have been used to shape the spectral distribution of radiation emitted by low-pressure fluorescent sunlamps, eliminating harmful UV-C radiation in large-scale greenhouse or field experiments. These fluorescent sunlamps were mainly Westinghouse FS-40 and Philips TL 40/12. Plants can be subjected to this artificial radiation in the field, where a constant proportion of UV-B radiation is either added in a modulated fashion after the ambient solar input is monitored or is added in fixed amounts over a specific period of time.[21,22] In greenhouses Mylar plastic films are used as a cover for the lamps; as a result, the UV-B component of the artificial light sources is absorbed entirely. Plants grown under these conditions are regarded as controls. However, this experimental design leaves the control plants without any UV-B radiation at all, an unrealistic situation for plants grown outdoors under a natural solar spectrum. Recently, a supplemental ultraviolet-B radiation system with UV-B 313 (Q-panel) was described for open-top field chambers.[23]

Since the spectral energy distributions differ between solar and artificial UV-B radiation sources, this radiation is weighted according to its biological effectiveness. Commonly used weighting functions are the generalized plant action spectrum and/or the DNA action spectrum.[1,24] The problems with this and other weighting functions were described by Caldwell et al.[25]

One could do without weighting functions if radiation sources were used that perfectly simulate various ozone depletion scenarios, except one needs to compare radiations of different geographical locations. Tevini et al. demonstrated a technique which eliminated the requirement of weighting functions.[26] UV-transmissable Plexiglas cuvettes were used to cover two identical growth chambers in an experiment carried out at a southern latitude (Portugal) with naturally high ambient levels of solar UV-B radiation. As ozone passed through the cuvette on top, the ambient UV-B-radiation was reduced, simulating the reduced UV-B radiation found in more northern latitudes. Plants grown under these conditions were considered as controls. The second cuvette on top only contained normal air, and plants within this growth chamber received ambient UV-B radiation which was higher compared to the control. The advantage of this technique lies in the adaptability of simulating natural solar UV-B radiation of many latitudes and altitudes.

Another modulation system continuously monitors solar UV-B fluences, provides a constant, proportional UV-B supplement, and is controlled by a true condition closed-loop feedback system, where the same sensor is used for both control and feedback.[27] This gives the best spectral match with regard to cloud cover, temperature, and solar angle.

EFFECTS ON PLANT GROWTH; COMPETITION; AND FLOWERING

Plant Growth

It has been shown that plant height and leaf area are reduced in UV-B-sensitive plants to various degrees.[22,28-30] For leaf area and hypocotyl length of cucumbers a fluence response relationship could be demonstrated when plants were grown in growth chambers under enhanced artificial UV-B radiation (Table 1).[31] A decrease of leaf area and stem length can also be induced solely by natural UV-B radiation with increasing daily fluence when the ozone filter technique is used. Where 12% O_3 depletion was simulated (equivalent to a 25% increase of solar UV-B radiation), continuous reductions of growth rates could be observed throughout the development up to 4 weeks of sunflower and

corn plants receiving higher levels of natural UV-B.[32] Growth reductions
following UV-B radiation are associated with alterations in cell division
and/or cell elongation. The existence of interaction with the growth regulator indole-3-acetic acid (IAA) has been demonstrated in sunflower
seedlings.[33]

The UV-dependent destruction of IAA and the formation of growth-
inhibiting IAA photoproducts results in reduced hypocotyl growth of
sunflower seedlings. Furthermore, the action of peroxidases functioning
as IAA oxidase might also inhibit elongation of sunflower seedlings as
the cell wall extensibility of the hypocotyl epidermis is reduced.[34] In
cucumber seedlings a single 6–8 hr exposure reduced the hypocotyl
elongation rate by 50%.[35] This inhibition was perceived mainly through
the cotyledons, indicating the action of a special UV-B photoreceptor
which has yet to be identified. Phytochrome and UV-A-blue receptors
may not be involved, since a mutant deficient in stable phytochrome
also shows hypocotyl reduction.[35]

Greenhouse studies with soybean cultivar "Essex" simulating a 25%
O_3 depletion showed that UV-B effects depend on the growth stage of
the plants, which were most sensitive to UV-B radiation during the
transition from vegetative to reproductive stage.[36] Plant height, leaf area,
and total dry weight were also reduced at the end of the vegetative and
reproductive phases, when plants were subjected to intermediate levels
of UV-B radiation (ca. 16% O_3 depletion).

The effects of UV-B radiation on rice (*Oryza sativa*), one of the most
important tropical crop plants, have been investigated by Teramura et
al.[37] A total of 16 cultivars from different geographical regions were
grown in greenhouses for 12 weeks under conditions simulating a 20%
ozone depletion above the equator (15.7 kJ m^{-2} day^{-1} UV-B$_{BE}$). The
results imply a significant decrease in total biomass with increased UV-
B radiation for about one third of all cultivars. In these sensitive plants
tiller number and leaf area were significantly reduced. Furthermore, only
a weak relationship existed between changes in photosynthesis and
biomass with increasing UV-B radiation, although photosynthetic capacity declined from some cultivars. A 20% increase of total biomass
occurred in one rice cultivar as a response to enhanced UV-B radiation.
Generally, effects of UV-B radiation are damaging; however, in some
cases the radiation has a stimulating effect which can not be explained
easily. Lydon et al. carried out field studies involving six soybean cultivars.[22] They simulated 16% and 25% O_3 depletion (related to a clear
summer day at Gainesville, Florida) and could demonstrate that UV-B
fluence-dependent reductions of relative growth rate, height, and net
assimilation rate occurred as a result of the irradiation conditions. Experiments on wheat and wild oat showed reductions in plant height and
blade length.[38] These responses were not associated with a reduction of
photosynthesis; it remained unchanged. Data on the effects of UV-B

radiation upon gymnosperms are few. These plants, however, seem to be sensitive to UV-B as well, at least in the seedling and sapling stages.[39] In greenhouses, *Pinus contorta, Pinus resinosa,* and *Pinus taeda* showed reduced seedling height dependent on UV-B fluence.[40,41] In a multiseasonal study, seeds of loblolly pine (*Pinus taeda*) from seven different locations were grown under natural and supplemental levels of UV-B radiation.[42] The supplemental irradiation simulated ozone depletions of 16% and 25% over Beltsville, Maryland, (39°N), U.S.

UV-B effects varied among seed sources during the first year. Plants grown from two of the seven seed origins showed reductions in growth following a single irradiation season. After 3 years of irradiation, plant biomass was reduced by 20% in three of the seven seed sources in response to a simulation of 16% ozone depletion on world tree populations. In some cases reductions of biomass could be observed in spite of unaffected photosynthesis. Reasons could be a decreased allocation of biomass into leaf tissue and/or direct effects of UV-B radiation on needle growth. Considering the long-term growth of trees, the need for multiple-season research is apparent in order to gain knowlege about the potential consequences of ozone depletion.

Competition

Competition for growth between weeds and crops is generally the most important problem for agriculture. Seven competing pairs of agricultural crops and associated weeds were grown in the field under increased levels of UV-B radiation, and it could be shown that the weeds *Avena fatua* and *Aegilops cylindrica* outcompeted *Triticum aestivum.*[43]

Species pairs occurring in natural ecosystems, such as *Poa pratensis* and *Geum macrophylum,* grown under conditions simulating a 40% ozone depletion resulted in a greater advantage of one over the other — in this case, *Geum* over *Poa.* Morphological changes are probably the reason for this competitive shift.[45] It was demonstrated that wild oat showed reduced stem and leaf blade length compared to wheat under enhanced UV-B levels, and it could also be shown that in both species photosynthesis was not affected.[46] These experiments imply that changes in growth form can have ecologically significant consequences even if plants are not depressed in overall growth by increased UV-B radiation. Furthermore, a change in competitive balance may have important impacts on mixed-crop agriculture as well as on species composition and biodiversity of natural ecosystems.[47]

Flowering

Flint and Caldwell demonstrated that the wall of anthers filters out over 98% of incident UV-B and protects pollen.[48] UV-B-absorbing compounds are contained within the pollen wall and it is therefore well protected during pollination, too. After the transfer to the stigma the pollen tube might be susceptible, especially binucleate types with longer time courses for germination and penetration compared to trinucleate types.[49] Indirect evidence for the impact of UV-B on pollen germination was drawn from in vitro experiments on 10 species.[50-53]

Germination of *Petunia hybrida* and *Vicia villosa* was inhibited by 65% within 1 hr, while that of *Tradescantia* clone 4430, *Brassica oleracea*, *Papaver rhoeas*, or *Cleome lutea* was inhibited by 33% within 3 hr following irradiances of 50 to 70 mW m^{-2} UV-B.[50] Furthermore, it could be demonstrated in three of four species that in vitro germination was partly inhibited by UV-B irradiation of high elevations or low latitudes.[53] The lack of in vitro experiments at present makes it somewhat difficult to assess the general impact of UV radiation on plant pollen.

Since the ovaries hide the ovules well, the latter can be considered sufficiently protected against solar UV-B radiation. Several scientists investigated UV-B effects on flowering, and it could be demonstrated that exclusion of UV-B radiation by Mylar plastic films or glass stimulated flowering as shown for *Melilotus*, *Trifolium dasyphyllum*, and *Tagetes*.[54-56] The inhibition of photoperiodic flower induction dependent on UV-B fluence rate and fluence could be demonstrated for the long day plant *Hyoscyamus niger*.[57] A 20% decrease of flowering resulted from irradiation with 100 mW m^{-2} UV-B, and a 50% reduction resulted from 300 mW m^{-2} UV-B compared to plants merely irradiated with white light. The suppression of flowering is correlated with changes in gibberellic acid content.

However, significant effects on flowering, tasseling, or heading could not be found for *Petunia*, *Zea mays*, and *Sorghum bicolor*, respectively.[58] It is thought that UV-B could also act on timing of flower production as shown for bean plants.[59]

If appearance of the natural insect pollinators was not to coincide with the flowering of the plants, this could have marked consequences for the biodiversity of natural ecosystems.

EFFECTS ON PLANT FUNCTION

Photosynthesis and Transpiration

When high UV-B irradiances were used in combination with low levels of white light, such as commonly found in growth chambers, effects on photosynthesis, measured as CO_2 assimilation, were generally deleterious in UV-B-sensitive plants.[60] However, even in the presence of higher levels of white light found in greenhouses and the field, reductions in photosynthesis of up to 17% were reported in the UV-B-sensitive soybean cultivar "Essex" when supplied with UV-B equivalent to a 16% ozone depletion.[61,62] Solar UV-B also reduced net photosynthesis in sunflower and corn seedlings by about 15% when a 12% ozone depletion was simulated by using the new ozone technique.[63] It is presently unknown whether photosynthesis is reduced in a fluence-dependent manner. It seems likely that the effect of enhanced solar UV radiation on photosynthesis increases during development in sunflower seedlings.[63] In a field experiment carried out over 3 years Naidu et al. examined the effects of supplemental UV-B radiation (280–320 nm) on different aged needles of *Pinus tadea* L., simulating a 25% ozone depletion at Beltsville, MD (39°N).[64] It could be demonstrated that only the youngest needles showed a decrease of photosynthetic activity in unprotected needles, indicating transient damage to photosynthesis. Instantaneous measures such as chlorophyll fluorescence induction characteristics and apparent quantum yield remained unaffected by UV-B radiation in needles of any age.

However, a 12–20% decrease in total biomass could be demonstrated, as well as a decrease in needle length. It is thought that the overall growth reductions probably occurred as a result of reduced total leaf surface and not as a result of decreased photosynthetic capacity. One reason for the reduction of plant photosynthesis might be stomatal closure induced by enhanced UV-B, as demonstrated in cucumber seedlings and for *Eragrostis* leaves.[65,66] Furthermore, it was shown that the abaxial leaf sides of sunflower seedlings, not directly exposed to UV-B radiation, exhibit stomatal closure with a time delay, indicating a fluence response.[67]

The action spectrum for stomatal closure of *Eragrostis* leaves peaks below 290 nm, whereas radiation longer than 313 nm is nearly ineffective.[68] Stomatal closure may be caused by a loss of turgor pressure mediated through ion leakage from the guard cells, as demonstrated with $^{86}Rb^+$ ions in epidermal strips of bean leaves.[69] On the other hand, no effects on leaf gas exchange were found in grasses like wheat and wild oat even when high supplemental UV-B (simulating a 40% O_3 reduction) was supplied in the field.[46] Transpiration was reduced in some UV-sensitive seedlings such as cucumber grown under artificial UV-B (6000-W xenon lamp) in growth chambers.[65] However, in sunflower seedlings grown under ambient solar UV radiation in Portugal, transpiration was unchanged or increased with age compared to those receiving a reduced fluence.[63] The time course for stomatal closure was rapid at low UV-B fluences, and stomatal opening was slow at higher UV-B fluences.[67] In addition to stomatal responses, photosynthetic activity of photosystem II is also reduced in many plant species. This was demonstrated in intact radish and pea leaves,[70,71] in isolated chloroplasts,[5,72,73] thylakoids,[74] and photosystem II (PSII) membrane fragments.[12]

One often reported change under enhanced UV-B is the reduction of the variable fluorescence F_v.[5,72,75] In isolated chloroplasts, this reduction is not accompanied by a reduction of the ground-level fluorescence F_o

as has been found in intact leaves.[70] The reduction of F_v accounts for a decreased efficiency of the PSII reaction center, which becomes ineffective in reducing Q_A, the primary acceptor of PSII. In leaves a decrease of F_o was found after long-term irradiation with enhanced UV-B.[70] This was attributed to the formation of a dissipative sink in the PSII reaction center. This was not the case in the chloroplasts isolated from these leaves when the chlorophyll content was adjusted to the same level in the samples. The decrease in F_o might therefore be a cause of the enhanced chlorophyll content per leaf area, which causes reabsorption of chlorophyll fluorescence and thus reduces fluorescence intensity. Cen and Bornman investigated the effect of different light levels on the responses to enhanced UV-B. Only under the lowest PAR applied (230 μmol m^{-2} s^{-2}), the supplemental UV-B irradiation of 2.12 μmol m^{-2} s^{-2} decreased the F_v/F_o ratio. With a PAR of 700 μmol m^{-2} s^{-2} the fluorescence parameters were unaffected.[76] Chlorophyll content was decreased under enhanced UV-B and low light only.

With more natural conditions, e.g., by use of the ozone technique, the effects of enhanced UV-B irradiation on chlorophyll induction characteristics are also less pronounced or absent.[77] The drastic effects found under low white light or with high differences in the UV-B between control and irradiated samples seem to be counteracted by more efficient photorepair and adaptations to high light stress. One possible mechanism could be the higher ability to recover from photoinhibition, meaning that the replacement of destroyed D1 protein is enhanced if the plants are adapted to higher levels of white light. Another mechanism is the accumulation of UV-protective pigments in the epidermal layer of plant leaves. By measuring changes in the F_m/F_o ratio and the Rfd (vitality index of leaves; ratio of fluorescence decrease to steady-state fluorescence) value it was shown that the accumulation of flavonoids in the epidermal layer of rye leaves could protect the photosynthetic apparatus against damage induced by an increase in UV-B irradiation if the plants were preadapted to UV-B.[78] Plants not adapted to UV-B and thus not having accumulated flavonoids were significantly reduced in their photosynthetic capacity by a 3-hr irradiation under damaging UV-B. In oat there was no change in fluorescence signals because of the high concentration of flavonoids already present in the plants grown without UV-B. By covering the leaves of *Vigna sinensis*, Kulandeivelu et al. concluded that the effect of UV-B on photosynthetic activity depends on the direct absorption of UV-B by the leaf tissue.[79]

In vitro studies on isolated chloroplasts indicate that the UV-B radiation-induced damage to photochemical reactions is greater in C_3 plants (*Dolichoas lablab, Phaseolus mungo,* and *Triticum vulgare*) than in C_4 plants (*Amaranthus gangeticus, Zea mays,* and *Pennisetum typhoides*). Such differences are associated with the changes in polypeptide compositon of the thylakoids.[80] Several studies have shown that the activity of the stromal

key enzyme, ribulose bisphosphate carboxylase (Rubisco), is reduced.[71,81,82] In pea leaves, the reduction in soluble protein was accompanied by reduced Rubisco activity and by lower concentrations of small
and large subunits. In contrast to a relatively slow decline of total soluble
protein and Rubisco (within days), the levels of the RNA transcripts for
the subunits were reduced within hours.[83] In all studies very high UV
irradiances were used, which may not be relevant in nature. Whether
the reduction of net photosynthesis is due to reduced Rubisco or other
functional disorders as described above is still an open question. Interestingly, two cultivars of rice showed different responses with respect
to increased UV-B radiation. In cultivar IR36 the predominate limitation
of photosynthesis was the capacity to regenerate ribulose bisphosphate,
whereas for the cultivar Fujiyama 5 the primary photosynthetic decrease
appeared to be related to a decline in apparent carboxylation efficiency.[84]
Photosynthesis under higher temperature in combination with enhanced
solar UV-B was investigated by Mark.[82] Photosynthetic rates of sunflower seedlings are much higher under 32°C maximum temperature
during the daily temperature course than under 28°C, indicating that
temperature increases that are expected in the future could ameliorate
UV-B-induced reductions in net photosynthesis normally found.

Studies in growth chambers with the ozone filter for attenuating solar
UV-B radiation showed significant reductions in net photosynthesis
(measured under saturating light conditions) on a leaf area and whole
plant basis in sunflower seedlings, grown for 3 weeks at a daily maximum temperature of 28°C or 32°C under a 20% higher UV-B daily fluence
compared to controls (54.4 kJ m^{-2} day^{-1} vs. 45.3 kJ m^{-2} day^{-1}). These
represent average values from May 1990 to August 1990 and are approximately equivalent to a 10% ozone depletion. In contrast, net photosynthesis was lower in maize seedlings only during the earliest stages
of development at both temperatures.[85]

EFFECTS ON PLANT COMPOSITION AND PLANT PROTECTION

Photosynthetic Pigments and other Lipids

Tevini et al. demonstrated in growth chamber studies that the destruction of chlorophylls was a function of UV-B fluence rate and fluence
only in UV-sensitive plants such as barley, bean, and cucumber.[29] In
these sensitive plants carotenoids as well as membrane lipids such as
galacto- and phospholipids had been affected in the same way. In cucumber cotyledons it was shown that the percentage of fatty acid composition of galacto- and phospholipids was slightly changed to the dis-
advantage of linolenic acid when 20% ozone depletion was simulated.
Furthermore, lipid perioxidation was increased, indicating that membranes are also targets of increased UV-B.[86] Under solar UV-B radiation

(Portugal) simulating a 12% ozone depletion, chlorophyll content was reduced with respect to the whole plant. An increase could be observed when chlorophyll content was based upon leaf area in spite of reductions of the overall area, indicating thicker leaves with more chlorophyll per leaf area.[87]

Tevini and Steinmüller investigated the effects of UV-B radiation on the surface lipids of cucumber seedlings and found that the homologue distribution of alkanes and alcohols (the main wax compounds) was altered to homologues with shorter chain lengths.[88] This alteration did not occur as a result of photooxidation but as a direct UV-B impact on wax biosynthesis. Positive effects of increased UV-B radiation were found in essential oil production in several herb plants such as basil, thyme, and marjoram.[89]

UV-Protection

UV-absorbing pigments, particularly phenylpropanoids, accumulate in leaves of most higher plants following irradiation with UV-B.[4,90,91] These compounds are usually contained within the upper epidermal layer of leaves. Under solar radiation the relatively UV-B-sensitive plant *Rumex patienta* possesses a higher epidermal UV transmittance compared to the more resistant species *Rumex obtusifolius*.[92] Effects of UV-B on leaf optical properties were also measured in the tissues with fiber optics.[93] Phenylpropanoids such as cinnamoyl esters, flavones, flavonol, isoflavonoids, and anthocyanins esterified with cinnamic acids represent these UV-absorbing compounds.[94-96] Anthocyanins accumulate in many plant species under enhanced UV-B radiation but only absorb weakly in the UV-B region except when esterified with cinnamic acids. Therefore, they can only be regarded as UV screens at either very high concentrations or in complex compounds. Rye and oat were used in an experiment, and it could be shown that the UV fluence- and wavelength-dependent accumulation of isovitexin derivatives in the epidermal layer of rye seedlings prevented damage to chloroplast function. When screening pigments did not accumulate the photosynthetic function was low.[78] Since large amounts of UV-absorbing pigments accumulate during the early development of oat seedlings, their photosynthetic apparatus appears to be better protected against UV-B damage than rye seedlings.[97] This inherently higher flavonoid production seems to be constitutive in nature since it occurs also in the absence of UV-B irradiation. *Aquilegia caerulea* present in alpine habitats and *Aquilegia canadensis* growing at lower altitudes also showed an increased flavonoid content induced by UV-B radiation.[98] The UV-B-free control plants of the alpine species accumulated higher amounts of flavonoids compared to *A. canadensis* after UV-B irradiation. It appears that plants genetically adapted to higher UV-B radiation conditions can increase their adaptation capacity. Apart from the phenylpropanoids, other products of the shikimic acid pathway such as furanocoumarins, polyketides, and terpenoids such as cannabinoid accumulate following increased UV-B radiation.[99,100] Alterations in their concentration might affect the plants' resistance to herbivores because many of these compounds are toxic as well as the selective power in the evolution of *Cannabis* chemotypes.[101]

Photorepair

Photoreactivation is another important protective mechanism which plants have evolved. DNA photolyase can repair the UV-induced production of DNA pyrimidine dimers. An increase of this enzyme following increased UV-B irradiation was demonstrated in *Arabidopsis* and also in bean seedlings via phytochrome under irradiation conditions of visible light.[102,103] This inducibility means that the de novo synthesis of DNA photolyase itself is a target for UV damage. Hence, increasing UV-B radiation might reduce the repair capacity of the cell, which is anticipated from stratospheric ozone depletion.

EFFECTS ON YIELD

Due to the artificial nature of the environment in growth chambers, data on plant yield must ideally be collected outdoors in carefully designed field studies. Of particular concern in most growth chambers and greenhouses is the low level of visible radiation (PAR) supplied to the plants. The effectiveness of UV-B radiation is magnified when given levels of radiation which are below the saturation level of photosynthesis. The reasons for this phenomenon are not completely known; however, it is thought that natural UV protective mechanisms do not become fully developed in low levels of visible light.

Since the last comprehensive review on yield, very few additional field studies, mainly with soybean cultivars, have been performed.[104] Earlier results on about 25 plant species illustrate the degree of technical difficulty and uncertainty surrounding the estimates of UV-B effects on yield. Many of these studies were conducted with filtered UV-B sources simulating relatively high ozone reduction rates.[105,106] In a German field study using filtered lamps and simulating 10% and 25% ozone reductions, no UV-B effects were demonstrated in three cabbage cultivars, nor in lettuce and rape. Since flavonoid contents increased in most plants, there might have been a UV-B effect on food quality; however, this was not specifically tested.[107] Biggs et al. grew 10 crop species in Gainesville, Florida (290°N) and found yield reductions between 5% and 90% in half of them, among them crops like wheat (-5%), potato (-21%), and squash (-90%), whereas rice, peanut, and corn were unaffected.[105,106] This brief summary indicates a high degree of interspecific variability complicated further by differences in artificial light sources, climate, soil quality, day length, etc.

In addition to this interspecific variability, there is a high degree of intraspecific variability among cultivars.[28,108] Twenty-three soybean cultivars were grown in a greenhouse and, of these, six were selected for a comparative field study. Results from the greenhouse and the field indicate that the cultivar "Forrest" was the most tolerant, whereas "Shore" and "York" were the most susceptible to UV-B, based upon a combination of responses including plant height, leaf area, total dry weight, and seed yield. Only "York" had a significant 25% reduction in yield when exposed to a simulated 16% ozone reduction. Although "James", "Forrest", and "Essex" demonstrated a similar level of yield reduction, they were not statistically significant. During the next 5 years, only "Essex" and "Williams" were grown in the field under both a 16 and 25% ozone depletion simulation. These two cultivars were chosen because they are widely grown in the U.S. and had demonstrated contrasting UV-B sensitivities. Except for 1983 and 1984, yield in "Essex" was reduced by 20–25%, while a 10–22% higher yield was found in "Williams" when simulating a 25% ozone reduction.[109,110] At a 16% ozone reduction, no consistently significant relationship could be found in "Essex" or "Williams". 1984 and 1983 field trials may not be representative of typical years since both years were abnormally dry and hot, and yields in the controls were already reduced by up to 80%. This leads to another phenomenon, that UV-B effects are partially masked when growth is already impacted by other stresses. In another field study with six soybean varieties simulating a 32% enhancement of UV-B irradiance no influence on seed yield was detected.[111] Currently, not enough is known about the reasons for these large UV-B response differences among cultivars. Ideally, we need to understand the genetic bases (heritability) of UV tolerance and sensitivity. Once this is known, we could estimate the possibility of using conventional breeding practices to minimize the potential impacts of UV damage. At present, plant breeders have not yet considered UV sensitivity as a selective factor. This has resulted in development of cultivar "Essex" which appears to be quite sensitive to UV-B radiation. "Essex" is a newer cultivar which is replacing the UV-tolerant cultivar "Williams" in many areas of the U.S.

UV RADIATION AND ABIOTIC AND BIOTIC FACTORS

Water Stress

In assessing the effect of UV radiation on plants, it is important to keep in mind that other factors may ameliorate or aggravate the response to UV radiation. Thus the response of the plant to multiple biotic and abiotic factors should be investigated for a more accurate assessment of the impact of global climate changes.

Among the most common stresses experienced by plants growing in the field are water and mineral deficiencies. Interactions of other environmental factors with UV-B radiation have been extensively reviewed.[60] Water stress in combination with enhanced UV-B (simulating a 12% O_3 depletion) adversely affected water loss in cucumber cotyledons. Stomatal resistance of water-stressed control plants receiving ambient levels of UV-B radiation displayed the normal diurnal pattern with high increases during midday, whereas plants irradiated with enhanced levels of UV-B lost their capacity to close stomata with increasing UV-B fluence.[65] Radish seedlings were much less sensitive to UV-B radiation under water stress than cucumber and had higher leaf flavonoid contents, possibly protecting seedlings by absorbing UV in the leaf epidermis, thereby protecting underlying tissues.[90] Well-watered "Essex" soybean, grown in the field under enhanced UV-B (simulating a 25% O_3 depletion) showed reductions in growth, dry weight, and net photosynthesis, but no significant UV-B effect could be detected in water-stressed plants.[61] Furthermore, photosynthetic recovery after water stress was shown to be greater and more rapid in UV-B-irradiated soybean plants and to be associated with lower stomatal conductances instead of internal water relations.[112,113] Phosphorus deficiency was also examined in the soybean cultivar "Essex" under enhanced UV-B artificially supplied in a greenhouse and equivalent to a 16% ozone reduction.[62] It was clearly shown that UV-B did not produce any additional damage to growth and photosynthesis in P-deficient plants. However, enhanced UV-B reduced net photosynthesis by about 20% in plants well-supplied with phosphate. Information on the interactions between mineral deficiency and UV-B radiation are limited to small-scale experimental studies; therefore, we currently do not know the applicability of these studies to natural field conditions.

Temperature

In addition to higher levels of UV-B radiation, increases in temperature due to the greenhouse effect are also anticipated in our future environment. The following study simulated a 4°C difference in the daily temperature course in combination with enhanced solar UV-B radiation.[82]

Seedlings of four plant species (sunflower, maize, rye, and oat) were grown for 3 weeks in growth chambers (placed in Portugal at 38°N) using the ozone filter technique, which simulated a 20% UV-B radiation difference between the chambers, and with daily maximum temperatures of 32°C or 28°C. Growth of seedlings (measured as plant height, leaf area, and dry weight) was greater at 32°C than at 28°C, except for oat seedlings, which did not grow well at higher temperatures. Leaf area and size of 3-week-old sunflower seedlings irradiated with a 20% higher UV-B level than the controls were significantly reduced at both temparture regimes. Maize and rye seedlings grown at the higher temperature regime (32°C) could compensate for the growth reduction normally found at 28°C. Dry weight reduction typically found at 28°C in sunflower and maize did not occur at 32°C. Oat and rye seedlings responded differently; oat seedlings suffered from the higher temperature, whereas rye did not. These results indicate that higher temperature regimes can ameliorate UV-B effects on at least some but not all plant species.

Heavy Metals

The rise in toxic pollutants, including heavy metals, from both industrialized and developing countries is cause of concern. Plants in particular may be adversely affected by the additional stresses beyond enhanced UV-B radiation. This approach to multiple effects is important because even low fluences of UV-B radiation in addition to another factor may substantially affect the plant.

When seedlings of Norway spruce (*Picea abies* L. Karst) were exposed to UV-B$_{BE}$ (biologically effective UV-B radiation) of only $6.17 \, kJ \, m^{-2} day^{-1}$ together with 5 mMol cadmium chloride for 10 weeks, rates of net photosynthesis decreased by 33% in plants under the combined treatment of enhanced UV-B radiation and cadmium (relative to controls). The enhanced levels of UV-B radiation and cadmium applied simultaneously also decreased dry weight, height of seedlings, and chlorophyll content to a greater extent than found for UV treatment given alone.[114] Therefore, unless the effects of simultaneous multiple stresses are taken into account, one may underestimate the different environmental pressures on plants.

Carbon Dioxide and Temperature

Current atmospheric levels of CO_2 may double from 340 ppm to 680 ppm by the middle of the next century. A number of field and greenhouse experiments have shown that growth and photosynthesis in a wide range of cultivated and native plant species will be substantially altered by a CO_2 doubling. However, few studies have examined the combined effects of increases in CO_2 and UV-B radiation. Wheat, rice, and soybean were grown in a factorial greenhouse utilizing two levels of CO_2 (350 ppm and 650 ppm) and two levels of UV-B (8.8 and 15.7 kJ m^{-2} UV-B$_{BE}$), simulating a 10% O_3 depletion at Singapore during the seasonal maximum.[115] Seed yield and total plant biomass increased significantly in all three species when grown in elevated CO_2. However, with concurrent increases in UV-B, these CO_2-induced increases remained in soybean, but were eliminated in rice and wheat. Therefore, the combined effects of CO_2 and UV-B are species specific, but do indicate that UV-B may modify CO_2-induced increases in photosynthesis and yield. Recently, further examinations were carried out on the interactions of two rice cultivars, IR-36 and Fujiyama-5, under similar combined UV-B radiation and CO_2 conditions described as above.[84] An analysis of gas exchange and chlorophyll fluorescence data indicated that the predominant limitation to photosynthesis with increased UV-B radiation was the capacity to regenerate RuBP in IR-36 and a decline in carboxylation efficiency in Fujiyama-5. Therefore, increased CO_2 may not compensate for the direct effects which UV-B has on photosynthesis in rice. This was not confirmed in sunflower seedlings grown under higher solar UV-B (equivalent to 12% ozone depletion, using the ozone filter technique) combined with double CO_2 concentration (680 μL L^{-1}) and 4°C higher daily temperature course (t_{max} = 32°C instead of 28°C.) The net photosynthetic rates of these plants were 10% higher than those of plants receiving higher temperature and UV-B (Tables 2 and 3). In contrast, maize seedlings had slightly lower photosynthetic rates.[85] This indicates that C_4 plants might not profit from elevated CO_2 levels compared to C_3 plants possessing photorespiration, which is suppressed by elevated CO_2.

Plant Disease

Inspection studies showed that certain diseases may become more severe in plants exposed to enhanced UV-B radiation, possibly by an interaction of these factors. Sugar beet (*Beta vulgaris*) plants infected with *Cercospora beticola* and receiving 6.9 kJ m^{-2} day^{-1} UV-B$_{BE}$ had large reductions in leaf chlorophyll content as well as in fresh and dry weight of total biomass.[116] There was also an increase in free radicals under the combined treatments.

In another study, three cucumber (*Cucumis sativus*) cultivars were exposed to a daily UV-B dose of 11.6 kJ m^{-2} UV-B$_{BE}$ in a greenhouse before and/or after infection with *Colletotrichum lagenarium* or *Cladosporium cucumerinum* and then analyzed for disease development.[117] Two of the three cultivars were disease resistant, the third was disease susceptible. Preinfection treatment with UV-B radiation led to greater disease development in the susceptible cultivar and in one of the disease-resistant cultivars. Post-infection treatment did not alter disease development. The increased disease development in UV-B irradiated plants was found only on the cotyledons and not on other leaves, suggesting that the effects of UV-B radiation on disease development in cucumber vary according to the cultivar, timing of UV-B exposure, and tissue type.

Table 2 Growth, Chlorophyll Content, and Gas Exchange of 18-Day-Old Sunflower Seedlings Grown at Ambient and Elevated Temperature and CO_2 with Ambient and Reduced UV-B

	A	B	%	C	%	D	%
Growth							
Fresh weight (g)	2.57 a	2.36 b	−8	2.56 ab	0	2.37 ab	−8
Dry weight (mg)	277.20 a	236.40 b	−14	290.40 ac	+5	328.60 c	+19
Size (cm)	16.77 a	13.23 b	−27	16.53 a	−1	16.15 a	−4
Leaf area (cm²)	34.34 a	31.00 b	−17	38.97 c	+14	35.42 ac	+3
Chlorophyll							
Chl (mg/cm²)	23.12 a	27.47 b	+19	25.30 ab	+9	23.17 a	0
Chl (mg/plant)	775.80 a	846.60 a	+9	955.30 a	+23	843.50 a	+9
Photosynthesis							
NP (mmol CO_2 m^{-2} s^{-1})	15.46 a	17.32 b	+12	14.59 a	−6	15.39 a	−1
NP (mmol CO_2 plant^{-1} s^{-1})	50.98 a	46.06 b	−10	50.64 ab	−1	55.63 a	+9
NP (mmol CO_2 g^{-1} chl^{-1} s^{-1})	71.98 a	57.93 b	−20	55.91 b	−22	72.30 a	0
Gas exchange							
DR (mmol CO_2 m^{-2} s^{-1})	0.94 a	1.08 b	+15	0.88 a	−6	0.91 a	−3
TR (mmol H_2O m^{-2} s^{-1})	2.33 a	2.64 ab	+13	2.07 b	−11	1.91 b	−18
TR (mmol H_2O plant^{-1} s^{-1})	7.65 a	7.15 a	−7	7.16 a	−6	6.87 a	−10
Wue	6.77 a	7.01 a	+4	7.54a	+11	10.03 b	+48

Note: % = percentage change relative to the control; means with the same letter are not significantly different at the 95% confidence level according to an ANOVA. NP = net photosynthesis; DR = dark respiration; TR = transpiration; Wue = water use efficiency.

control	28°C	340 ppm CO_2
+25% UV-B	28°C	340 ppm CO_2
+25% UV-B	32°C	340 ppm CO_2
+25% UV-B	32°C	680 ppm CO_2

CONCLUSIONS

Because of technical difficulties in conducting UV-B experiments which have a sense of realism to them, many of the earlier studies show quite conflicting responses. For instance, many greenhouse studies excluded UV-B entirely from the controls, which is unrealistic in nature. Many studies applied unrealisticly high ozone reduction rates, sometimes using unprotected UV-B (and UV-C) radiation sources. The wattage of irradiance is not sufficient to characterize the biological effectiveness of

TABLE 3 Growth Chlorophyll Content, and Gas Exchange of 18-Day-Old Maize Seedlings Grown at Ambient and Elevated Temperature and CO_2 with Ambient and Reduced UV-B

	A	B	%	C	%	D	%
Growth							
Fresh weight (g)	2.54 a	2.03 b	−20	2.78 a	+9	2.70 a	+6
Dry weight (mg)	289.10 a	221.00 b	−24	379.10 c	+31	382.30 c	+32
Size (cm)	33.51 a	28.30 b	−16	41.26 c	+23	37.78 d	+13
Leaf area (cm²)	83.42 a	65.01 b	−22	88.70 a	+6	87.76 a	+5
Chlorophyll							
Chl (mg/cm²)	14.82 a	17.13 b	+16	15.32 ab	+3	13.36 a	−10
Chl (mg/plant)	1046.30 a	1055.50 a	+1	1066.60 a	+2	984.80 a	−6
Photosynthesis							
NP (mmol CO_2 m^{-2} s^{-1})	9.44 a	8.98 a	−5	7.59 ab	−20	6.16 b	−35
NP (mmol CO_2 plant^{-1} s^{-1})	72.29 a	57.33 b	−21	70.55 a	−2	68.38 a	−5
NP (mmol CO_2 g^{-1} chl.$^{-1}$ s^{-1})	70.96 a	50.45 b	−29	67.86 a	−4	71.12 a	0
Gas exchange							
DR (mmol CO_2 m^{-2} s^{-1})	0.58 a	0.66 b	+14	0.61 ab	+5	0.53 a	−9
TR (mmol H_2O m^{-2} s^{-1})	1.01 a	0.95 a	−6	1.21 b	+20	0.45 c	−55
TR (mmol H_2O plant^{-1} s^{-1})	7.78 a	6.22 a	−20	11.38 b	+46	4.90 c	−37
Wue	9.49 a	9.44 a	−1	6.56 b	−31	14.74	+55

Note: % = percentage change relative to control; means with the same letter are not significantly different at the 95% confidence level according to an ANOVA. NP = net photosynthesis; DR = dark respiration; TR = transpiration; Wue = water use efficiency.

control	28°C	340 ppm CO_2
+25% UV-B	28°C	340 ppm CO_2
+25% UV-B	32°C	340 ppm CO_2
+25% UV-B	32°C	680 ppm CO_2

the radiation in use. Therefore, one must be cautious when interpreting these results. The use of an ozone cuvette to reduce solar radiation might solve this problem, but this is only applicable in small growth chambers placed in locations with high solar UV-B input. Refined plastic materials with absorption coefficients matching that of ozone might be developed to conduct more realistic greenhouse and field studies.

Plant responses to enhanced UV-B levels vary markedly within species and among species. Photorepair, accumulation of UV-absorbing pigments, and growth delay are potential adaptive mechanisms; however, only a few studies had demonstrated a direct relationship between these protective mechanisms and insensitivity to UV-B radiation. The accumulation of UV-absorbing compounds as well as growth reduction have been shown to be wavelength, fluence rate, and fluence dependent. However, growth reduction is not always correlated with reductions in photosynthesis, total biomass, or yield. Reductions in net photosynthesis on a whole-plant basis may also be due to overall growth reductions rather than to direct effects on photosynthetic function, although inhibition of photosystem II activity by UV-B has been demonstrated. Conclusions from growth chamber studies using low levels of white light, which limit photosynthesis in most plant species, are not applicable to the field or the greenhouse, where higher levels of photosynthetically active radiation are present. Differential growth response may also be involved in shifts in competitive balance between plant species, which have been demonstrated in selected species pairs. From the few competition studies which have been performed it is evident that there is a potential risk for changes in ecosystem composition in the future. Likewise, global agricultural yield is also potentially at risk, but very few studies have been conducted under realistic UV radiation conditions. Significant reductions in harvestable yield have been found in several soybean cultivars; however, other species might also be impacted but have just not been properly tested. Mechanistic studies are also providing improved insight into repair and tolerance processes in plants. Nevertheless, recent studies also indicate the complexities in which plant responses to UV-B may be modified by other environmental factors. These complications, and the very limited number of field studies which have been conducted with realistic UV-B supplements, greatly constrain quantitative predictions.

Most of the research to date deals with temperate-latitude agricultural species. Little is known at present about the manner in which agricultural and native plants at tropical latitudes cope with the intense solar UV-B flux already present in these regions, nor the degree to which these species can adapt to the still greater flux that would occur with ozone depletion.

RESEARCH NEEDS

An enormous amount of research is still needed to describe and evaluate the effects of enhanced UV-B on plants. Field validations on crop plants must be expanded to determine whether UV-B affects yield in other agriculturally important plants. Studies must be initiated to determine the impacts to natural ecosystems. Little is known of the effects of UV in other natural ecosystems such as natural forests, including tropical rain forests, meadows, savannas, tundra, and alpine areas. Furthermore, the UV-B effects on growth and reproductive cycles of lower plants, such as mosses, fungi, and ferns, have yet to be studied. It is

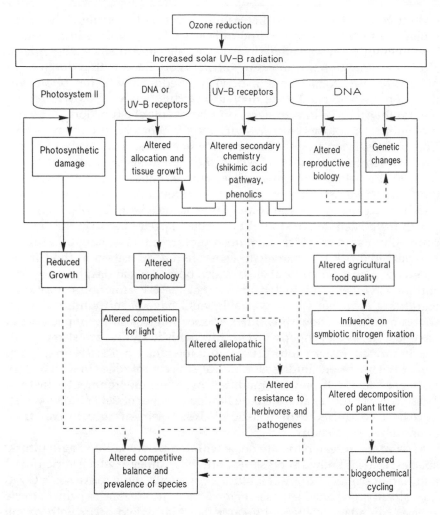

Figure 1   Potential consequences of ozone column decrease and corresponding
increase in solar UV-B radiation for higher plants at different levels
of integration from molecular photochemistry to ecosystems. Experimental evidence for interactions is indicated by solid lines; dashed
lines are for interactions where no direct experimental evidence is yet
available. Feedback loops indicate that the flavonoids and phenolics
that may be induced by increased UV-B can serve as filtering agents,
reducing the flux received by the photoreceptors and, thus, sometimes
reducing the response to increased UV-B.[47]

important to study natural plants since we rely on them to supply us
with new drugs, medicines, and other natural products, and they act
as a reservoir of genetic diversity for our modern crop breeding programs. Therefore, despite the fact that they have little economic value

now, natural plants could become quite important to us in the future. Figure 1 described the potential consequences of a decreased ozone column and the corresponding increase in solar UV-B radiation for higher plants at different levels of integration from molecular photochemistry to ecosystems.

During the next several decades other environmental changes will be superimposed upon the increases in UV-B radiation, such as increases in temperature and carbon dioxide concentration in the atmosphere. Increased CO_2 is generally thought to have a beneficial effect on plants. Therefore, it is necessary to know whether the generally deleterious UV-B effects may be compensated by changes in CO_2 and/or temperature. Temperature increases cause regional and global climate changes which may thus impact plant growth through altered water supplies. Most of the continental areas of the world may experience profound changes in the pattern of precipitation. Plant adaptation to stresses like water, temperature, and mineral deficiency must therefore be examined in combination with increased UV-B radiation. It will be increasingly important for plant breeders to select well-adapted varieties in areas where the climatic changes will be the greatest (i.e., temperate regions). Another area of worldwide interest is tropical rice growing regions, where almost nothing is known about how rice will be affected either under enhanced UV-B or under increased temperature and CO_2. Of increasing interest are man-made air pollutants such as ozone, sulfur dioxide, and nitrogen oxides, which already are known to have damaging effects on forests. More attention must be focused on whether the negative effects of these air pollutants may be aggravated by UV-B radiation.

ACKNOWLEDGMENTS

Work done by M. Tevini and co-workers was supported by a grant from the German BMFT. I am also grateful to Thomas Hietzker for his help in preparing the manuscript.

REFERENCES

1. Caldwell, M. M. "Solar UV Irradiation and the Growtn and Development of Higher Plants," in *Photophysiology, Vol. VI*, A. C. Giese, Ed. (New York: Academic Press, 1971), pp. 131–268.
2. Klein, R. "Plants and Near-Ultraviolet Radiation," *Bot. Rev.* 44:1–12 (1978).
3. Caldwell, M. M. "Plant Response to Solar Ultraviolet Radiation," in *Encyclopedia of Plant Physiology, Vol. 12A*, Physiological Plant Ecology I, O. L. Lange, P. S. Nobel, C. B. Osmond, and H. Ziegler, Eds. (Berlin: Springer-Verlag, 1981) pp. 169–197.

4. Wellmann, E. "UV Radiation: Definitions, Characteristics and General Effects," in *Encyclopedia of Plant Physiology, Vol. 16B*, New Series, Photomorphogenesis, W. Shropshire and H. Mohr, Eds. (Berlin: Springer-Verlag, 1983), pp. 745–746.

5. Iwanzik, W., M. Tevini, G. Dohnt, M. Voss, W. Weiss, P. Gräber, and G. Renger. "Action of UV-B Radiation on Photsynthetic Primary Reactions in Spinach Chloroplasts," *Physiol. Plant.* 58:401–407 (1983).

6. Teramura, A. H. "Effects of Ultraviolet-B Radiation on the Growth and Yield of Crop Plants," *Physiol. Plant.* 58:415–427 (1983).

7. Worrest, R. C. and M. M. Caldwell, Eds. *Stratospheric Ozone Reduction, Solar Ultraviolet Radiation and Plant Life*, NATO ASI Series G: Ecological Sciences, Vol. 8.

8. Caldwell, M. M. "Plant Life and Ultraviolet Radiation. Some Perspectives," *Science* 237:35–42 (1987).

9. Coohill, T. P. "Ultraviolet Action Spectra and Solar Effectiveness Spectra for Higher Plants," *Photochem. Photobiol.* 50:451–457 (1989).

10. Bornmann, J. F. "Target Sites of UV-B Radiation in Photosynthesis of Higher Plants," *Photochem. Photobiol. B* 4:145–158 (1989).

11. Tevini, M. and A. H. Teramura. "UV-B Effects on Terrestrial Plants," *Photochem. Photobiol.* 50:479–487 (1989).

12. Renger, G., M. Völker, H. J. Eckert, R. Fromme, S. Hohm-Veit, and P. Gräber. "On the Mechanisms of Photosystem II Deterioration by UV-B Irradiation," *Photochem. Photobiol.* 49:97–105 (1989).

13. Krupa, S. V. and R. N. Kickert. "The Greenhouse Effect Impacts of Ultraviolet-B (UV-B) Radiation, Carbon Dioxide (CO_2), and Ozone (O_3) on Vegetation," *Environ. Pollut.* 61:263–393 (1989).

14. UNEP, "Environmental Effects Panel Report," J. C. van der Leun, M. Tevini, and R. C. Worrest, Eds., United Nations Environmental Program, Nairobi, Kenya (1989).

15. UNEP, "Environmental Effects of Ozone Depletion: 1991 Update," J. C. van der Leun, M. Tevini, and R. C. Worrest, Eds., United Nations Environmental Program, Nairobi, Kenya (1991).

16. Teramura, A. H. "Effects of Ultraviolet-B Irradiances on Soybean. I. Importance of Photosynthetically Active Radiation in Evaluating Ultraviolet-B Irradiance Effects on Soybean and Wheat Growth," *Physiol. Plant.* 48:333–339 (1980).

17. Warner, C. W. and M. M. Caldwell. "Influence of Photon Flux Density in the 400–700 nm Waveband on Inhibition of Photosynthesis by UV-B (280–320 nm) Irradiation in Soybean Leaves: Separation of Indirect and Immediate Effects," *Photochem. Photobiol.* 38:341–346 (1983).

18. Mirecki, R. M. and A. H. Teramura. "Effects of Ultraviolet-B Irradiance on Soybean. V. The Dependence of Plant Sensitivity on the Photosynthetic Photon Flux Density During and After Leaf Expansion," *Plant Physiol.* 74:475–480 (1985).

19. Wellmann, E., V. Steinmetz, G. Beha, G. Buchholz, E. Karlsen, B. Langer, R. Lembke, U. Schneider-Ziebert, and M. Steiert. *UV-B Wirkungen auf Pflanzen: Charakterisierung von UV-Schutzmechanismen und UV-spezifischen Photomorphosen; Dosis-Wirkungsbeziehungen für UV-Primärschäden*, BPT-Bericht 5/91, GSF München (1991).

20. Wellmann, E. "Specific Ultraviolet Effects in Plant Development," *J. Exp. Bot. (Suppl.)* 32:42 (1991).
21. Caldwell, M. M., W. G. Gold, G. Harris, and C. W. Ashurst. "A Modulated Lamp System for Solar UV-B (280–320 nm) Supplementation Studies in the Field," *Photochem. Photobiol.* 37:479–485 (1983).
22. Lydon, J., A. H. Teramura, and E. G. Summers. "Effects of Ultraviolet-B Radiation on the Growth and Productivity of Field Grown Soybean," in *Stratospheric Ozone Reduction, Solar Ultraviolet Radiation and Plant Life*, R. C. Worrest and M. M. Caldwell, Eds. (Berlin: Springer-Verlag, 1986), pp. 313–325.
23. Booker, F. L., E. L. Fiscus, R. B. Philbeck, A. S. Heagle, and W. W. Heck. "A Supplemental Ultraviolet-B Radiation System for Open-Top Field Chambers," *J. Environ.* 21:56–61 (1992).
24. Setlow, R. B. "The Wavelength in Sunlight Effective in Producing Skin Cancer: A Theoretical Analysis," *Proc. Natl. Acad. Sci. U.S.A.* 71:3363–3365 (1974).
25. Caldwell, M. M., L. B. Camp, C. W. Warner, and S. D. Flint. "Action Spectra and Their Key Role in Assessing Biological Consequences of Solar UV-B Radiation Change," in *Stratospheric Ozone Reduction, Solar Ultraviolet Radiation and Plant Life*, NATO ASI Series G: Ecological Sciences, Vol. 8, R. C. Worrest and M. M. Caldwell, Eds. (Berlin: Springer-Verlag, 1986), pp. 87–112.
26. Tevini, M., U. Mark, and M. Saile. "Plant Experiments in Growth Chambers Illuminated with Natural Sunlight," in *Environmental Research with Plants in Closed Chambers*, H. D. Payer, T. Pfirrmann, and P. Mathy, Eds., *Air Poll. Res.* 26:240–251 (1990).
27. Yu, W., A. H. Teramura, and J. H. Sullivan. "Model YMT & UV-B Modulation System Manual of Operation," Final Report submitted to the U.S. Environmental Protection Agency, Corvallis, Oregon (1991).
28. Biggs, R. H., S. V. Kossuth, and A. H. Teramura. "Response of 19 Cultivars of Soybeans to Ultraviolet-B Irradiance," *Physiol. Plant.* 53:19–26 (1981).
29. Tevini, M., W. Iwanzik, and U. Thoma. "Some Effects of Enhanced UV-B Radiation on the Growth and Composition of Plants," *Planta* 153:388–394 (1981).
30. Murali, N. S. and A. H. Teramura. "Intraspecific Differences in *Cucumis sativus* to Ultraviolet-B Radiation," *Physiol. Plant.* 68:673–677 (1986).
31. Tevini, M. and W. Iwanzik. "Effects of UV-B Radiation on Growth and Development of Cucumber Seedlings," in *Statospheric Ozone Reduction, Solar Ultraviolet Radiation and Plant Life*, NATO Series G: Ecological Sciences, Vol. 8, R. C. Worrest and M. M. Caldwell, Eds. (Berlin: Springer-Verlag, Heidelberg, 1986), pp. 271–285.
32. Tevini, M., J. Braun, G. Fieser, U. Mark, J. Ros, and M. Saile. "Effekte solarer und künstlicher UV-B-Strahlung auf Wachstum, Funktion und Zusammensetzung von Nutzpflanzen," BPT-Bericht 5/90, GSF München (1990).
33. Tevini, M., J. Braun, P. Grusemann, and J. Ros. "UV-Wirkungen auf Nutzpflanzen," in *Lauffener Sem. Beitr.* 3/88, Akad. Naturforsch. Landschaftspflege (ANL), Laufen/Salzach (1989), pp. 38–51.

34. Ros, J. "On the Effect of UV-Radiation on Elongation Growth of Sunflower Seedlings (*Helianthus annus* L.)," in *Karlsr. Beitr. Entw. Ökophysiol. 8*, M. Tevini, Ed. (1990), pp. 1–157.

35. Ballaré, C. L., P. W. Barnes, and R. E. Kendrick. "Photomorphogenetic Effects of UV-B-Radiation on Hypocotyl Elongation in Wild Type and Stable Phytochrome-Deficient Mutant Seedlings of Cucumber," *Physiol. Plant.* 83:652–658 (1991).

36. Teramura, A. H. and J. H. Sullivan. "Soybean Growth Responses to Enhanced Levels of Ultraviolet-B Radiation Under Greenhouse Conditions," *Am. J. Bot.* 74:975–979 (1987).

37. Teramura, A. H., L. H. Ziska, and A. E. Sztein. "Changes in Growth and Photosynthetic Capacity of Rice with Increased UV-B Radiation," *Physiol. Plant.* 83:373–383 (1991).

38. Barnes, P. W., P. W. Jordan, W. G. Gold, S. D. Flint, and M. M. Caldwell. "Competition, Morphology and Canopy in Wheat (*Tricium aestivum* L.) and Wild Oat (*Avena fatua* L.) Exposed to Enhanced Ultraviolet-B Radiation," *Funct. Ecol.* 2:319–330 (1988).

39. Kossuth, S. V. and R. H. Biggs. "Ultraviolet-B Radiation Effects on Early Seedling Growth of *Pinaceae* species," *Can. J. For. Res.* 11:243–248 (1981).

40. Sullivan, J. H. and A. H. Teramura. "Effects of Ultraviolet-B Irradiation on Seedling Growth in the *Pinaceae*," *Am. J. Bot.* 75(2):225–230 (1988).

41. Sullivan, J. H. and A. H. Teramura. "Field Study of the Interaction Between Solar Ultraviolet-B Radiation and Drought on Photosynthesis and Growth in Soybean," *Plant Physiol.* 92:141–146 (1989).

42. Sullivan, J. H. and A. H. Teramura. "The Effects of UV-B Radiation on Loblolly Pine. Growth of Field-Grown Seedlings," *Trees* 6:115–120 (1991).

43. Gold, W. G. and M. M. Caldwell. "The Effects of Ultraviolet-B Radiation on Plant Competition in Terrestrial Ecosystems," *Physiol. Plant.* 58:435–444 (1983).

44. Fox, F. M. and M. M. Caldwell. "Competitive Interaction in Plant Populations Exposed to Supplementary Ultraviolet-B Radiation," *Oecologia* 36:173–190 (1978).

45. Barnes, P. W., S. D. Flint, and M. M. Caldwell. "Morphological Responses of Crop and Weed Species of Different Growth Forms to Ultraviolet-B Radiation," *Am. J. Bot.* 77:1354–1360 (1990).

46. Beyschlag, W., P. W. Barnes, S. D. Flint, and M. M. Caldwell. "Enhanced UV-B Irradiation Has No Effect on Photosynthetic Characteristics of Wheat (*Tricium aestivum* L.) and Wild Oat (*Avena fatua* L.) Under Greenhouse and Field Conditions," *Photosynthetica* 22:516–525 (1988).

47. Caldwell, M. M., A. H. Teramura, and M. Tevini. "The Changing Solar Ultraviolet Climate and the Ecological Consequences for Higher Plants," *Trends Ecol. Evol.* 4:363–366 (1989).

48. Flint, S. D. and M. M. Caldwell. "Influence of Floral Optical Properties on the Ultraviolet Radiation Environment of Pollen," *Am. J. Bot.* 70:1416–1419 (1983).

49. Flint, S. D. and M. M. Caldwell. "Comparative Sensitivity of Binucleate and Trinucleate Pollen to Ultraviolet Radiation. A Theoretical Perspective," in *Stratospheric Ozone Reduction, Solar Ultraviolet Radiation and Plant Life,* R. C. Worrest and M. M. Caldwell, Eds. (Berlin: Springer-Verlag, 1984), pp. 211–222.

50. Campbell, W. F., M. M. Caldwell, and W. B. Sisson. "Effect of UV-B Radiation on Pollen Germination," in *Impacts of Climatic Change on the Biosphere,* CIAP Monogr. 5. (Washington, D.C.: U.S. Department of Transportation, 1975), pp. 227–276.

51. Chang, D. C. N. and W. F. Campbell. "Responses of *Tradescantia* Stamen Hairs and Pollen to UV-B Irradiation," *Environ. Exp. Bot.* 16:195–199 (1976).

52. Caldwell, M. M., R. Robberecht, S. Holman, R. Nowak, L. B. Camp, S. D. Flint, G. Harris, and A. H. Teramura. "Higher Plant Responses to Elevated Ultraviolet Irradiance," Annual Report 1978, NAS-9-14871, NASA, Department of Range Science & Ecology Center, Utah State University, Logan, Utah (1979).

53. Flint, S. D. and M. M. Caldwell. "Partial inhibition of In Vitro Pollen Germination by Simulated Solar Ultraviolet-B Radiation," *Ecology* 65:792–795 (1984).

54. Kasperbauer, L. W. and W. E. Loomis. "Inhibition of Flowering by Natural Daylight on an Inbred Strain of *Melilotus,*" *Crop. Sci.* 5:193–194 (1983).

55. Caldwell, M. M. "Solar Ultraviolet Radiation as an Ecological Factor for Alpine Plants," *Ecol. Monogr.* 38:243–268 (1968).

56. Klein, R. M., P. C. Edsall, and A. C. Gentile. "Effects of Near Ultraviolet and Green Radiations on Plant Growth," *Plant Physiol.* 40:903–906 (1965).

57. Rau, W., H. Hoffmann, A. Huber-Wille, U. Mitzka-Schnabel, and E. Schrott. *Die Wirkung von UV-B auf photoregulierte Entwicklungsvorgänge bie Pflanzen* (Munich: Gesellschaft für Strahlen- und Umweltforschung mbH, BPT-Bericht, 1988).

58. Hart, R. H., G. E. Carlson, H. H. Klueter, and H. R. Carns. "Response of Economically Valuable Species to Ultraviolet Radiation," in *Climatic Impacts Assessment Program (CIAP),* Monography 5, D. S. Nachtway, M. M. Caldwell, and R. H. Biggs, Eds. (U.S. Department of Transportation, Report No. DOT-TST-75-55, Springfield, VA, 1975), pp. 263–275.

59. Saile-Mark, M. and M. Tevini. Unpublished results (1992).

60. Teramura, A. H. "Interaction Between UV-B Radiation and Other Stresses in Plants," in *Stratospheric Ozone Reduction, Solar Ultraviolet Radiation and Plant Life,* NATO ASI Series, Series G: Ecological Sciences, Vol. 8, R. C. Worrest and M. M. Caldwell, Eds. (Berlin: Springer, 1986), pp. 327–343.

61. Murali, N. S. and A. H. Teramura. "Effectiveness of UV-B Radiation on the Growth and Physiology of Field-Grown Soybean Modified by Water Stress," *Photochem. Photobiol.* 44:215–219 (1986).

62. Murali, N. S. and A. H. Teramura. "Intensity of Soybean Photosynthesis to Ultraviolet-B Radiation Under Phosphorus Deficiency," *J. Plant Nutr.* 10:501–515 (1987).

63. Tevini, M., U. Mark, G. Fieser, and M. Saile. "Effects of Enhanced Solar UV-B Radiation on Growth and Function of Crop Plant Seedlings," in *Current Topics in Plant Biochemistry and Physiology, Vol. 10.* (Columbia, MO: University of Missouri, 1991) pp. 13–31.

64. Naidu, S. L., J. H. Sullivan, A. H. Termaura, and E. H. DeLucia. "The Effects of Ultraviolet Radiation on Photosynthesis of Different Needle Age Classes in Field Grown Loblolly Pine," in *Current Topics in Plant Biochemistry and Physiology, Vol. 10* (Columbia, MO: University of Missouri, 1991), p. 304.

65. Teramura, A. H., M. Tevini, and W. Iwanzik. "Effects of Ultraviolet-B Irradiance on Plants During Mild Water Stress. I. Effects on Diurnal Stomatal Resistance," *Physiol. Plant.* 57:175–180 (1983).

66. Negash, L. and L. O. Björn. "Stomatal Closure by Ultraviolet Radiation," *Physiol. Plant.* 66:360–364 (1986).

67. El-Sarout, S. "On the Effects of UV Radiation on Stomata and Transpiration of Selected Plants," in *Karlsr. Beitr. Entw. Ökophysiol. 10*, M. Tevini, Ed. (1991), pp. 1–118.

68. Negash, L. "Wavelength-Dependence of Stomatal Closure by Ultraviolet Radiation in Attached Leaves of *Eragrostis tef*: Action Spectra Under Backgrounds of Red and Blue Lights," *Plant Physiol. Biochem.* 25:753–760 (1987).

69. Negash, L., P. Jensen, and L. O. Björn. "Effect of Ultraviolet Radiation on Accumulation and Leakage of ^{86}Rb$^+$ in Guard Cells of *Vicia faba*," *Physiol. Plant.* 69:200–204 (1987).

70. Tevini, M. and W. Iwanzik. "Inhibition of Photosynthetic Activity in Radish Seedlings," *Physiol. Plant.* 58:395–400 (1983).

71. Strid, A., W. S. Chow, and J. M. Anderson. "Effects of Supplementary Ultraviolet-B Radiation on Photosynthesis in *Pisum sativum*," *Biochim. Biophys. Acta* 1020:260–268 (1990).

72. Noorudeen, A. M. and G. Kulandaivelu. "On the Possible Site of Inhibition of Photosynthetic Electron Transport by Ultraviolet-B (UV-B) Radiation," *Physiol. Plant.* 55:161–166 (1982).

73. Tevini, M. and K. Pfister. "Inhibition of Photosystem II by UV-B Radiation," *Z. Naturforsch.* 40c:129–133 (1985).

74. Tevini, M., P. Grusemann, and G. Fieser. *Assessment of UV-B Stress by Chlorophyll Fluorescence Analysis. Applications of Chlorophyll Fluorescence*, H. K. Lichtenthaler, Ed. (Dordrecht: Kluwer Academic Publishers, 1988), pp. 229–238.

75. Bornman, J. F., L. O. Björn, and H. E. Akerlund. "Action Spectrum for Inhibition by Ultraviolet Radiation of Photosystem II Activity in Spinach Thylakoids," *Photochem. Photobiophys.* 8:305–313 (1984).

76. Cen, Y.-P. and J. F. Bornman. "The Response of Bean Plants to UV-B Radiation Under Different Irradiances of Background Visible Light," *Botanika* 41:1489–149 (1990).

77. Tevini, M., U. Mark, G. Fieser, and M. Saile. "Effects of Enhanced Solar UV-B Radiation on Growth and Function of Selected Crop Plant Seedlings," in *Photobiology*, E. Riklis, Ed. (New York: Plenum Press, 1991), pp. 635–649.

78. Tevini, M., J. Braun, and G. Fieser. "The Protective Function of the Epidermal Layer of Rye Seedlings Against Ultraviolet-B Radiation," *Photochem. Photobiol.* 53:329–333 (1991).

79. Kulandeivelu, G., S. Maragatham, and N. Nedunchezhian. "On the Possible Control of Ultraviolet-B Induced Response in Growth and Photosynthetic Activities in Higher Plants," *Physiol. Plant.* 76:398–404 (1989).

80. Kulandeivelu, G., N. Nedunchezhian, and K. Annamalaninathan. "Ultraviolet-B (280–320 nm) Radiation Induced Changes in Photochemical Activities and Polypeptide Components of C_3- and C_4 Chloroplasts," *Photosynthetica* 25:333–339 (1992).
81. Vu, C. V., L. H. Allen, and L. A. Garrad. "Effects of Enhanced UV-B Radiation (280–320 nm) on Ribulose-1,5-Bisphosphate Carboxylase in Pea and Soybean," *Environ. Exp. Bot.* 24:131–143 (1984).
82. Mark, U. "On the Effect of Increased Artificial and Solar UV-B Radiation in Combination with Increased Temperature and Carbon Dioxide Concentration on Growth and Gas Exchange of Selected Crop Plants," *Karlr. Beitr. Entw. Ökophysiol.* 11, M. Tevini, Ed. (1992), pp. 1–220.
83. Jordan, B. R., J. He, W. S. Chow, and J. H. Anderson. "Changes in mRNA levels and Polypeptide Subunits of Ribulose, 1,5-Bisphosphate Carboxylase in Response to Supplemental Ultraviolet-B-Radiation," *Plant Cell Environ.* 15:91–98 (1992).
84. Ziska, L. H. and A. H. Teramura. "Modification of CO_2 Enhancement of Growth and Photosynthesis in Rice (*Oryza sativa*), Modification by Increased Ultraviolet-B Radiation," *Plant Physiol.* 99:473–48 (1992).
85. Tevini, M. and U. Mark. "Effects of Enhanced UV-B and Temperature on Growth and Function in Crop Plants," International Congress on Photobiology, Kyoto, Japan, Sept. 1992.
86. Kramer, G. F., H. A. Norman, D. T. Krizek, and R. Mirecki. "Influence of UV-B Radiation on Polyamines, Lipid Perioxidation and Membrane Lipids in Cucumber," *Photochemistry* 30:2101–2108 (1991).
87. Tevini, M., J. Ros, U. Mark, and T. Hietzker. "UV-B Effects on Terrestrial Plants," in *Plant Photoreceptors and Photo Perception*, Proceedings, Cambridge, 20–23 Sept. 1992, in press.
88. Tevini, M. and D. Steinmüller. "Influence of Light, UV-B Radiation and Herbicides on Wax Biosynthesis of Cucumber Seedlings," *J. Plant Physiol.* 131:111–121 (1987).
89. Roth, B. "The Essential Oils of Selected Spices: Composition and Biosynthesis of the Oils during Development and after Artificial UV-Radiation," *Karlsr. Beitr. Entw. Ökophysiol.* 12, M. Tevini, Ed. (1992), pp. 1–24.
90. Tevini, M., W. Iwanzik, and A. H. Teramura. "Effects of UV-B Radiation on Plants During Mild Water Stress. II. Effects on Growth, Protein and Flavonoid Content," *Z. Pflanzenphysiol.* 110:459–467 (1983).
91. Beggs, C. J., U. Schneider-Ziebert, and E. Wellmann. "UV-B Radiation and Adaptive Mechanisms in Plants, in *Stratospheric Ozone Reduction, Solar Ultraviolet Radiation and Plant Life*, NATO ASI Series G: Ecological Sciences, Vol. 8, R. C. Worrest and M. M. Caldwell, Eds. (Berlin: Springer-Verlag, 1986), pp. 235–250.
92. Robberecht, R. and M. M. Caldwell. "Leaf UV Optical Properties of *Rumex patentia* L. and *Rumex obtusifolia* L. in Regard to a Protective Mechanism Against Solar UV-B Radiation Injury," in *Stratospheric Ozone Reduction, Solar Ultraviolet Radiation and Plant Life*, NATO ASI Series G: Ecological Sciences, Vol. 8, R. C. Worrest and M. M. Caldwell, Eds. (Berlin: Springer-Verlag, 1986), p. 251.

93. Bornmann, J. F. and T. C. Vogelmann. "Effects of UV-B Radiation on Leaf Optical Properties Measured with Fibre Optics," *J. Exp. Bot.* 42:547–554 (1991).

94. Wellmann, E. "Regulation der Flavonoidbiosynthese durch ultraviolettes Licht und Phytochrome in Zellkulturen und Keimlingen von Petersilie (*Petroselinum hortense* Hoffm.)", *Ber. Dtsch. Bot. Ges.* 87:267–273 (1974).

95. Beggs, C. J., A. Stolzer-Jehle, and E. Wellmann. "Isoflavonoid Formation as an Indicator of UV Stress in Bean (*Phaseolus vulgaris* L.) Leaves. The Significance of Photorepair in Assessing Potential Damage by Increased Solar UV-B Radiation," *Plant Physiol.* 79:630–634 (1985).

96. Braun, J. and M. Tevini. "Regulation of UV-Protective Pigment Synthesis in the Epidermal Layer of Rye Seedlings (*Secale cereale* L. cv. Kustro)," *Photochem. Photobiol.* 57:318–323 (1993).

97. Braun, J. "The Protective Function of Phenolic Compounds of Rye and Oat Seedlings against UV-B Radiation and Their Biosynthetic Regulation," *Karlsr. Beitr. Entw. Ökophysiol.* 9, M. Tevini, Ed. (1991), pp. 1–237.

98. Larson, R. A., W. J. Garrison, and R. W. Carlson. "Differential Responses of Alpine and Non-alpine *Aquilegia* Species to Increased UV-B Radiation," *Plant Cell Environ.* 13:983–987 (1990).

99. Zangerl, A. R. and M. R. Berenbaum. "Furanocoumarins in Wild Parsnip: Effect of Photosynthetically Active Radiations, Ultraviolet Light and Nutrients," *Ecology* 68:516–520 (1987).

100. Lydon, J., A. H. Teramura, and C. B. Coffman. "UV-B Radiation Effects on Photosynthesis, Growth and Cannibinoid Production of Two *Cannabis sativa* chemotypes," *Photochem. Photobiol.* 46:201–206 (1987).

101. Pate, D. W. "Possible Role of Ultraviolet Radiation in Evolution of *Cannabis* Chemotypes," *Econ. Bot.* 37:396–405 (1983).

102. Pang, Q. and J. B. Hays. "UV-B-Inducible and Temperature-Sensitive Photoreactivation of Cyclobutane Pyrimidine Dimers in *Arabidopsis thalina*," *Plant Physiol.* 95:536–543 (1991).

103. Langer, B. E. and E. Wellman. "Phytochrome Induction of Photoreactivation in *Phaseolus vulgaris* L. Seedlings," *Photochem. Photobiol.* 52:861–864 (1990).

104. Teramura, A. H. "Ozone Depletion and Plants," in *Assessing the Risks of Trace Gases That Can Modify the Stratosphere, Vol. VIII,* U.S. EPA report, 1987, pp. 1–117.

105. Biggs, R. H. and S. V. Kossuth. "Effects of Ultraviolet-B Radiation Enhancement under Field Conditions on Potatoes, Tomatoes, Corn, Rice, Southern Peas, Peanuts, Squash, Mustard and Radish," in *UV-B Biological and Climatic Effects Research* (BACER), Final Report, U.S. EPA, Washington, D.C. (1978).

106. Biggs, R. H., P. G. Webb, L. A. Garrard, T. R. Sinclair, and S. H. West. "The Effects of Enhanced Ultraviolet-B Radiation on Rice, Wheat, Corn, Soybean, Citrus and Duckweed," Year 3 interim report. Environmental Protection Agency Report 808075-03, U.S. EPA, Washington, D.C. (1984).

107. Dumpert, K. and T. Knacker. "A Comparison of the Effects of Enhanced UV-B Radiation on Some Crop Plants Exposed to Greenhouse and Field Conditions," *Biochem. Physiol. Pflanz.* 180:599–612 (1985).

108. Teramura, A. H. and N. S. Murali. "Intraspecific Differences in Growth and Yield of Soybean Exposed to Ultraviolet-B Radiation Under Greenhouse and Field Conditions," *Environ. Exp. Bot.* 26:89–95 (1986).

109. Teramura, A. H. and J. W. Sullivan. "Effects of Ultraviolet-B Radiation in Soybean Yield and Seed Quality," *Environ. Poll.* 53:416–469 (1988).

110. Teramura, A. H., J. H. Sullivan, and J. Lydon. "Effects of UV-Radiation on Soybean Yield and Seed Quality: A Six Year Field Study," *Physiol. Plant.* 80:5–11 (1990).

111. Sinclair, T. R., O. N. Diaye, and R. H. Biggs. "Growth and Yield of Field Grown Soybean in Response to Enhanced Exposure to UV-B Radiation," *J. Environ. Qual.* 19:478–481 (1990).

112. Teramura, A. H., M. C. Perry, J. Lydon, M. S. McIntosh, and E. G. Summers. "Effects of Ultraviolet-B Radiation on Plants During Mild Water Stress. III. Effects on Photosynthetic Recovery and Growth in Soybean," *Physiol. Plant.* 60:484–492 (1984).

113. Teramura, A. H., I. N. Forseth, and J. Lydon. "Effects of UV-B Radiation on Plants During Mild Water Stress. 4. The Insensitivity of Soybean *Glycine max* Cultivar Essex Internal Water Relations to UV-B Radiation," *Physiol. Plant.* 62:384–389 (1984).

114. Dubé, L. S. and J. F. Bornman. "The Response of Young Spruce Seedlings to Simultaneous Exposure of Ultraviolet-B Radiation and Cadmium," *Plant Physiol. Biochem.* 30:761–767 (1992).

115. Teramura, A. H., J. H. Sullivan, and L. H. Ziska. "Interaction of Elevated UV-B Radiation and CO_2 on Productivity and Photosynthetic Characteristics in Wheat, Rice, and Soybean," *Plant Physiol.* 94:470–475 (1990).

116. Panagopoulus, I., J. F. Bornman, and L. O. Björn. "Response of Sugar Beet Plants to Ultraviolet-B (280–320 nm) Radiation and *Cercospora* Leaf Spot Disease," *Physiol. Plant.* 84:140–145 (1991).

117. Orth, A. B., A. H. Teramura, and H. D. Sisler. "Effects of UV-B Radiation on Fungal Disease Development in *Cucumis sativus*," *Am. J. Bot.* 77:1188–1192 (1990).

118. Green, A. E. S., K. R. Cross, and L. A. Smith. "Improved Analytical Characterization of Ultraviolet Skylight," *Photochem. Photobiol.* 31(1):59–65 (1980).

6

Effects of Enhanced Solar Ultraviolet Radiation on Aquatic Ecosystems

Donat-P. Häder

UV-B AND THE AQUATIC ECOSYSTEM

Reduction of the Ozone Layer and Increase in Solar Ultraviolet Radiation

Recent measurements have indicated that the predicted reductions in stratospheric ozone concentrations have begun to materialize. The most prominent example is the Antarctic ozone hole which opens up during the local spring starting in September through December, when the ozone concentration decreases by more than 50% to below 150 Dobson units (1 Dobson unit = 0.01 mm path length) over an area the size of the continental U.S.[1-3] In addition, there is growing concern about a potential development of another ozone hole over the northern polar regions because of high chlorine concentrations in the Arctic atmosphere. However, not only polar regions are affected, since there is a measurable decrease in the ozone concentration on a global basis. Due to increasing pollution and aerosol concentrations over the industrialized northern hemisphere, which partially balances the effect of decreasing stratospheric ozone concentrations, satistically significant increases in UV-B radiation have not been measured in many areas of the northern hemisphere; one of the exceptions is a study by Blumthaler and Ambach,[4] who found significant increases in UV-B radiation on the moun-

0-87371-911-5/93/$0.00 + $.50
© 1993 by Lewis Publishers

tain of Jungfraujoch in southern Germany. In contrast, in the southern hemisphere an average increase by about 6% has been measured.[5]

Spectral Distribution of UV-B Radiation in the Water Column

The attenuation of solar radiation on the water column strongly depends on the wavelength:[6] short- and long-wavelength radiation is absorbed more strongly than green and blue radiation. UV-B is also strongly absorbed. However, the transparency of water to ultraviolet radiation is also largely affected by the type of water, which has been classified into several types.[7] Coastal waters with high turbidity and large concentrations of gelbstoff allow UV-B to penetrate only a few decimeters or meters.[8,9] In contrast, in clear oceanic waters UV-B has been found to penetrate dozens of meters,[10] and in Antarctic waters 1% of the solar UV-B impinging on the surface has been measured at a depth of 65 m.[11]

During a recent cruise the downwelling radiation has been measured in Antarctic waters using a light and ultraviolet submenible spectroradio (LUVSS) instrument.[12] This instrument has a 0.2 nm resolution from 250 to 350 nm and a 0.8 nm resolution from 350 to 700 nm. It is installed on a remote-operated vehicle which dives to a certain depth and measures data while moving upward in the water column. Since it is independent from the host vessel the measurements are not perturbed. Calculating the ratio of UV-B to total flux gave results consistent with the total ozone mapping system (TOMS) as well as balloon data and surface data from the Palmer National Science Foundation Monitoring Station. The data even allowed researchers to determine when the ozone hole vortex was over the measurement site and when it was not. Phytoplankton productivity was found to be limited by UV-B and inhibition increased linearly with increasing dose. A 15–20% inhibition of photosynthesis could be measured in surface samples after a 7–12 h incubation period compared to 40–60% inhibition in samples from a depth of 5 m. This higher inhibition in subsurface samples may be due to UV-A-dependent photoregulatory processes. Differences could clearly be determined between measurements inside and outside the ozone hole.[12]

THE AQUATIC ECOSYSTEMS

The observed effects of solar and increased UV-B radiation on phytoplankton organisms have caused growing concern for aquatic ecosystems.[13-20] This chapter will concentrate on the measured and predicted effects of increased solar ultraviolet radiation on aquatic microorganisms, including phytoplankton and zooplankton in both freshwater and marine habitats. It will also concentrate on the expected consequences of UV-related phytoplankton losses including changes in species composition, global climate changes and decreases in food production for human consumption.

While this chapter includes effects of ultraviolet radiation on freshwater systems, the most severe effects are expected in the marine habitats because of their immense size, which exceeds the terrestrial habitats almost by a factor of two. The area of freshwater habitats is only 0.5% that of marine habitats.

The photosynthetic production of organic biomass on our planet has been estimated to incorporate about 2×10^{11} tons of carbon annually. Terrestrial ecosystems — forests, savannas, crop plants, etc. — produce about half of that biomass and incorporate about 100 gigatons of carbon annually, while the other half (104 gigatons carbon annually) is due to the primary producers (phytoplankton) in the oceans[21] (Figure 1). In contrast, the standing crop of phytoplankton is rather small compared to terrestrial systems. Because of the large productivity of the marine phytoplankton ecosystem even a small percentage decrease in the biomass productivity of these organisms due to an increased exposure to solar UV-B radiation may have dramatic effects both on the intricate ecosystem itself and on humans, who depend on this system in many ways.

Primary Producers

Phytoplanktonic microorganisms depend on solar energy for their growth and metabolism, and therefore it is not surprising that they are not equally distributed in the water column.[22,23] Most organisms dwell in the top layers of the water column, the euphotic zone, which depending on the transparency of the water extends from a few decimeters to several dozen meters. A useful measure for the depth of the euphotic zone is the attenuation of photosynthetically active radiation (PAR) to 1% (= 2 O.D.) of the incident radiation, which is called one attenuation unit. This is about the depth where photosynthesis is balanced by respiration. The actual depth of one attenuation unit may range from a few feet to several hundred feet depending on the turbidity of the water.[24] The highest concentration of organisms is not found immediately close to the water surface since the cells are affected by too high irradiances at the surface, but most cells are distributed within the euphotic zone and only a few organisms are found in the subsequent attenuation zones (Figure 2).

Because of their position within the euphotic zone close to the surface the cells are exposed to high levels of solar irradiation. Since the unicellular phytoplankton cells do not have protective layers such as an epidermis they are likely to be affected by the short-wavelength irradiation. There are two pieces of evidence that even current levels of radiation affect the organisms:

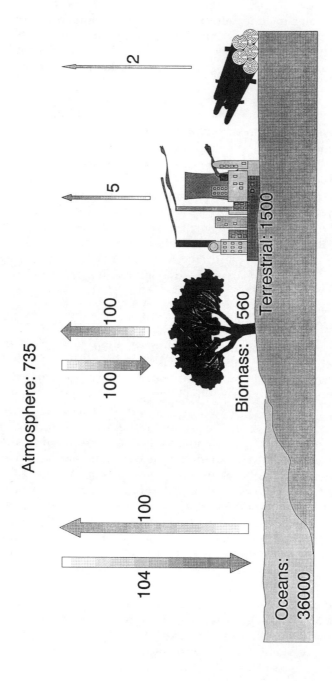

Figure 1 Global carbon cycles in terrestrial and aquatic ecosystems (all numbers in gigatons). Also shown are the emissions from anthropogenic sources as well as the sizes of important carbon reservoirs. (Modified from Houghton and Woodwell, 1989.)

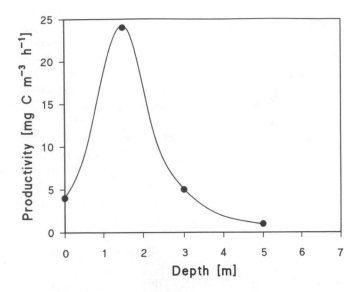

Figure 2   Distribution of phytoplankton in the water column as indicated by the incorporation of carbon. (Modified from Cabrera and Montecino, 1987.)

1. The large algal blooms in the oceans as well as in freshwater habitats occur after the winter, when permissive temperatures allow growth and frequent cell divisions. However, these blooms disappear when the level of solar irradiation increases during its summer maximum. Often there is a second smaller algal bloom in autumn, when the UV-B levels have decreased, provided that the temperature is still high enough and that there are sufficient nutrients in the water.

2. The concentration of phytoplankton is not uniform in the oceans of the globe. Rather, the density — as measured as the number of cells per volume or concentration of chlorophyll — is highest in the cir-cumpolar regions with their low UV-B levels, while the density is 100 to 1000 times smaller in the equatorial waters, where the UV-B levels are much higher. The ratio of UV-B:UV-A:PAR is much higher in tropical seas than in any other ocean areas.[25] Of course, other factors, such as nutrient concentration, temperature, salinity, etc., may also affect growth and abundance of phytoplankton. Pseudo-color satellite photographs showing the phytoplankton concentra-tions reveal one exception to the general pattern: there are large concentrations of phytoplankton in the upwelling areas on the con-tinental shelves[26] with a high turbidity and gelbstoff concentration which may attenuate the ultraviolet radiation.

Phytoplankton and the Biological Food Web

Phytoplanktonic organisms are the primary producers of biomass in both freshwater and marine ecosystems and are thus at the base of the intricate biological food web within the aquatic habitat. The biomass they produce is utilized by the primary consumers (zooplankton) such as unicellular organisms and then passed to the nekton (free-swimming organisms), including krill, mollusk, fish and crab larvae, which in turn are consumed by organisms of the next level in the food web. The end consumers are large fish, birds and mammals, including humans.

The transition from one level to the next reduces the amount of biomass by a factor of about 10; i.e., 1000 g of phytoplankton yield 100 g of larvae, which produce 10 g of small fish which eventually yield 1 g of large fish. Since the consumers follow the primary producers they are exposed to the same radiation regime as the phytoplankton, which may affect them directly. In addition, they are affected indirectly when the productivity of the primary producers is decreased by high UV-B irradiation.

UV-B EFFECTS ON PHYTOPLANKTON

The first measurements of UV-B sensitivity were performed in the laboratory using a number of test systems, the biochemistry and behavior of which had been established beforehand. These systems allowed the detection and quantification of UV-B stress-induced changes experimentally. However, the behavior of laboratory strains often significantly differs from that of natural populations. Furthermore, artificial radiation sources, which have been used frequently to study the effects on microorganisms, produce a spectrum that deviates significantly from natural solar radiation both quantitatively and qualitatively. While laboratory investigations are necessary and important to reveal the mechanisms of UV-B damage and repair, ecologically relevant data can only be gathered by studying the effects of solar radiation of different irradiances on natural populations. Therefore, recently, research has been extended to ecologically important algal groups, such as dinoflagellates, cryptophyceae and diatoms.

The Antarctic is specifically productive in phytoplankton, and the famous surgeon and botanist J. D. Hooker, who traveled with Sir James Clark Ross on the *Erebus* and *Terror* expedition to the Antarctic, wrote that the diatoms "occured in such countless myriads as to stain the sea everywhere of a pale ochreous brown, in some cases causing the surface of the ocean, from the locality of the ships, as far as [the] eye could reach, to assume a pale brown colour."[125] In addition to the free-swimming phytoplankton, there is a large flora in the pack ice, which also stains the ice brown. These ice algae are supposed to be an important inoculum for the phytoplankton communities during the spring bloom after the ice melts.[36] One of the first investigations carried out on Antarctic phytoplankton was performed in 1987 by El Sayed, who studied the effect of ambient and enhanced ultraviolet radiation on natural phytoplankton populations taken from the water or from melted ice. The organisms were kept in tanks outside the Palmer station laboratory under ambient light conditions. In one tank the phytoplankton was exposed to natural light including UV-A and UV-B, while in the second tank both UV-A and UV-B were excluded. In a third tank UV-B was reduced, and in a fourth the level of UV-B radiation was enhanced by 50% using sunlamps (which is roughly equivalent to a 25% ozone depletion). The experiments showed that phytoplankton productivity was two to four times higher in the tank where UV-A and UV-B were excluded. Pigmentation was also affected, and the cells looked pale as compared to the irradiated cells. In contrast, in some phytoplankton the amount of carotenoids, believed to reduce the effects of excessive radiation, increased under moderate UV stress (see below). The main species in the population was *Navicula glacei*, which produced mainly α- and β-carotene as well as zeaxanthin.

In spite of forming major components of the phytoplankton communities, the nanoplankton, defined by its small size (below 20 μm in diameter), and picoplankton (smaller than 2 μm) are not yet well studied. Specifically in the Antarctic these groups are major links in the food web on which the herbivorous zooplankton and krill feed. In order to evaluate the potential hazards of enhanced solar UV-B radiation on the phytoplankton community, the effects of short-wavelength radiation on both movement and orientation, as well as on physiological and biochemical parameters, need to be understood and quantified.

UV-B EFFECTS ON MOTILITY AND ORIENTATION

Many phytoplankton organisms are motile and actively move to and maintain a specific position in their habitat. Organisms with no active propelling structures such as flagella or cilia often utilize buoyancy to adjust their position within the water column and move up and down by changing their specific density using osmotic mechanisms or gas vacuoles. As the light intensity changes in a circadian pattern which in addition is modulated by a varying cloud cover the optimal zones move up and down in the water column, and consequently the cells have to constantly readjust their positions. Some dinoflagellates have been reported to undergo daily movements of up to 15 m.[27] On top of the active movements the cells are relocated within the mixing layer,[25,28] the size of which depends on the wind and wave conditions.

The cells actively move to and maintain a specific depth within the water column using very precise orientation strategies based on external signals[29] such as light and gravity,[30-32] chemical[33] and temperature gradients,[34] as well as the magnetic field of the earth.[35]

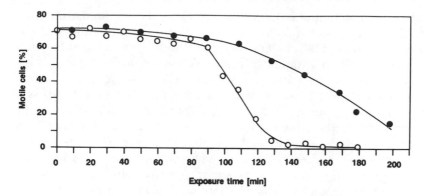

Figure 3   Percentage of motile *Cryptomonas maculata* after exposure to solar radiation (open circles) and under a cuvette with artifically produced
ozone (closed circles).[42]

To cope with the constantly changing conditions in their environment
the organisms must permanently respond to the available cues and readjust their position. Thus, if increased UV-B radiation inhibits motility or
the ability of the cells to respond to the external stimuli, this would
negatively affect their chances for growth and survival. And indeed there
is growing evidence that most phytoplankton studied so far are currently
under UV-B stress even at ambient levels.

INHIBITION OF MOTILITY AND ORIENTATION

Effects of Ultraviolet Radiation on Motility

As mentioned in the introductory section, planktonic organisms are
not evenly distributed in a body of water but rather use a number of
complex strategies to optimize their vertical position. Motility in flagellates has recently been shown to be impaired by both artificial and
solar radiation.[37-41] When exposed to solar radiation the percentage of
motile organisms decreases within a few hours in the marine organism
Cryptomonas maculata (Figure 3).[42] A similar behavior was found in a
freshwater *Cryptomonas*[43] as well as in a number of other flagellates.[44,45]
Simultaneously, the linear velocity of the remaining motile cells decreases drastically (Figure 4). Neither of these two effects is due to thermal stress by the infrared component of solar radiation since the experiments were carried out in temperature-controlled growth chambers
with double-layered Plexiglas tops developed by Tevini (see Chapter 5),
which allow solar radiation to penetrate.

Most of the inhibition is due to the UV-B component of solar radiation
since artificial ultraviolet radiation, which did not contain any visible
radiation, had similar effects.[46-48] Also, reducing the short-wavelength

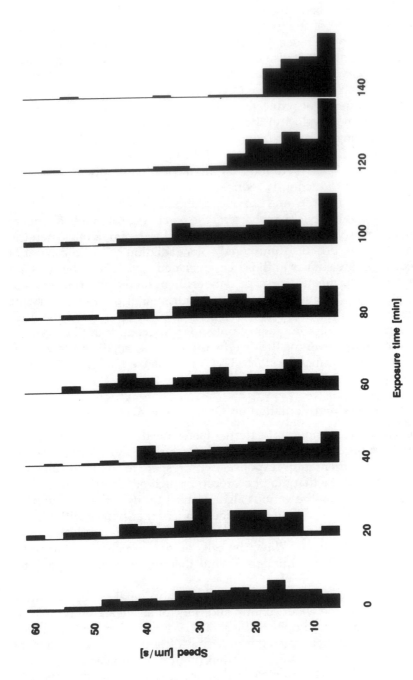

Figure 4 Effect of exposure time to solar radiation on the velocity distribution of *Cryptomonas maculata*.[42]

component of solar radiation by means of UV-B-absorbing cutoff filters (Schott WG series) or by inserting a layer of artificially produced ozone in the top cuvette of the growth chamber over the organisms allowed the organisms to tolerate solar radiation significantly longer. However, it needs to be stated that also UV-A and even visible radiation can affect motility in many phytoplankton systems when they are exposed to unfiltered radiation for a prolonged period of time.

As a consequence of reduced motility (both percentage of motile organisms and linear velocity) the organisms are impaired in their capability of adapting to the changing parameters in their environment so that they are either exposed to too bright light intensities, which may photobleach the cells, or to too dim intensities, where their photosynthetic biomass production is reduced. In both situations the ability of the populations to grow and survive is diminished.[31,49-51]

In gliding filamentous cyanobacteria the percentage of motile filaments and their linear velocity have also been found to be impaired when the organisms are exposed to unfiltered solar radiation.[52-54] The ecological consequences are similar to those in flagellated organisms: the cells are deprived of their means to escape dark areas or too bright irradiation in exposed areas. This may be even more detrimental than in eukaryotic cells since most cyanobacteria have been found to be adapted to rather low fluence rates (on the order of only a few percent of unfiltered solar radiation) and are eventually killed by intensities exceeding a few thousand lux.[55-57] In addition to UV-B, UV-A and visible radiation also exert a negative effect on these organisms.

Effects of Ultraviolet Radiation on Orientation Mechanisms

The single most important external factor for the orientation of phytoplanktonic organisms in the water column may be light.[29,30,58,59] Action spectra for the orientation responses with respect to the light direction (phototaxis) indicate that the photoreceptor pigments employed for this purpose vary among the various algal groups, though most use various bands in the visible and long-UV range to orient themselves with respect to light. None of the organisms studied so far possesses a photoreceptor active in the UV-B band. Thus, the cells do not perceive this radiation — a situation similar to humans — and therefore cannot escape detrimental radiation.

In addition, the responses to visible radiation, vital for optimization of the position in the water column and thus for survival of phytoplanktonic populations, are impaired by solar UV-B radiation. In both freshwater and marine flagellates the precision of orientation is affected by even short exposure to solar radiation (Figure 5). Similar effects have been found in artificial ultraviolet radiation, indicating that the solar UV-B radiation exerts the strongest inhibition, even though effects by UV-A and visible radiation cannot be excluded.

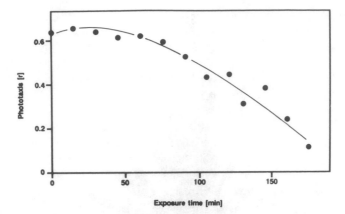

Figure 5 Effect of solar radiation on the precision of orientation in *Peridinium gatunense*.[45]

Peridinium gatunense is an interesting and important flagellate from Lake Kinneret. During its bloom it produces more than 300 g of fresh weight per square meter[60] and dominates all other species by representing 99.5% of the total biomass. Since Lake Kinneret is the most important freshwater reservoir in Israel, the fate of these phytoplankton under increased levels of UV-B may be important. If the cells are sensitive to increased UV-B radiation they may be replaced by another, more tolerant species. If this happens to be one of the numerous poisonous dinoflagellates, the freshwater supply of the country as well the fishing industry in the lake may be at stake.

The organism shows an interesting pattern of orientation:[61] it moves to the surface using positive phototaxis at low fluence rates, with an optimum at 1 klx. At fluence rates exceeding 16 klx the cells move in a diaphototactic manner (perpendicular to the incident sun rays), which causes the cells to remain at a specific water depth. A similar behavior has been found in a marine *Peridinium* (Figure 6). The precision of orientation decreases dramatically when the cells are exposed to solar or artificial ultraviolet radiation[45,48] (Figure 7).

The freshwater flagellate *Euglena* shows positive phototaxis at low fluence rates and negative phototaxis at higher ones.[34] Both responses are affected by UV-B radiation;[37,39] however, negative phototaxis is impared more than positive phototaxis, so that the cells move closer to the surface under increased UV-B radiation, which is detrimental for the cells. When the UV-B component of solar radiation is removed by inserting a UV-B-absorbing cutoff filter or UV opaque glass, the cells oriented themselves for a much longer period of time. This organism is an interesting test system since the molecular mechanism of orientation has been revealed to some extent. The photoreceptor is supposed to be located in the paraflagellar body (PFB), a swelling at the basis of the

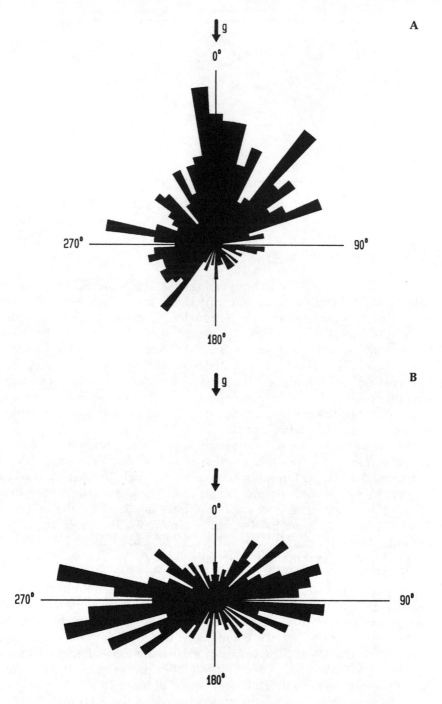

Figure 6   Phototactic orientation of the marine *Peridinium faeroense* (A) at 1750 $\mu E\ m^{-2}\ s^{-1}$ and (B) at 6600 $\mu E\ m^{-2}\ s^{-1}$.[80]

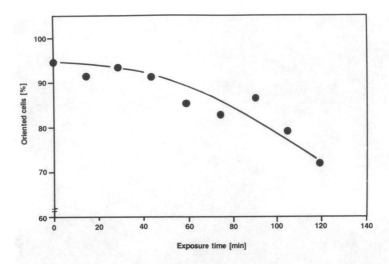

Figure 7   Inhibition of phototaxis in *Peridinium gatunense* by artificial UV-B irradiation.[48]

emerging flagellum, still inside the reservoir (Figure 8). The second flagellum does not leave the reservoir and is attached to the long one near the PFB. Microphotographs taken in a fluorescence microscope reveal a blue fluorescence of the PFB when excited by UV irradiation (370 nm) and a green fluorescence when excited at 450 nm, indicating the presence of two independent photoreceptor systems.

Recently Gualtieri and co-workers[63] refined a method originally developed by Rosenbaum and Child[64] which allowed them to isolate the flagella from the cells so that the PFBs were still attached to the flagella.[65] Fluorescence spectroscopy revealed the presence of both pterins and flavins in the PFB.[66] Biochemical analysis using sodium dodecyl sulfate polyacrylamide gel electrophoresis (SDS PAGE) on a Smartsystem showed that there were four proteins in the flagella with the PFBs attached which were lacking in flagella without PFBs.[67] Further separation of the proteins on a fast protein liquid chromatography (FPLC) using an anion exchange column (MonoQ) also revealed the presence of the four proteins, the molecular weight of which could be determined by subsequent SDS PAGE to be between 27 and 33.5 kDa. The protein fractions separated on the column still retained their chromophoric groups. Fluorescence spectroscopy showed that all four proteins carried a pterin and the 33.5-kDa protein had an additional flavin. Thus, the molecular apparatus for phototaxis seems to operate similar to the photosynthetic apparatus, with antenna pigments absorbing at shorter wavelengths and a reaction center (flavin) which undergoes the photochemical reaction leading to the signal transduction chain.

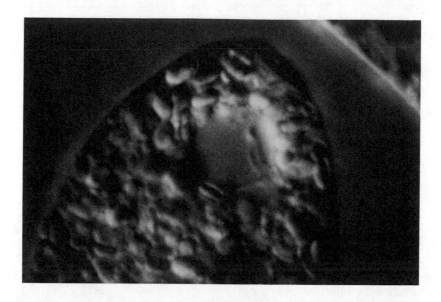

Figure 8   Front end of the green flagellate *Euglena grailis* with the reservoir containing the bases of the two flagella, the longer of which holds the paraflagellar body (PFB), a swelling at the basis of the emerging flagellum, still inside the reservoir. The second flagellum does not leave the reservoir and is attached to the long one near the PFB.[67]

Isoelectric focussing (IEF) also showed the four proteins in addition to the α- and β-subunits of tubulin, which can also be detected by SDS PAGE. In *Astasia*, which does not show phototaxis and which does not contain a PFB, only the two tubulin bands were visible. Pretreatment of the cells with UV-B reduced the amount of PFB proteins, which accounted for the loss of phototaxis after excessive UV radiation.[68] But the tubulin bands were also affected, which explains the effect of UV radiation on motility. The IEF strips can be used to run two-dimensional (2D) gels with SDS PAGE in the second dimension. After this treatment the PFB proteins can be identified by comparison with a sample taken from *Astasia* (with no PFB proteins). 2D gel analysis of cells exposed to UV-B shows a significant reduction of PFB proteins (Figure 9).

In the absence of a light stimulus many organisms have been found to orient themselves with respect to the gravitational field of the earth.[69-72] Unlike the photoreceptor, which has recently been analyzed (see above), the gravireceptor has not been identified in phytoplanktonic organisms. It has even been proposed that the orientation is brought about by a passive physical process: the cell is supposed to be tail heavy so that the front end with the flagella points upward, which would take the cells toward the surface of the water column if they are not reoriented by other stimuli. However, gravitaxis has also been found to be impaired

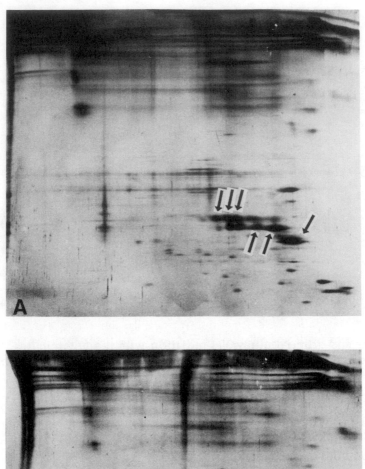

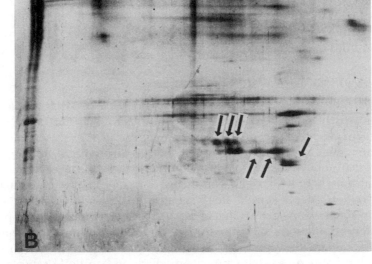

Figure 9 Two-dimensional gel electrophoresis of flagellar and PFB proteins (A) before and (B) after exposure to UV-B.

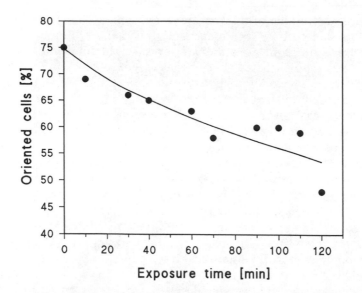

Figure 10   Effect of solar UV-B on the precision of gravitactic orientation in *Peridinium gatunense*.[75]

by solar and artificial ultraviolet radiation within a few minutes,[74] and prolonged exposure of several hours completely disturbs the orientation so that the cells swim randomly (Figure 10). One interesting effect was found in freshwater and marine dinoflagellates: after excessive UV irradiation the cells stop moving and, since they are heavier than water, they sediment in the water column to a lower depth. This behavior may be an effective escape mechanism by which the cells quickly move away from too bright solar radiation.[75,76]

Resulting Movement Patterns

Many flagellates use phototaxis and/or gravitaxis as antagonistic responses, which allow the cells to concentrate in a horizontal band. This band fluctuates vertically in the water column as the environmental conditions, such as the light intensity, change throughout the day.[30,31]

In order to follow the vertical movement patterns of microorganisms a vertical transparent Plexiglas column of 1 m length was constructed with 18 outlets evenly spaced along its length. It was filled either with organism suspensions grown in a growth chamber or with natural phytoplankton populations and then immersed in a natural body of water. After thermal equilibration samples were taken at regular time intervals from outlets using a peristaltic pump which could handle 18 samples in parallel.[77] The data were analyzed using a fully automatic image analysis system programmed to determine the cell densities in the samples.[78] Larger columns are being used for marine populations.

The vertical migrations of the marine dinoflagellate *Prorocentrum micans* are controlled by both phototaxis and gravitaxis.[76] Phototaxis was studied at three different ages and at several light intensities. High irradiances caused the cells to show negative phototaxis and low irradiances yielded positive phototaxis. The precision of negative phototaxis reached a maximum in the early afternoon, while the precision of positive phototaxis was found to peak in the morning and at night. The cells also showed a pronounced negative gravitactic orientation, which had a maximum in precision in the early afternoon. The degree of gravitaxis was found to be constant over time when the cells were confined to a closed cuvette for up to 9 h. As a consequence of the orientation strategies populations of *Prorocentrum micans* showed daily vertical migrations in a 3-m Plexiglas column and accumulated in the top layers in the afternoon, while they were almost randomly distributed during the rest of the day. However, this avoidance response is not sufficient to protect the organisms from enhanced UV-B levels.[79]

Phototaxis and gravitaxis were also studied in the marine dinoflagellates *Amphidinium caterea* and *Peridinium faeroense* at several culture ages.[80] *Peridinium faeroense* showed a positive gravitaxis and *A. caterea* a negative one, the precision of which varied depending on the time of day. While no obvious phototaxis could be observed in *A. caterea*, *P. faeroense* showed a pronounced positive phototaxis at low and intermediate fluence rates and a diaphototaxis (perpendicular to the light beam) at high fluence rates (see above). As a consequence of the orientation mechanisms *P. faeroense* exhibited vertical migrations in a 3-m water column and was found near the surface in the late morning hours and late afternoon; this organism was more randomly distributed during the rest of the day. In contrast, *A. caterea* failed to show vertical migrations.

Since the orientation mechanisms are impaired by UV-B radiation, these important regulation and adaptation strategies fail and the cells lose their capability to orient themselves within the water column. This failure adversely affects the phytoplankton communities.

DEVELOPMENT AND METABOLISM

During the developmental cycle of phytoplankton the sensitivity to solar UV-B radiation changes since the organisms are more vulnerable at some stages than in others. This can be due both to a higher sensitivity and to a more exposed position in the water column. Sublethal doses of UV-B radiation cause a retardation of growth and cell division and thus a loss in biomass. Since some species are more tolerant than others, another consequence is a change in the species composition of phytoplankton in a community.[14,15,81,82] This in turn affects the subsequent links in the food web, since both a loss of organic material and a change in the species composition decrease the availability of food. Changes in the species composition also bear the risk of the development of toxic algal blooms (such as dinoflagellates or cyanobacteria), which have been found to cause poisoning in fish, mussels, crabs and other primary and secondary consumers, including man.

General Metabolism

UV-B radiation affects many physiological and biochemical reactions in microorganisms. At lower doses the radiation impairs growth and the endogenous rhythms found in many microorganisms.[16] Since aromatic amino acids absorb strongly in the UV-B range, proteins are specifically destroyed by the radiation, although at sublethal doses these may be regenerated. Higher doses have been demonstrated to affect membranes and to increase the ion permeability, which eventually causes irreversible damage. Often UV-B effects are amplified by additional stress factors such as salinity and temperature.[83]

Photosynthesis

While no systematic and long-term measurements are available in any of the major phytoplankton habitats, recent preliminary investigations in Antarctic waters have indicated a reduction in photosynthesis by as much as 25% in the top 10 to 20 m due to increased UV-B radiation. Photosynthetic CO_2 incorporation has been measured in situ at various depths in UV-transparent and UV-opaque containers, respectively. It is interesting to note that UV-A had an effect similar to that of UV-B;[19,85] however, only UV-B will be enhanced as a consequence of ozone depletion. Also, the ATP content in Antarctic phytoplankton significantly decreased in the presence of the ozone hole.[86,87] Similar photosynthetic inhibition has been detected in macroalgae at their natural depth.[88,89] UV-B-dependent losses in Antarctic phytoplankton may be significant on a global basis since 10–20% of the global primary production is estimated to be located in the southern oceans.[36]

Target investigations in the laboratory have shown multiple targets of short-wavelength radiation. One of the targets is the herbicide binding protein associated with photosystem II, which causes the electron transport to be affected.[90,91] Another site of action is the water-splitting machinery of the photosynthetic apparatus. The reaction center of photosystem II is damaged by ultraviolet radiation and the integrity of the membranes has been found to be altered, accompanied by a decrease in the lipid content.

Prolonged exposure to UV-B also causes the photosynthetic pigments to be bleached,[92,93] which can be seen even by the naked eye in some phytoplankton organisms.[23,50] In contrast to higher plants, most phytoplankton are not capable of tolerating excessive solar radiation and the organisms die within a few days when exposed to unfiltered sunlight. In an experiment where the cells were forced to stay in a layer of about 10 mm of water, the accessory pigments, responsible for light harvesting in photosynthesis, were bleached within 15 min. Absorption spectra measured at regular time intervals showed that in the marine *Cryptomonas maculata* the accessory biliprotein pigments were bleached first. Next, the carotenoids were found to be bleached; they are thought to have a role in protection from reactive oxygen species produced under excessive radiation. Finally, the chlorophylls were permanently damaged within hours at constant exposure. These effects are primarily due to the UV-B component of solar radiation since they can be reproduced using an artificial ultraviolet radiation source, which emits about 5 W m^{-2} in the UV range.

In vivo fluorescence measurements are also a useful tool to study detrimental effects of UV-B radiation. Fluorescence is a process in which part of the excitation energy is lost by a radiative process rather than being used for photochemical reactions. Thus, the energy emitted by the photosynthetic pigments as fluorescence is wasted as it is not available for conversion of light energy into biochemical energy. Under unstressed conditions about 8% of the excitation energy is lost this way in a phytoplankton population. After a short exposure to UV-B radiation a strong increase in fluorescence can be detected, indicating that the excitation energy cannot be utilized by the photosynthetic apparatus effectively. After longer exposure times the fluorescence decreases again since the absorbing pigments are progressively destroyed by the radiation, as also indicated by absorption spectra discussed above. This effect can be seen in *Cryptomonas* where the fluorescence emitted by the biliproteins increases during the first few minutes of UV-B radiation. Simultaneously, the emission maximum shifts to shorter wavelengths, indicating that the polymeric phycobilins start to disintegrate first into hexamers and subsequently into trimers and monomes (Figure 11). Similar results have been found in natural plankton communities by using spectroscopic data from satellite measurements;[94] this may be a tool in the future to quantify phytoplankton photosynthetic capacity in the oceans and to verify the predicted losses in biomass productivity.

As a consequence of the deleterious processes described above, the photosynthetic oxygen production decreases due to exposure to enhanced UV-B radiation.[19,95,96] This effect can be observed on a much faster time scale than the loss of pigmentation or protein, indicating changes in the structural composition of the photosynthetic apparatus. On example for the rapid decrease in photosynthesis is the cyanobacterium *Phormidium* (a strain isolated from Lake Baikal), in which oxygen production decreases within minutes when exposed to solar radiation (Figure 12). In addition to the UV-B component, this effect, however, may be due to other spectral bands in solar radiation.

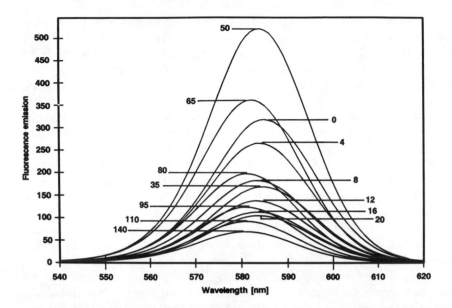

Figure 11   Fluorescence spectra from *Cryptomonas maculata* in vivo measured
after increasing exposure times to solar radiation (numbers at the
curves, in minutes). While the excitation monochromator scanned
the spectral range the emission monochromator was synchronously
adjusted to wavelengths 20 nm longer.[95]

Nitrogen Assimilation

Nitrogen fixation is an important prerequisite for growth because of
its requirement in protein synthesis. The key enzyme for nitrogen assimilation is the nitrogenase, which is activated by light and inactivated
by UV-B radiation. Also, other enzymes which incorporate the nitrogen
into carbon skeletons and produce amino acids are affected by ultraviolet
radiation in a number of ecologically important phytoplanktonic organisms.[97-99]

Higher plants are not able to assimilate atmospheric nitrogen. They
rely on nitrite or nitrate taken up by the roots. In contrast, some prokaryotic organisms, such as cyanobacteria and root nodule bacteria, are
capable of utilizing atmospheric nitrogen and converting it into a form
that can be utilized by higher plants which live in a loose or tight symbiosis with the prokaryotes. Therefore, cyanobacteria play an important
role in providing nitrogen for higher plants, e.g., in tropical rice paddies,[100] where it has been assumed that the annual nitrogen fixation by
cyanobacteria amounts to about 35 million tons. By comparison, artificial
nitrogen fertilizer production with the Haber-Bosch process amounts to
30 million tons annually. In crop areas in the temperate zones cyanobacteria also contribute a significant amount of nitrogen, which has been

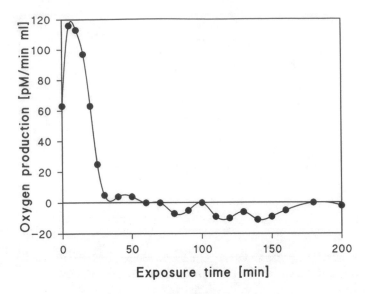

Figure 12 Photosynthetic oxygen production affected by solar radiation in the cyanobacterium *Phormidium uncinatum* (strain isolated from Lake Baikal).

estimated to amount to 1 kg per hectare per year.[101] On the basis of 3.3 billion ha of arable land on our globe this amounts to 36 million tons of atmospheric nitrogen annually.[102] Under optimal conditions the nitrogen incorporation can reach far higher numbers, e.g., in the tropic *Azolla-Anabaena* symbiosis.[103]

TARGETS OF UV-B RADIATION

DNA and Proteins

Most action spectra measured so far indicate that short-wavelength UV-B radiation below 300 nm is more effective than longer wavelength radiation. Only a few action spectra are available for specific UV-B damage effects in microorganisms. Figure 13 shows the action spectrum for the inhibition of motility in the photosynthetic flagellate *Euglena*. It shows a major peak at about 270 nm, a smaller one at 305 nm and a shoulder at 290 nm. Comparing the action spectrum with the solar emission spectrum, calculated for a temperate latitude of 50°N in mid-summer using a computer program,[104] shows that under natural conditions only a fraction of the UV-B sensitivity of the organism coincides with the solar radiation. However, if the algae were transfered to the equator — enhancing the ultraviolet radiation — the integral over the product of the two curves would increase by 22%. Thus, any decrease in the ozone

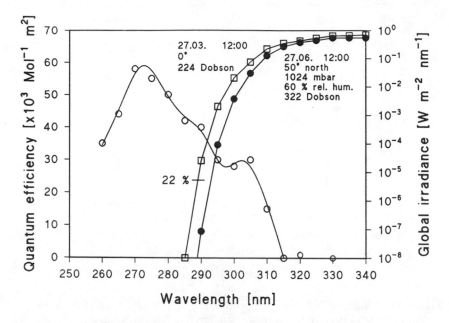

Figure 13   Action spectrum for the inhibition of motility in the photosynthetic
flagellate *Euglena* in comparison to the solar emission spectrum for
a location in central Europe and at the equator.[74]

layer, which results in an increase in the UV-B component, is bound to
have adverse effects on the organisms.

A comparison of the measured action spectra of UV-B-induced damage
with the absorption spectrum of DNA has strengthened the initial idea
that the genetic material of the cell is the main UV-B target, which has
been confirmed for some microorganisms.[105] The damage and repair of
DNA in Antarctic species is currently being investigated at Palmer Station.

In contrast, some UV-B responses have been found not to be mediated
by DNA based on the observation that ultraviolet radiation-impaired
motility decreased measurably within 10 min, which is too short to
account for protein resynthesis mediated by DNA.[96] In addition, photoreactivation could not be observed. This light-dependent repair mechanism is mediated by the activity of the enzyme photolyase, which
removes thymine dimers produced by highly energetic UV radiation.
The enzyme is activated by long-wavelength UV-A or visible radiation.[106]
A similar result was found in gliding cyanobacteria, in which UV-B-
induced inhibition of motility was both very fast and could not be pho-
torepaired.[52]

Photodynamic Effects

Photodynamic responses are another potential mechanism by which ultraviolet radiation affects living cells.[107] A chromophore molecule absorbs a high-energy photon. Excess excitation energy may be used by either of two mechanisms that involve oxygen (type II photodynamic reaction)[108] or other acceptors of the triplet energy (type I photodynamic reaction).[109] Both mechanisms are known to destroy membranes and other cellular components.

While these mechanisms play a role in some UV-B-induced types of damage in microorganisms,[110] photodynamic reactions could be excluded in others. Specific diagnostic reagents such as quenchers and scavengers are available for singlet oxygen and free radicals.[107,108,111,112] Neither the UV-B-induced inhibition of motility in cyanobacteria nor that in green flagellates was relieved by the application of these drugs, which are supposed to quench singlet oxygen or free radicals, indicating that these damages were mediated by a mechanism other than photodynamic reactions.[52]

If DNA can be excluded as a major UV-B target and, likewise, photodynamic reactions have been found not to be involved in the inhibition mechanism in some responses, it can be speculated that ultraviolet radiation damages intrinsic components of the photoreceptor and motor apparatus. This hypothesis is supported by the biochemical analysis described above for the photoreceptor proteins as well as for the photosynthetic apparatus.

DEFENSIVE MECHANISMS AGAINST INCREASED UV-B RADIATION

Theoretically, a straightforward mechanism to protect against enhanced solar UV-B radiation could be to move to lower levels within the water column with lower UV-B doses. However, as indicated above, most organisms studied to date do not possess a sensor for UV-B. Furthermore, even if they would have the opportunity to move to lower levels, they would have lower productivity since the PAR is also reduced at lower levels. A second possibility is the production and incorporation of UV-B-absorbing substances, which has been found to be a key defensive mechanism in higher plants exposed to even greater UV-B radiation. In fact, a group of UV-B-absorbing substances has been found in phytoplankton; these are mycosporine-like amino acids.[113-115] Interestingly, these substances are even taken up by the consumers in the following levels of the food web. Since *Phaeocystis pouchetii*, one of the most abundant Antarctic species, produces large concentrations of these substances, it has been speculated that in the face of increasing UV-B levels this organism may have an advantage over the diatoms, thus changing the species composition and the pelagic trophic interactions as well as the vertical carbon flux.[116] Most of the mycosporines, however, have an absorption maximum in the UV-A and only smaller absorption in the UV-B. In addition, one important aspect which needs to be clarified is whether the production of these UV-absorbing substances is induced by UV-B radiation. Only if this is the case can an increased production of mycosporine-like amino acids compensate for increased levels of UV-B.

There is one proven example of UV-B-induced shielding substances: some cyanobacteria have been found to produce scytonemin, which absorbs in the UV-B region and is incorporated into the slime sheath of the organisms. The production of this substance is induced by UV-B, and it has been found to actively prevent, e.g., the UV-B-dependent bleaching of chlorophyll.[117]

PRIMARY AND SECONDARY CONSUMERS

Any reduction in the biomass production necessarily causes losses in the next trophic levels,[118,119] leading, e.g., to losses in fisheries yield.[120,121] In addition, various experiments have demonstrated that UV-B radiation causes damage to early developmental stages of fish, shrimp, crab and other animals that are essential components of the marine food web. The most obvious effects are decreased reproductive capacity, growth or survival.[122] Even at ambient levels solar UV-B radiation is an important limiting ecological factor, although maybe not as important as light, temperature or nutrient level. However, the results indicate that even small increases of UV-B exposure could result in significant damages and changes in the consumer ecosystem.[123] Coral reefs are also known to be affected by a number of stress factors, including sedimentation, pollution and temperature increases. Increased UV-B may be an additional stress factor which pushes the population past its threshold.

Since about 30% of the world's animal protein for human consumption has been estimated to come from the sea, substantial UV-B-induced damage in the larval stages of fish, shrimp and other animals will affect the global food supply.

EFFECTS ON ZOOPLANKTON

Marine invertebrates differ greatly in their sensitivity to UV-B radiation. For instance, one small crustacean has been found to suffer about 50% mortality at fluence rates even below those currently present at the sea surface. In contrast, some shrimp larvae tolerate dose rates greater than those predicted even for a 16% ozone depletion at the surface of the water column. The DNA-weighted daily dose calculated to cause mortality in larval shrimp amounts to 15 J m^{-2} assuming a daily exposure of 3 h,[124] which is close to the UV-B dose measured near the surface in spring at mid-latitudes; during the summer these doses are easily exceeded. The adult crustacean *Thysanoessa raschii*, in contrast, has a threshold sensitivity of 51 J m^{-2} day^{-1} under similar conditions,[124] which is higher than the calculated thresholds for existing and anticipated ozone levels in spring. However, in summer the dose at similar latitudes exceeds 150 J m^{-2} day^{-1} on clear days even without ozone depletion. Assuming a 16% ozone depletion over temperate pelagic waters, a 50% mortality cumulative radiation dose for about half the species examined would be reached in summer at a depth of 1 m in less than 5 days.

UV-B has been shown to kill the most common copepod, *Acartia clausii*, and also to reduce fecundity in the surviving organisms. Similar effects were reported on shrimp-like crustaceans and crab larvae in the Pacific Northwest. In contrast, data on UV-B sensitivity are not available in Antarctic krill and other crustaceans. Freshwater crustaceans are also affected by solar UV-B. However, it is interesting to note that *Daphnia* species from an alpine lake (where the UV-B radiation is higher than in lowland lakes) are more intensely colored and tolerate higher UV-B doses.[9]

Benthic (bottom-dwelling) organisms are also susceptible to UV-B radiation. It could be shown that egg cleavage in sea urchin eggs is impaired by ultraviolet radiation.[125] Marine organisms associated with coral reefs, such as sponges, bryozoans and tunicates, are likewise affected. Production of melanins seems to aid in tolerating solar UV-B radiation since, e.g., several colored corals withstand high levels of this radiation by production of the protective pigments S-320. Corals differ in their UV-B sensitivity depending on the depth at which they have been growing,[9] and the amount of the UV-absorbing pigment decreases with depth.[126,127]

EFFECTS ON FISHERIES

Increased UV-B radiation will affect fisheries by two mechanisms: directly by affecting eggs and larvae, and through indirect effects on the food chain on which the larvae feed. The bulk of the world's marine harvest of fish, shellfish and crustaceans consists of species that have eggs and larvae which develop at or near the sea surface,[128] where they are exposed to high levels of UV-B radiation. Enhanced solar UV-B radiation directly reduces the growth and survival of larval fish.[129]

Anchovy larvae on the North American Pacific coastal shelf occur at a time of high radiation levels — between June and August, with a maximum in July. In the shelf areas the larvae are restricted to the upper 0.5 m. A 16% ozone reduction could lead to large increases in larval mortality.[129] Experiments have shown that larvae 2, 4 and 12 days old would be expected to face 50, 82 and 100% mortality, respectively. Nixon has suggested that yield in fisheries increases in a power-law fashion with increases in primary production: fisheries yield increases as productivity raised to the 1.55 power.[120] Therefore, a 5% decrease in primary production, which is assumed for a 16% ozone depletion, will cause reductions in fish yield of approximately 7%, which, if it occurred on a global basis, would represent a loss of about 6 million tons of fish per year.

CONSEQUENCES OF UV-B DAMAGE IN AQUATIC ECOSYSTEMS

Loss in Biomass Production and Effects on Food Web

It is more difficult to determine the biomass production in aquatic ecosystems than in terrestrial systems. Up to now sporadic measurements have been available and only very few have concerned the loss in productivity as a consequence of increased UV-B radiation, e.g., in Antarctic waters during the occurrence of the ozone hole. However, because of the size of the marine ecosystems it can be predicted that even a small loss has noticeable adverse effects. While the standing crop of phytoplankton is rather small as compared to terrestrial systems, its productivity equals or exceeds it. The global biomass production by phytoplanktonic organisms can be calculated as 6×10^{14} kg. An estimated loss of 10% would far exceed the gross national product of all countries in the world, assuming any reasonable price for biomass on the market, such as $1 U.S. per kilogram. However, our present knowledge is far too limited to predict exact losses and damages on a global basis.

A loss in primary productivity of 5% has been estimated to result in a 6–9% reduction in fisheries catch.[130] Further reductions may result from the predicted global warming, since changes in water temperature can be expected to alter the geographical distribution and abundance of commercially important fish. Further research is needed to improve our understanding of how stratospheric ozone depletion could influence the aquatic ecosystems. The available information suggests that the likelihood of a significant impact resulting from UV-B exposure on marine environments is real, even if the direct and indirect effects on the marine ecosystem itself and the resources significant to man cannot yet be fully quantified.

Change in Species Composition

A very significant effect of increased solar ultraviolet radiation on aquatic ecosystems may be a change in the species composition.[122] A change in community composition at the base of the food web may produce instabilities within ecosystems that affect higher trophic levels.[131] The generation time of marine phytoplankton is in the range of hours to days, while the genetic adaptation of species occurs within rather long time spans. Since the anthropogenic increase in ambient levels of solar UV-B irradiance will occur over a period of decades the genetic adaptation within species may not be fast enough to adapt during this time period. Alternatively, changes within the species composition will be the result of increased UV-B stress, which will lead to altered patterns of predation, competition, diversity and trophic dynamics.

Increase in Atmospheric CO_2 Concentration Resulting from a Reduced Sink Capacity

The atmospheric CO_2 undergoes a natural cycle in which about 200 Gt of carbon are incorporated in terrestrial and aquatic photosynthetic organisms annually.[21] The same amount is released during decomposition of organic material. This balance is disturbed by the additional release of 5 Gt of carbon by fossil fuel consumption and 2 Gt of carbon by tropical deforestation. The excess CO_2 builds up in the atmosphere and is assumed to be the cause of the greenhouse warming of the earth. The phytoplankton in the oceans is a major biological sink for atmospheric CO_2.[132] A decrease in the phytoplankton populations will increase the atmospheric CO_2 concentration and advance its buildup, since the CO_2 not taken up by the oceans will remain in the atmosphere. This factor is not yet accounted for by the current climate change models. A hypothetical 10% decrease in phytoplankton productivity would result in an additional amount of atmospheric CO_2 equal to that resulting from fossil fuel burning. This effect would have long-term consequences for the global climate and would enhance the predicted sea level rise.[133]

Loss in Nitrogen for Higher Plants

The role of cyanobacteria in nitrogen fixation, especially in tropical rice paddies, has been mentioned above. A significant decrease in nitrogen fixation by prokaryotic microorganisms is bound to affect growth and productivity of higher plants. The costs to compensate for this loss with artificial nitrogen fertilizer will be substantial.

DMS Production and Cloud Condensation

Many algal groups are known to produce dimethylsulfoniopropionate as an antifreeze and osmotic regulator. By an enzymatic reaction dimethylsulfide (DMS) is cleaved and is emitted into the water.[134] From there it diffuses into the atmosphere. In the Antarctic, *Phaeocystis* has been reported to be the principal producer of DMS. Oxidation of DMS forms methane sulfonate and sulfate particles which are thought to be cloud condensation nuclei (CCN). DMS emissions are thought to account for about half of the global flux of biogenic sulfur into the atmosphere;[135-137] 40 million tons of sulfur are released by this mechanism annually, which equals about 50% of sulfur emissions from anthropogenic sources. As a consequence of phytoplankton decrease, the amount of DMS and, thus, the availability of sulfur as CCN may change and thereby affect the global albedo, the cloud cover and surface temperature. The contribution of the Antarctic *Phaeocystis* to the total flux of DMS into the atmosphere has been estimated to be 10%.[138]

CONCLUSIONS

Despite the obvious lack of quantitative data, there is ample evidence that both primary producers and consumers in aquatic habitats are under considerable UV-B stress at current ultraviolet radiation levels. Any decrease in the ozone layer could have detrimental effects on the ecosystems. Because of the enormous size of the systems, even a minor loss in productivity would have substantial impacts on a global scale. Ecosystems have a buffer capacity to tolerate moderate stresses. When this capacity is exceeded beyond the threshold, the system responds with disproportionately large changes. Our knowledge of the system is still too limited to predict this breaking point. While current data suggest that predicted increases in UV-B radiation could have significant negative effects in the marine environment, uncertainties regarding the magnitude of these effects remain large. Extrapolating laboratory findings to the open sea is difficult and uncertain, and the nearly complete absence of data on long-term effects and ecosystem responses make predictions vague. Additional information is needed in several areas before more reliable assessments of risk are possible. The information required includes biological action spectra for marine species based on dose-response data in key representatives of phytoplankton, zooplankton, ichthyoplankton and shallow-water benthos. Furthermore, the molecular mechanisms for UV-B damage need to be determined for ecologically important species. To assess potential damages, a predictive 3-D model, based on the spectral distribution of UV-B in the water column as a function of latitude and season,[139,140] as well as the biological sensitivity of key plankton species, would be a valuable tool to estimate the losses in biomass production and CO_2 increase. Up to now no predictive model has existed but one is being developed presently.[141] The downwelling spectral irradiance in the UV-B range will depend on the solar zenith angles and the ability of UV to penetrate the water column.[142] Other factors to be considered are seasonal abundance and vertical distribution of organisms as well as vertical mixing. Another problem is the lack of historical data on oceanic productivity, so it is difficult to estimate current and future losses.[145] The current picture can possibly be described by stating that while there is some information available on selected habitats and ecosystems we still lack the global knowledge to fully evaluate the potential hazards by UV-B radiation on aquatic ecosystems.[146-150]

REFERENCES

1. Bidigare, R. R. "Potential Effects of UV-B Radiation on Marine Organisms of the Southern Ocean: Distributions of Phytoplankton and Krill During Austral Spring," *Photochem. Photobiol.* 50:469–477 (1989).
2. Lubin, D., J. E. Frederick, C. R. Booth, T. Lucas, and D. Neuschuler. "Measurements of Enhanced Springtime Ultraviolet Radiation at Palmer Station, Antarctica," *Geophys. Res. Lett.* 16:783–785 (1989).
3. Karentz, D. and L. H. Lutze. "Evaluation of Biologically Harmful Ultraviolet Radiation in Antarctica with a Biological Dosimeter Designed for Aquatic Environments," *Limnol. Oceanogr.* 35:549–561 (1990).
4. Blumthaler, M. and W. Ambach. "Indication of Increasing Solar Ultraviolet-B Radiation Flux in Alpine Regions," *Science* 248:206–208 (1990).
5. Madronich, S., L. O. Björn, M. Iliyas, and M. M. Caldwell. "Changes in Biologically Active Ultraviolet Radiation Reaching the Earth's Surface," Environmental Effects Panel Report, United Nations Environmental Program (1991), pp. 1–13.
6. Jerlov, N. G. "Light — General Introduction," in *Marine Ecology, Vol. 1*, O. Kinne, Ed. (1970), pp. 95–102.
7. Jerlov, N. G. "Ultraviolet Radiation in the Sea," *Nature (London)* 116:111–112 (1950).
8. Smith, R. C. and K. S. Baker. "Penetration of UV-B and Biologically Effective Dose-Rates in Natural Waters," *Photochem. Photobiol.* 29:311–323 (1978).
9. Siebeck, O. and U. Böhm. *Untersuchungen zur Wirkung der UV-B-Strahlung auf kleine Wassertiere* (Munich: BPT Bericht, Gesellschaft für Strahlen- und Umweltforschung, 1987), p. 84.
10. Baker, K. S. and R. C. Smith. "Spectral Irradiance Penetration in Natural Waters," in *The Role of Solar Ultraviolet Radiation in Marine Ecosystems*, J. Calkins, Ed. (New York: Plenum Press, 1982), pp. 233–246.
11. Gieskes, W. C. and G. W. Kraay. "Transmission of Ultraviolet Light in the Weddell Sea. Report on the First Measurements Made in Antarctic," *Biomass Newsletter* 12:12–14 (1990).
12. Smith, R. C., B. B. Prezelin, K. S. Baker, R. R. Bidigare, N. P. Boucher, T. Coley, D. Karentz, S. MacIntyre, H. A. Matlick, D. Menzies, M. Ondrusek, Z. Wan, and K. J. Waters. "Ozone Depletion: Ultraviolet Radiation and Phytoplankton Biology in Antarctic Waters," *Science* 255:952–959 (1992).

13. Worrest, R. C., D. L. Brooker, and H. van Dyke. "Results of a Primary Productivity Study as Affected by the Type of Glass in the Culture Bottle," *Limnol. Oceanogr.* 25:360–364 (1980).

14. Worrest, R. C., K. U. Wolniakowski, J. D. Scott, D. L. Brooker, B. E. Thompson, and H. van Dyke. "Sensitivity of Marine Phytoplankton to UV-B Radiation: Impact upon a Model Ecosystem," *Photochem. Photobiol.* 33:223–227 (1981).

15. Worrest, R. C., B. E. Thompson, and H. van Dyke. "Impact of UV-B Radiation upon Estuarine Microcosms," *Photochem. Photobiol.* 33:861–867 (1981).

16. Worrest, R. C. "Review of Literature Concerning the Impact of UV-B Radiation upon Marine Organisms," in *The Role of Solar Ultraviolet Radiation in Marine Ecosystems*, J. Calkins, Ed. (New York: Plenum Press, 1982), pp. 429–457.

17. Lorenzen, C. J. "UV Radiation and Phytoplankton Photosynthesis," *Limnol. Oceanogr.* 24:1117–1120 (1979).

18. Calkins, J. and T. Thordardottir. "The Ecological Significance of Solar UV-B Radiations on Aquatic Organisms," *Nature* 283:563–566 (1980).

19. Smith, R. C., K. S. Baker, O. Holm-Hansen, and R. Olson. "Photoinhibition of Photosynthesis in Natural Waters," *Photochem. Photobiol.* 31:585–592 (1980).

20. Maske, H. "Daylight Ultraviolet Radiation and the Photoinhibition of Phytoplankton Carbon Uptake," *J. Plankton Res.* 6:351–357 (1984).

21. Houghton, R. A. and G. M. Woodwell. "Global Climatic Change," *Sci. Am.* 260:18–26 (April 1989).

22. Häder, D.-P. "Effects of Enhanced Solar Ultraviolet Radiation on Aquatic Ecosystems," in *Biophysics of Photoreceptors and Photomovements in Microorganisms*, F. Lenci, F. Ghetti, G. Colombetti, D.-P. Häder, and P.-S. Song, Eds. (New York: Plenum Press, 1991), pp. 157–172.

23. Häder, D.-P. and R. C. Worrest. "Effects of Enhanced Solar Ultraviolet Radiation on Aquatic Ecosystems," *Photochem. Photobiol.* 53:717–725 (1991).

24. El Sayed, S. Z., F. C. Stephens, R. R. Bidigare, and M. Ondrusek. "Effect of Ultraviolet Radiation on Antarctic Marine Phytoplankton," in *Antarctic Ecosystems, Ecological Change and Conservation*, K. R. Kerry and G. Hempel, Eds. (Berlin: Springer-Verlag, 1990), pp. 379–385.

25. Smith, R. "Ozone, Middle Ultraviolet Radiation and the Aquatic Environment," *Photochem. Photobiol.* 50:459–468 (1989).

26. Viollier, M., D. Tanré, and P. Y. Deschampes. "An Algorithm for Remote Sensing of Water Color from Space," *Boundary-Layer Meteorol.* 18:247–267 (1980).

27. Burns, N. M. and F. Rosa. "In Situ Measurements of the Settling Velocity of Organic Carbon Particles and Ten Species of Phytoplankton," *Limnol. Oceanogr.* 2:855–864 (1980).

28. Ignatiades, L. "Photosynthetic Capacity of the Surface Microlayer during the Mixing Period," *J. Plankton Res.* 12:851–860 (1990).

29. Nultsch, W. and D.-P. Häder. "Photomovement in Motile Microorganisms II," *Photochem. Photobiol.* 47:837–869 (1988).

30. Häder, D.-P. "Phototaxis and Gravitaxis in *Euglena gracilis*," in *Biophysics of Photoreceptors and Photomovements in Microorganisms*, F. Lenci, F. Ghetti, G. Colombetti, D.-P. Häder, and P.-S. Song, Eds. (New York: Plenum Press, 1991), pp. 203–221.

31. Häder, D.-P. "Strategy of Orientation in Flagellates," in *Photobiology. The Science and Its Applications*, E. Riklis, Ed. (New York: Plenum Press, 1991), pp. 497–510.

32. Bean, B. "Microbial Geotaxis," in *Membranes and Sensory Transduction*, G. Colombetti and F. Lenci, Eds. (New York: Plenum Press, 1984), pp. 163–198.

33. MacNab, R. M. "Biochemistry of Sensory Transduction in Bacteria," in *Sensory Perception and Transduction in Aneural Organisms*, G. Colombetti, F. Lenci, and P.-S. Song, Eds. (New York: Plenum Press, 1985), pp. 31–46.

34. Poff, K. L. "Temperature Sensing in Microorganisms," in *Sensory Perception and Transduction in Aneural Organisms*, G. Colombetti, F. Lenci, and P.-S. Song, Eds. (New York: Plenum Press, 1985), pp. 299–307.

35. Esquivel, D. M. S. and de Barros, H. G. P. L. "Motion of Magnetotactic Microorganisms," *J. Exp. Biol.* 121:153–163 (1986).

36. Voytek, M. A. "Addressing the Biological Effects of Decreasing Ozone in the Antarctic Environment," *Ambio* 19:52–61 (1990).

37. Häder, D.-P. "Effects of UV-B on Motility and Photobehavior in the Green Flagellate, *Euglena gracilis*," *Arch. Microbiol.* 141:159–163 (1985).

38. Häder, D.-P. "The Effect of Enhanced Solar UV-B Radiation on Motile Microorganisms," in *Stratospheric Ozone Reduction, Solar Ultraviolet Radiation and Plant Life*, R. C. Worrest and M. M. Caldwell, Eds. (Berlin: Springer-Verlag, 1986), pp. 223–233.

39. Häder, D.-P. "Effects of Solar and Artificial UV Irradiation on Motility and Phototaxis in the Flagellate, *Euglena gracilis*," *Photochem. Photobiol.* 44:651–656 (1986).

40. Häder, D.-P. and M. Häder. "Inhibition of Motility and Phototaxis in the Green Flagellate, *Euglena gracilis*, by UV-B Radiation," *Arch. Microbiol.* 150:20–25 (1988).

41. Häder, D.-P. and M. Häder. "Ultraviolet-B Inhibition of Motility in Green and Dark Bleached *Euglena gracilis*," *Curr. Microbiol.* 17:215–220 (1988).

42. Häder, D.-P. and M. Häder. "Effects of Solar and Artificial UV Radiation on Motility and Pigmentation in the Marine *Cryptomonas maculata*," *Environ. Exp. Bot.* 31:33–41 (1991).

43. Häder, D.-P. and M. Häder. "Effects of Solar Radiation on Photoorientation, Motility and Pigmentation in a Freshwater *Cryptomonas*," *Bot. Acta* 102:236–240 (1989).

44. Häder, D.-P. and M. A. Häder. "Effects of Solar UV-B Irradiation on Photomovement and Motility in Photosynthetic and Colorless Flagellates," *Environ. Exp. Bot.* 29:273–282 (1989).

45. Häder, D.-P., M. Häder, S.-M. Liu, and W. Ullrich. "Effects of Solar Radiation on Photoorientation, Motility and Pigmentation in a Freshwater *Peridinium*," *BioSystems* 23:335–343 (1990).

46. Häder, D.-P. and M. A. Häder. "Effects of Solar and Artificial Radiation on Motility and Pigmentation in *Cyanophora paradoxa*," *Arch. Microbiol.* 152:453–457 (1989).

47. Häder, D.-P. and M. Häder. "Effects of UV Radiation on Motility, Photoorientation and Pigmentation in a Freshwater *Cryptomonas*," *J. Photochem. Photobiol. B* 5:105–114 (1990).

48. Häder, D.-P., S.-M. Liu, M. Häder, and W. Ullrich. "Photoorientation, Motility and Pigmentation in a Freshwater *Peridinium* Affected by Ultraviolet Radiation," *Gen. Physiol. Biophys.* 9:361–371 (1990).

49. Häder, D.-P. "Einfluß von UV-B-Strahlung auf die Photoorientierung von Flagellaten," *Laufener Sem. Beitr.* 3:67–73 (1989).

50. Häder, D.-P., R. C. Worrest, and H. D. Kumar. "Aquatic Ecosystems," UNEP Environmental Effects Panel Report (1989), pp. 39–48.

51. Worrest, R. C. and D.-P. Häder. "Effects of Stratospheric Ozone Depletion on Marine Organisms," *Environ. Conserv.* 16:261–263 (1989).

52. Häder, D.-P., M. Watanabe, and M. Furuya. "Inhibition of Motility in the Cyanobacterium, *Phormidium uncinatum*, by Solar and Monochromatic UV Irradiation," *Plant Cell Physiol.* 27:887–894 (1986).

53. Häder, D.-P. and M. Häder. "Effects of Solar Radiation on Motility, Photomovement and Pigmentation in Two Strains of the Cyanobacterium, *Phormidium uncinatum*," *Acta Protozool.* 29:291–303 (1990).

54. Donkor, V. and D.-P. Häder. "Effects of Solar and Ultraviolet Radiation on Motility, Photomovement and Pigmentation in Filamentous, Gliding Cyanobacteria," *FEMS Microbiol. Ecol.* 86:159–168 (1991).

55. Häder, D.-P. "Photomovement," in *The Cyanobacteria*, P. Fay and C. van Baalen, Eds. (Amsterdam: Elsevier, 1987), pp. 325–345.

56. Häder, D.-P. "Photosensory Behavior in Procaryotes," *Microbiol. Rev.* 51:1–21 (1987).

57. Häder, D.-P. "Signal Perception and Amplification in Photoresponses of Cyanobacteria," *Biophys. Chem.* 29:155–159 (1988).

58. Foster, K. W. and R. D. Smyth. "Light Antennas in Phototactic Algae," *Microbiol. Rev.* 44:572–630 (1980).

59. Häder, D.-P. "Ecological Consequences of Photomovement in Microorganisms," *J. Photochem. Photobiol. B.* 1:385–414 (1988).

60. Serruya, C. *Lake Kinneret* (The Hague: Dr. W. Junk b. v., 1978).

61. Liu, S.-M., D.-P. Häder, and W. Ullrich. "Photoorientation in the Freshwater Dinoflagellate, *Peridinium gatunense* Nygaard," *FEMS Microbiol. Ecol.* 73:91–102 (1990).

62. Häder, D.-P., G. Colombetti, F. Lenci, and M. Quaglia. "Phototaxis in the Flagellates, *Euglena gracilis* and *Ochromonas danica*," *Arch. Microbiol.* 130:78–82 (1981).

63. Gualtieri, P., L. Barsanti, and G. Rosati. "Isolation of the Photoreceptor (Paraflagellar Body) of the Phototactic Flagellate *Euglena gracilis*," *Arch. Microbiol.* 145:303–305 (1986).

64. Rosenbaum, J. L. and F. M. Child. "Flagellar Regeneration in Protozoan Flagellates," *J. Cell Biol.* 34:345–346 (1967).

65. Gualtieri, P., L. Barsanti, and V. Passarelli. "Absorption Spectrum of a Single Isolated Paraflagellar Swelling of *Euglena gracilis*," *Biochim. Biophys. Acta* 993:293–296 (1989).

66. Galland, P., P. Keiner, D. Dörnemann, H. Senger, B. Brodhun, and D.-P. Häder. "Pterin- and flavin-like fluorescence associated with isolated flagella of *Euglena gracilis*," *Photochem. Photobiol.* 51:675–680 (1990).

67. Brodhun, B. and D.-P. Häder. "Photoreceptor Proteins and Pigments in the Paraflagellar Body of the Flagellate, *Euglena gracilis*," *Photochem. Photobiol.* 52:865–871 (1990).

68. Häder, D.-P. and B. Brodhun. "Effects of Ultraviolet Radiation on the Photoreceptor Proteins and Pigments in the Paraflagellar Body of the Flagellate, *Euglena gracilis*," *J. Plant Physiol.* 137:641–646 (1991).

69. Roberts, A. M. "Geotaxis in Motile Micro-organisms," *J. Exp. Biol.* 53:687–699 (1970).

70. Kessler, J. O. "Hydrodynamic Focusing of Motile Algal Cells," *Nature (London)* 313:218–220 (1985).

71. Fenchel, T. and B. J. Finlay. "Photobehavior of the Ciliated Protozoon *Loxodes*: Taxic, Transient, and Kinetic Responses in the Presence and Absence of Oxygen," *J. Protozool.* 33:139–145 (1986).

72. Taneda, K. "Geotactic Behavior in *Paramecium caudatum*. I. Geotaxis Assay of Individual Specimen," *Zool. Sci.* 4:781–788 (1987).

73. Brinkmann, K. "Keine Geotaxis bei *Euglena*," *Z. Pflanzenphysiol.* 59:12–16 (1968).

74. Häder, D.-P. and S.-M. Liu. "Motility and Gravitactic Orientation of the Flagellate, *Euglena gracilis*, Impaired by Artificial and Solar UV-B Radiation," *Curr. Microbiol.* 21:161–168 (1990).

75. Häder, D.-P. and S.-M. Liu. "Effects of Artificial and Solar UV-B Radiation on the Gravitactic Orientation of the Dinoflagellate, *Peridinium gatunense*," *FEMS Microbiol. Ecol.* 73:331–338 (1990).

76. Eggersdorfer, B. and D.-P. Häder. "Phototaxis, Gravitaxis and Vertical Migrations in the Marine Dinoflagellate, *Prorocentrum micans*," *Eur. J. Biophys.* 85:319–326 (1991).

77. Häder, D.-P. and K. Griebenow. "Versatile Digital Image Analysis by Microcomputer to Count Microorganisms," *EDV Med. Biol.* 18:37–42 (1987).

78. Häder, D.-P. and K. Griebenow. "Orientation of the Green Flagellate, *Euglena gracilis*, in a vertical column of water," *FEMS Microbiol. Ecol.* 53:159–167 (1988).

79. Yoder, J. A. and S. S. Bishop. "Effects of the Mixing-Induced Irradiance Fluctuations on Photosynthesis of Natural Assemblages of Coastal Phytoplankton," *Mar. Biol.* 90:87–93 (1985).

80. Eggersdorfer, B. and D.-P. Häder. "Phototaxis, Gravitaxis and Vertical Migrations in the Marine Dinoflagellates, *Peridinium faeroense* and *Amphidinium caterii*," *Acta Protozool.* 30:63–71 (1991).

81. McLeod, G. C. and J. McLachlan. "The Sensitivity of Several Algae to Ultraviolet Radiation of 2537," *Physiol. Plant.* 12:306–309 (1959).

82. Worrest, R. C., H. van Dyke, and B. Thomson. "Impact of Enhanced Simulated Solar Ultraviolet Radiation upon a Marine Community," *Photochem. Photobiol.* 27:471–478 (1978).

83. Döhler, G. "Effect of UV-B Radiation on the Marine Diatoms *Lauderia annulata* and *Thalassiosira rotula* Grown in Different Salinities," *Mar. Biol.* 83:247–253 (1984).

84. Holm-Hansen, O. "UV Radiation in Antarctic Waters: Effect on Rates of Primary Production," in *Proceedings of Workshop on Response of Marine Phytoplankton to Natural Variations in UV-B Flux* (LaJolla, CA: Scripps Institution of Oceanography, May 1990), Appendix G.

85. Mitchell, B. G. "Action Spectra of Ultraviolet Photoinhibition of Antarctic Phytoplankton and a Model of Spectral Diffuse Attenuation Coefficients," in *Proceedings of Workshop on Response of Marine Phytoplankton to Natural Variations in UV-B Flux* (LaJolla, CA: Scripps Institution of Oceanography, May 1990), Appendix H.

86. Vosjan, J. H., G. Döhler, and G. Nieuwland. "Effect of UV-B Irradiance on the ATP Content of Microorganisms of the Weddell Sea, Antarctica," *Neth. J. Sea Res.* 25:391–394 (1990).

87. Karentz, D., J. E. Cleaver, and D. L. Mitchell. "DNA Damage in the Antarctic," *Nature* 350:28 (1991).

88. Bittersmann, E., A. R. Holzwarth, G. Agel, and W. Nultsch. "Picosecond Time-Resolved Emission Spectra of Photoinhibited and Photobleached *Anabaena variabilis*," *Photochem. Photobiol.* 47:101–105 (1988).

89. Nultsch, W., J. Pfau, and K. Huppertz. "Photoinhibition of Photosynthetic Oxygen Production and Its Recovery in the Subtidal Red Alga *Polyneura hilliae*, *Bot. Acta* 103:62–67 (1990).

90. Renger, G., M. Völker, H. J. Eckert, R. Fromme, S. Hohm-Veit, and P. Gräber. "On the Mechanisms of Photosystem II Deterioration by UV-B Irradiation," *Photochem. Photobiol.* 49:97–105 (1989).

91. Tevini, M., A. H. Teramura, G. Kulandaivelu, M. M. Caldwell, and L. O. Björn. "Terrestrial Plants," UNEP Environmental Effects Panel Report (1989), pp. 25–37.

92. Nultsch, W. and G. Agel. "Fluence Rate and Wavelength Dependence of Photobleaching in the Cyanobacterium *Anabaena variabilis*," *Arch. Microbiol.* 144:268–271 (1986).

93. Häder, D.-P., E. Rhiel, and W. Wehrmeyer. "Ecological Consequences of Photomovement and Photobleaching in the Marine Flagellate *Cryptomonas maculata*," *FEMS Microbiol. Ecol.* 53:9–18 (1988).

94. Jeffrey, S. W. and G. F. Humphrey. "New Spectrophotometric Equations for Determining Chlorophylls a, b, c_1 and c_2 in Higher Plants, Algae and Natural Phytoplankton," *Biochem. Physiol. Pflanz.* 167:191–194 (1975).

95. Zündorf, I. and D.-P. Häder. "Biochemical and Spectroscopic Analysis of UV Effects in the Marine Flagellate *Cryptomonas maculata*," *Arch. Microbiol.* 156:405–411 (1991).

96. Häberlein, A. and D. P. Häder. "UV Effects on Photosynthetic Oxygen Production and Chromoprotein Composition in the Freshwater Flagellate *Cryptomonas S2*," *Acta Protozool.*, 31:85–92 (1992).

97. Döhler, G., R. C. Worrest, I. Biermann, and J. Zink. "Photosynthetic $^{14}CO_2$ Fixation and ^{15}N-Ammonia Assimilation during UV-B Radiation of *Lithodesmium variabile*," *Physiol. Plant.* 70:511–515 (1987).

98. Döhler, G. and M.-R. Alt. "Assimilation of ^{15}N-Ammonia during Irradiance with Ultraviolet-B and Monochromatic Light by *Thalassiosira rotula*," *C. R. Acad. Sci. Ser. D* 308:513–518 (1989).

99. Döhler, G. "Effect of UV-B (290–320 nm) Radiation on Uptake of ^{15}N-Nitrate by Marine Diatoms," in *Inorganic Nitrogen in Plants and Microorganisms. Uptake and Metabolism.* W. R. Ullrich, C. Rigano, A. Fuggi, and J. P. Aparicio, Eds. (Berlin: Springer-Verlag, 1990), pp. 359–354.

100. Kumar, A. and H. D. Kumar. "Nitrogen Fixation by Blue-Green Algae" in *Plant Physiology Research*, S. P. Seu, Ed. (New Dehli: Society for Plant Physiology and Biochemistry, 1st International Congress of Plant Physiology, Feb. 15–22, 1988).

101. Richter, G. *Stoffwechselphysiologie der Pflanzen* (Stuttgart: Thieme, 1988), p. 653.

102. Crosson, P. R. and N. J. Rosenberg. "Strategies for Agriculture," *Sci. Am.* 261:78–85 (1989).

103. Newton, J. W. and J. F. Cavins. "Altered Nitrogenous Pools Induced by the *Azolla-Anabaena-Azollae* Symbiosis," *Plant Physiol.* 58:798–799 (1976).

104. Björn, L. O. and T. M. Murphy. "Computer Calculation of Solar Ultraviolet Radiation at Ground Level," *Physiol. Veg.* 23:555–561 (1985).

105. Yammamoto, K. M., M. Satake, H. Shinagawa, and Y. Fujiwara. "Amelioration of the Ultraviolet Sensitivity of an *Escherichia coli* recA Mutant in the Dark by Photoreactivating Enzyme," *Mol. Gen. Genet.* 190:511–515 (1983).

106. Hirosawa, T. and S. Miyachi. "Inactivation of Hill Reaction by Long-Wavelength Ultraviolet Radiation (UV-A) and Its Photoreactivation by Visible Light in the Cyanobacterium, *Anacystis nidulans*," *Arch. Microbiol.* 135:98–102 (1983).

107. Ito, T. "Photodynamic Agents as Tools for Cell Biology," in *Photochemical and Photobiological Reviews, Vol. 7*, K. C. Smith, Ed. (New York: Plenum Press, 1983), pp. 141–186.

108. Maurette, M.-T., E. Oliveros, P. P. Infelta, K. Ramsteiner, and A. M. Braun. "Singlet Oxygen and Superoxide: Experimental Differentiation and Analysis," *Helv. Chim. Acta* 66:722–733 (1983).

109. Spikes, J. D. "Photosensitization," in *The Science of Photobiology*, K. C. Smith, Ed. (New York: Plenum Press, 1977), pp. 87–112.

110. Häder, D.-P. and M. A. Häder. "Effects of Solar Radiation on Motility in *Stentor coeruleus*," *Photochem. Photobiol.* 54:423–428 (1991).

111. Merkel, P. B., R. Nilsson, and D. R. Kearns. "Deuterium Effects on Singlet Oxygen Lifetimes in Solution. A New Test of Singlet Oxygen Reactions," *J. Am. Chem. Soc.* 94:1030–1031 (1972).

112. Spikes, J. D. and R. Straight. "The Sensitized Photooxidation of Biomolecules, an Overview," in *Oxygen and Oxy-Radicals in Chemistry and Biology*, M. A. J. Rodgers and E. L. Powers, Eds. (New York: Academic Press, 1981), pp. 421–424.

113. Carreto, J. J., M. O. Carignana, G. Daleo, and S. G. de Marco. "Occurrence of Mycosporine-like Amino Acids in the Red Tide Dinoflagellate *Alexandrium excavatum*. UV-Photoprotective Compounds," *J. Plankton Res.* 12:909–921 (1990).

114. Karentz, D., F. S. Mc Euen, M. C. Land, and W. C. Dunlap. "Survey of Mycosporine-like Amino Acid Compounds in Antarctic Marine Organisms: Potential Protection from Ultraviolet Exposure, *Mar. Biol.* 108:157–166 (1991).

115. Raven, J. A. "Responses of Aquatic Photosynthetic Organisms to Increased Solar UVB," *J. Photochem. Photobiol. B*, 9:239–244 (1991).

116. Marchant, H. J., A. T. Davidson, and G. J. Kelly. "UV-B Protecting Pigments in the Marine Alga *Phaeocystis pouchetti* from Antarctica," *Mar. Biol.* 109:391–395 (1991).
117. Garcia-Pichel, F. and R. W. Castenholz. "Characterization and Biological Implications of Scytonemin, a Cyanobacterial Sheath Pigment," *J. Phycol.* 27:395–409 (1991).
118. Holm-Hansen, O., G. B. Mitchell, and M. Vernet. "UV Radiation in Antarctic Waters: Effect on Rates of Primary Production," *Antarct. J. U.S.* 24:177–178 (1989).
119. Behrenfeld, M. M. S. "Primary Productivity in the Southeast Pacific: Effects of Enhanced Ultraviolet-B Radiation," M.S. Thesis, Oregon State University, Corvallis, Oregon (1989).
120. Nixon, S. W. "Physical Energy Inputs and the Comparative Ecology of Lake and Marine Ecosystems," *Limnol. Oceanogr.* 33:1005–1025 (1988).
121. Gucinski, H., R. T. Lackey, and B. C. Spence. "Fisheries," *Bull. Am. Fish. Soc.* 15:33–38 (1990).
122. "An Assessment of the Effects of Ultraviolet-B Radiation on Aquatic Organisms," in *Assessing the Risks of Trace Gases That Can Modify the Stratosphere*, EPA 400/1-87/001C, U.S. Environmental Protection Agency (1987), pp. 1–33.
123. Damkaer, D. M. "Possible Influence of Solar UV Radiation in the Evolution of Marine Zooplankton," in *The Role of Solar Ultraviolet Radiation in Marine Ecosystems*, J. Calkins, Ed. (New York: Plenum Press, 1982), pp. 701–706.
124. Damkaer, D. M. and D. B. Dey. "UV Damage and Photo-Reactivation Potentials of Larval Shrimp, *Pandalus platyceros*, and Adult Euphausiids, *Thysanoessa raschii*," *Oecologia* 60:169–175 (1983).
125. El Sayed, S. "Fragile Life Under the Ozone Hole," *Nat. Hist.* 97:73–80 (1988).
126. Maragos, J. E. "A Study of the Ecology of Hawaiian Reef Corals," Ph.D. Thesis, University of Hawaii (1972).
127. Jokiel, P. L. and H. R. York. "Solar Ultraviolet Photobiology of the Reef Coral *Pocillopora damicornis* and Symbiontic Zooxanthellae," *Bull. Mar. Sci.* 32:301–315 (1982).
128. Hardy, J. T. "The Sea Surface Microlayer: Biology, Chemistry and Anthropogenic Enrichment," *Progr. Oceanogr.* 11:307–328 (1982).
129. Hunter, J. R., S. E. Kaupp, and J. H. Taylor. "Assessment of Effects of UV Radiation on Marine Fish Larvae," in *The Role of Solar Ultraviolet Radiation in Marine Ecosystems*, J. Calkins, Ed. (New York: Plenum Press, 1982), pp. 459–497.
130. Hardy, J. and H. Gucinski. "Stratospheric Ozone Depletion: Implications for Marine Ecosystems," *Oceanogr. Mag.* 2:18–21 (1989).
131. Kelly, J. R. "How Might Enhanced Levels of Solar UV-B Radiation Affect Marine Ecosystems?," in Proceedings of EPA/UNEP International Conference on Health and Environmental Effects of Ozone Modification and Climate Change (July 1986).
132. Gaundry, A., P. Monfray, G. Polian, and G. Lanabert. "The 1982–1983 El Nino: A 6 Billion Ton CO_2 Release," *Tellus* 39B:209–213 (1987).
133. Schneider, S. H. "The Changing Climate," *Sci. Am.* 261:38–47 (1989).

134. Karsten, U., C. Wiencke, and G. O. Kirst. "The Effect of Light Intensity and Daylength on the β-Dimethylsulphoniopropionate (DMSP) Content of Marine Green Macroalgae from Antarctica," *Plant Cell Environ.* 12:989–993 (1990).

135. Charlson, R. J., J. E. Lovelock, M. O. Andreae, and S. G. Warren. "Oceanic Phytoplankton, Atmospheric Sulphur, Cloud Albedo and Climate," *Nature (London)* 326:655–661 (1987).

136. Andreae, M. O. "The Ocean as a Source of Atmospheric Sulphur Compounds," in *The Role of Air-Sea Exchange in Geochemical Cycling*, P. Buat-Mernard, Ed. (Dordrecht: Deidel, 1986), pp. 331–362.

137. Bates, T. S., R. J. Charlson, and R. H. Gammon. "Evidence for the Climatic Role of Marine Sulphur," *Nature*, 329:319–321 (1987).

138. Gibson, J. A. E., R. C. Garrick, H. R. Burton, and A. R. McTaggart. "Dimethylsulfide and the Algae *Phaeocystis pouchetii* in Antarctic Coastal Waters," *Mar. Biol.* 104:339–346 (1989).

139. Haltrin, V. I. "The Self-Consistent Two-Flow Approximation of the Transport Theory of Radiation," *Izv. Akad. Nauk SSSR Fiz. Atmos. Okeana* 21:589–597 (1985).

140. Haltrin, V. I. "Propagation of Light in the Depth of a Sea," in *Remote Sensing of the Sea and the Influence of the Atmosphere*, V. A. Urdenko and G. Zimmermann, Eds. (Moscow: GDR Academy of Sciences Institute of Space Research, 1985).

141. Haltrin, V. I. and V. A. Urdenko. "Scattering of Light in the Atmosphere and Remote Sensing of the Optical Characteristics of Sea Water," in *Remote Sensing of the Sea and the Influence of the Atmosphere*, V. A. Urdenko and G. Zimmermann, Eds. (Moscow: GDR Academy of Sciences Institute of Space Research, 1985).

142. El Sayed, S. Z. and V. I. Haltrin. "Modelling the Potential Effects of Increased Ultraviolet Radiation on Oceanic Productivity," *Photochem. Photobiol.*, submitted (1992).

143. Baker, K. S., R. C. Smith, and A. E. S. Green. "Middle Ultraviolet Radiation Reaching the Ocean Surface," *Photochem. Photobiol.* 32:367–374 (1980).

144. Cabrera, S. and V. Montecino. "Productividad Primaria en Ecosistemas Limnicos," *Arch. Biol. Med. Exp.* 20:105–116 (1987).

145. El-Sayed, S. Z. and F. C. Stephens. "Potential Effects of Increased Ultraviolet Radiation on the Productivity of the Southern Ocean," in *The Science of Global Change, The Impact of Human Activities on the Environment*, American Chemical Society Symposium Series 483, Chapter 9, D. A. Dunette and R. J. O'Brien, Eds., pp. 188–206.

146. Holligan, P., Ed. "Coastal Ocean Fluxes and Resources," in *The International Geosphere-Biosphere Programme: A Study of Global Change (IGBP) of the International Council of Scientific Unions (ICSU)* (Stockholm: ICSU, 1990), pp. 5–31.

147. Overbeck, J., G. Rheinheimer, W. Gunkel, W. E. Krumbein, and H. Weyland. "Stand und Perspektiven der Gewässermikrobiologie in der Bundesrepublik Deutschland," *Naturwissenschaften* 78:543–556 (1991).

148. Brown, P. C. and K. L. Cochrane. "Chlorophyll *a* Distribution in the Southern Benguela, Possible Effects of Global Warming on Phytoplankton and Its Implication for Pelagic Fish," *S. Afr. Tydskr. Wetenskap* 87:233–242 (1991).
149. El-Sayed, S. Z., F. C. Stephens, R. R. Bidigare, and M. E. Ondrusek. "Effect of Ultraviolet Radiation on Antarctic Marine Phytoplankton," in *Antarctic Ecosystems. Ecological Change and Conservation*, K. R. Kerry and G. Hempel, Eds. (Berlin: Springer-Verlag, 1990), pp. 379–385.
150. Carpenter, E. J. and K. Romans. "Major Role of the Cyanobacterium *Trichodesmium* in Nutrient Cycling in the North Atlantic Ocean," *Science* 254:1356–1358 (1991).

7

Polymer Materials

Anthony L. Andrady

INTRODUCTION

Near-ultraviolet radiation quanta have energies of about 3 to 4.3 eV which correspond to 72–97 kcal/mol. The predominant covalent bonds in most synthetic and natural polymeric materials are the C–H, C–C, and C–O linkages, with bond dissociation energies of 94–99 kcal/mol, 77–83 kcal/mol, and 76–79 kcal/mol, respectively, in aliphatic compounds. Other covalent bonds such as C–X (where X is a halogen), C–N, and O–O also occur in polymers and have lower bond dissociation energies, some even corresponding to the energy associated with quanta of visible light. Figure 1 shows the bond dissociation energies relevant to common polymers in relation to the energy content of monochromatic radiation. It is therefore not surprising that most polymeric materials undergo chemical reactions even on exposure to sunlight with only 5–7% ultraviolet radiation content. Higher energy, shorter wavelength UV radiation such as that found in the extraterrestrial solar spectrum is more effective in promoting chemical alteration of these materials. At high enough intensities UV-C radiation can rapidly ablate or etch polymer surfaces to a depth of several microns.[1]

The present review will focus on the nature of photoreactions that occur when organic polymers are exposed to UV radiation. This discussion is limited to general aspects of photodegradation and photoinitiated oxidation of common organic polymers, especially commodity

0-87371-911-5/93/$0.00 + $.50
© 1993 by Lewis Publishers

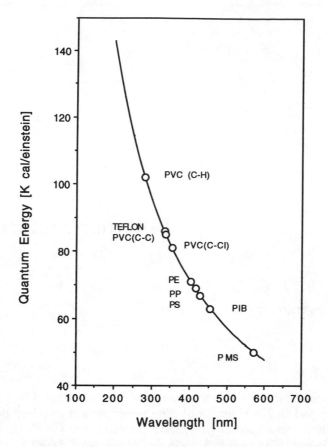

Figure 1 Bond dissociation energies of some common polymers in relation to
wavelength of UV-visible electromagnetic radiation.

thermoplastic materials, to illustrate the effect of UV radiation upon
polymers. The reader is directed to many excellent reviews for detailed
discussions on mechanisms and kinetics of the degradation processes.

LIGHT-MATERIAL INTERACTIONS

Occurrence of photochemical processes in organic molecules requires
that radiation of suitable energy be absorbed by the molecule (sometimes
called the Grotthus Draper law). Energy gained excites the molecule,
which may then undergo one or more photophysical processes. These
primary photophysical interactions of light with organic molecules are
conveniently summarized in the Jablonsky diagram shown in Figure 2.
The photons promote the molecule, which is in the ground state (S_0),
to a state of higher of energy. In almost all molecules the ground-state
electronic configuration involves electrons with opposing spin-angular

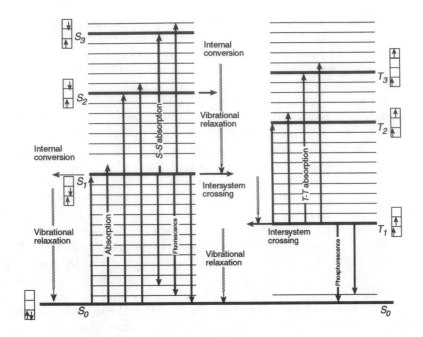

Figure 2 A modified Jablonsky energy diagram. See text for details.

moments which are paired in the molecular orbitals. Radiant energy supplied to the molecule may promote these electrons to higher energy levels while preserving the paired spins to yield excited singlet states generally indicated as (S_1), (S_2), (S_3), and so on depending on the energy level. Electrons in an excited singlet state no longer share the same orbital and are therefore able, without violating the Pauli exclusion principal, to adopt parallel spins, yielding triplet excited states, indicated by (T_1), (T_2), and so on. Each excited state has a definite energy and a finite lifetime associated with it. An $(S_1) \rightarrow (T_1)$ transition occurs by spin inversion via intersystem crossing as the direct excitation of a molecule from singlet to triplet excited state is a forbidden transition. Each photon absorbed by the molecule has a certain probability of populating either a singlet or a triplet state. Depending on the energy of photons absorbed, the molecule might be excited into a variety of vibrational levels within an excited sate. The resulting wide distribution of excited states achieved is reflected in the absorption spectrum of the molecule, which essentially maps the intensity of light absorption as a function of wavelength.

The fate of electronically excited singlet and triplet states of organic molecules depends upon the relative effectiveness of a set of competing photophysical processes. These involve several interesting unimolecular and bimolecular interactions, including both radiative and nonradiative photophysical processes. One of the pathways available to the molecule for losing the excess energy is by chemical reaction and is the basis of all light-induced structural changes obtained in organic molecules. A detailed discussion of the competing photophysical processes is outside the scope of this discussion. These include fluorescence (a radiative unimolecular reversion of excited singlet state to the ground state), a nonradiative internal conversion or vibrational relaxation into a lower excited state, phosphorescence (a radiative process involving a $(T_1) \rightarrow (S_0)$ transition), and delayed fluorescence (via the thermal reactivation of a triplet state into an excited singlet, followed by reversion to ground state). As the radiative processes can occur from different excited states of varying energy, the fluorescence and phosphorescence emissions from organic molecules tend to be polychromatic. Chemical reactions may also result from quenching of an excited state in a bimolecular collision. Such collisions may lead to the formation of excimers (essentially a dimer of the excited state and ground-state molecules of the same type) or exciplexes, which are similar associations but of different molecules. Both singlet and triplet excited state species are also quenched by molecular oxygen,[2] which has a triplet ground state. The lifetime of the lowest triplet excited state (T_1) of a molecule is generally about 10^5 times longer than that of the singlet excited state. Photochemical reactions therefore tend to involve the excited triplet states more often than the singlet states. These events lead to the possible primary photochemical reactions of the molecule. Products from the primary process such as radicals and ions may then undergo further reaction in a secondary photochemical process, yielding the familiar photodegradation products from organic molecules and polymers.

In polymers where the macromolecules are randomly oriented long chains, several chromophores may exist on the same molecule. Specially in solid polymers this allows for stronger interaction of the chromophores compared to that in compounds of lower molecular mass. Most studies on photophysical processes have been carried out in solution, and the findings therefore may not always apply to photodegradation of a solid polymer. Photodegradation in solid polymer systems is of greatest interest from a practical standpoint since polymers are mostly used as solids. Some of the features which make the photochemical processes in solid polymer systems more complex than those in liquid systems are as follows:

1. Even in the case of transparent but thick polymer sections, the irradiation is not uniform throughout the bulk of the polymer; each layer receives spectrally altered polychromatic radiation due to filtering by layers above it.[3] This is one reason that light-induced reaction are commonly limited to the surface layers in thick, solid polymer systems.[4]

2. Filled polymers (those containing powdered minerals dispersed within the matrix) afford even a more complex system, with selective ab-

sorption and reflection of radiation by fillers creating a heterogeneous illumination field within its bulk. Models of systems which absorb and scatter light simultaneously have been discussed.[5,6]

3. Plastics which are mostly in the glassy state (below the glass-rubber transition temperature, T_g) at ambient temperature provide a rigid matrix which can severely constrain the translational and/or rotational movements of the macromolecules. Chain segmental motion in glassy systems is also restricted, affecting the rate of bimolecular processes in the polymer. Furthermore, the free volume of the glassy polymer, which is determined by the pressure and the temperature (relative to T_g), controls the diffusion of quenchers of the excited states such as oxygen (as well as product species).[7]

4. A pair of radicals formed on photolysis of a bond may not effectively diffuse away from each other within a polymer matrix and may result in "cage" recombination, affecting the kinetics of photoreactions in the solid phase.[8]

5. Solubility as well as diffusivity of oxygen in solid polymer matrices is much lower than in liquids. In polyethylene, oxygen solubility is only about 10^{-3} mol/L.[2] In amorphous polymers, the rate of quenching of excited species occurs at 10^9–10^{10} mol/L,[2] and excited species with a lifetime shorter than about 10^8 s are not efficiently deactivated by oxygen. The crystalline domains within a semicrystalline polymer matrix, as with polypropylene,[9-11] are often impervious to oxygen.

6. Solid polymers irradiated under strain generally undergo faster photooxidation.[12]

Lifetimes of various radical species, the energy dispersive processes, and the kinetics of photoreactions in the case of solid polymer systems are therefore different from those of small organic molecules in solution.

Transmission of radiation through a homogeneous slab of polymer with no scattering losses either at surfaces or within its bulk is described by the Beer-Lambert law. The fraction of monochromatic radiation energy absorbed by such a medium is related to the concentration of chromophores and to the path length of the radiation within the medium:

$$\text{Log } I_t/I_0 = -\epsilon \cdot c \cdot \ell \tag{1}$$

where I_t and I_0 are the intensities of incident and transmitted radiation, respectively
c is the concentration (moles per liter) of the light-absorbing moiety
ℓ is the thickness (cm) of the slab

Proportionality coefficient ϵ is termed the molar extinction coefficient. It can be shown that for low levels of absorbance of the radiation

$$\text{Light absorbed, } I_a \propto c \cdot \epsilon \tag{2}$$

To ensure high yield of products from photoreactions, it is necessary to have high levels of absorption of radiation and consequently high concentrations of chromophores with large extinction coefficients.

PHOTOCHEMICAL REACTIONS OF POLYMERS

The effect of UV radiation on organic polymers is dependent upon the chemical nature of the polymeric species, the wavelength distribution of the UV source, the physical state of the polymeric substrate (solution, solid film, amorphous powder), and the gaseous environment in which the exposure is carried out. As the chemistry of light-induced processes is so dependent upon the structure of polymers, these effects are best discussed separately for different classes of polymers, emphasizing those commercially used within each class. Table 1 gives the characteristics of key polymers used extensively in packaging and building applications, which constitute large markets for thermoplastics (i.e., polymers which can be repeatedly formed into shapes by the application of heat), for the benefit of readers unfamiliar with polymers. Shown also are the repeat unit structure of the chain, the glass-rubber transition temperature, and volume usage of the polymer in the United States.

The sequence of chemical reactions which initiate the light-induced degradation of polymers is of particular interest. However, even in relatively simple polymers such as polyethylenes the photoinitiation is not completely understood. The complexity of the mechanisms leading to photodegradation in polymers is best illustrated by the following discussion on polyolefins. The ambiguity regarding the primary chromophore species, discussed below, is common with other commodity polymers (such as PVC) as well.

Photoinitiation of Polyolefins

Light-induced degradation of polyethylene, the most widely used thermoplastic, and polypropylenes has been extensively studied. Understandably, most reported studies dealt with the effects of exposure to UV radiation typically found in terrestrial sunlight. Pure polyolefins (polyethylenes and polypropylenes), being hydrocarbon polymers, lack the chromophores needed to absorb the UV radiation >290 nm present in sunlight. However, they do absorb solar UV radiation and display very low photostability[13] due to the presence of various impurities introduced during polymerization and processing of the polymer, which act as either photoinitiators or photosensitizers.

Absorption of light energy allows the photolysis of hydrocarbon bonds and the consequent formation of free radicals. These undergo a complex set of reactions very similar to that which occurs in the photothermal oxidation of simple hydrocarbons in liquid phase. This sequence of re-

Table 1 Plastics Used in Applications Where Exposure to Sunlight Might be Expected

Type of Plastic	Application	Tg (°C)	Usage (million lbs)[a]
Building Industry			
Poly(vinyl chloride) (rigid)	Siding		678
	Door/window		232
	Other		82
	Conduit	87	528
	Irrigation pipe		162
	Other pipe		2584
Poly(vinyl chloride) (plasticized)	Roofing		23
	Liners		26
	Wire-cable		432
	Weatherstrip		47
	Garden hose		60
Unsaturated polyester (thermoset)	Glazing		42
	Panels/siding		117
	Pipe		143
Polycarbonate (BPA-PC)	Glazing	150	103
	Fixtures		11

Table 1 (continued) Plastics Used in Applications Where Exposure to Sunlight Might be Expected

Type of Plastic		Application	Tg (°C)	Usage (million lbs)[a]
Packaging				
Polyethylene	—CH₂—CH₂—	Film	120	4224
		Containers		3611
Polypropylene	—CH₂—CH— CH₃	Film	10	586
Thermoplastic polyester (PET)	—O—(CH₂)₂—O—C(=O)—⟨benzene⟩—C(=O)—	Containers	69	995
Poly(vinyl chloride) (plasticized)	—	Film		318
		Containers		367
Housewares and Toys				
Polyethylene				1036
Polystyrene	—CH₂—CH—⟨benzene⟩			462
Polypropylene				242

[a] Based on 1989 statistics published in *Modern Plastics*, January 1990.

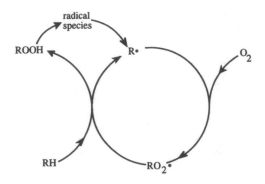

Termination: radical combination
radical disproportionation

Figure 3 Simplified basic autoxidation scheme. See text for details.

actions shown in Figure 3 is called the basic autoxidation scheme.[14] The generation of photolyzable hydroperoxides in the propagation cycle causes increased initiation, resulting in an autocatalytic process (one where the rate of oxidation increases with the extent). Ashby[15] reported energies of activation of 23–27 kcal/mol and 19.7 kcal/mol for thermal oxidation of polypropylene and polyethylene, respectively. The cyclic process uses up hydrocarbon and oxygen, yielding hydroperoxides and radical species. The chemical modification of the polymer by the reacted oxygen is quite low and should not affect the properties of the polymer significantly. However, polymer chain scission and cross-linking reactions that take place concurrently with the oxidation process drastically reduce the mechanical properties of the polymer, seriously limiting its outdoor lifetime.

The nature of the initiation reaction which yields the initial set of radicals for the reaction sequence continues to be controversial. Several candidate functionalities and impurity compounds have been proposed, and the more important of these are shown in Table 2.

Scott[16] proposed that for polyethylenes the hydroperoxides, the ketone functionalities, and the charge-transfer complexes with oxygen were the key mechanisms, in that order of importance. Carlsson and Wiles[17] reviewed the initiation mechanisms for polypropylene and proposed the relative contribution from different chromophores to be as follows:

Titanium residues $\sim$ (ROOH) > (C=O) > RO–OR >> (PP ... O_2)

While the relative contributions from different mechanisms are not definitively known, photoinitiation in polyolefins clearly involves at least the hydroperoxide and ketone groups formed either during manufac-

Table 2 Photoinitiating and Photosensitizing Chromophores in Polyolefins

Chromophore	Example	Origin[a]	References
1. Charge transfer complex with oxygen	(structures involving CH_2, $CH=CH_2$, and O_2 complex)	E	18–20
2. Unsaturation	(olefinic structures $=CH_2$)	M	21
3. Hydroperoxides	($-CH_2-CH-$, $O-OH$)	P,E	16,22,23
4. Ketones	($-CH_2-C-CH_2-$, $=O$; $-CH-CH_2-C=O$, CH_3)	P,E	22,24,25
5. Titanium residues	$TiO_2 + O_2 \longrightarrow\ ^1O_2\ \text{or}\ ^{\cdot}O{-}O^{\cdot}$	M,C	26–29
6. Hydrocarbon-O_2 reaction	$RH + O_2 \xrightarrow{h\nu}$ radicals $\longrightarrow\ ^1O_2 + RH$	E	30,31
7. Others (polynuclear aromatics)	–	E,P,M	32–34

[a] E = from environment; M = manufacture; C = Compounding ingredient; P = processing (such as extrusion, injection molding, and blow molding).

turing, processing, or during slow oxidation under ambient exposure conditions.

Hydroperoxides

Polymer hydroperoxides are generally regarded as the dominant photoinitiator of light-induced oxidation of polyolefins during the early stages of the process. In polyethylenes, allylic hydroperoxides, particularly the vinylidine hydroperoxides, initiate the photodegradation. The macroxy radicals formed on their dissociation can lead to the formation of ketonic carbonyl compounds, macroaldehydes, vinylidine alcohols, and macroradicals.[35,36] Solar wavelengths have sufficient energy to dissociate the O–O linkage and the polymer-oxygen linkage (but generally not the O–H bond) in the polymer hydroperoxide.[37,38] Having a relatively low absorption coefficient and being transparent to UV-A radiation $\lambda > 340$ nm, hydroperoxides are believed to dissociate for the most part as a result of energy transfer from excited chromophores present in the system. The presence of relatively lower levels of hydroperoxides in photooxidizing polyethylene compared to that in polypropylene has been pointed out;[39,40] upon photolysis polyethylene hydroperoxides might be converted into nonradical products including a carbonyl functionality. Shorter lifetimes and the lower concentrations of alkoxy radicals in polyethylenes (as deduced from electron spin resonance [ESR] studies[41]) limit the initiating effectiveness of the hydroperoxides in polyethylenes and are therefore expected to play less of a role as the primary initiator in polyethylene compared to polypropylene.

Alkyl hydroperoxides absorb in the UV range of $\lambda = 200$–300 nm and may undergo a unimolecular or bimolecular photolysis yielding free radicals.

$$ROOH \xrightarrow{h\upsilon} RO\cdot + \cdot OH$$

$$2\,ROOH \xrightarrow{h\upsilon} RO_2\cdot + RO\cdot + H_2O$$

The radicals formed in these reactions may react with another molecule of the hydroperoxide to yield radical species. Studies on photolysis of thermally generated polypropylene hydroperoxides found the reaction to have a high quantum efficiency of about four. Carbonyl functionalities are the main products of photolysis.[42,43]

An alternative mechanism of hydroperoxide photolysis proposed by Gugumus[44] is based on a bimolecular reaction between the hydroperoxide functionality and a neighboring macromolecular chain segment. Both secondary and tertiery hydroperoxides are postulated to undergo this reaction, which yields carbonyl groups as the main product but involves no radical formation or chain scission. Intramolecular reactions of this type involving a six-membered transition state can lead to chain scission.

Such intramolecular reactions, however, demand a degree of chain flexibility which might not always be available in the ambient temperature solid-phase oxidations of polyolefins, particularly those below T_g. There is some evidence that irradiation at wavelengths of $\lambda > 360$ nm (where Norrish II reactions do not occur) leads to vinyl group formation, suggesting that this nonradical mechanism for hydroperoxide decomposition is important in polyethylenes.

A mechanism for sensitized decomposition of hydroperoxides by interaction with a photoexcited carbonyl group via an exciplex formation has been proposed[45-47] on the basis of studies on polyisoprene hydroperoxides.

An excited carbonyl group may also abstract hydrogen from the hydroperoxide to yield a radical pair.[48] While both processes are mechanistically feasible and supported by some experimental evidence, their relative importance in polyolefin photooxidation is not known.

Ketones

Photolysis of ketones is well known and occurs via two accepted mechanisms: the Norrish I reaction, yielding free radical species, and the Norrish II reaction, which does not yield radicals.[49-52] The latter process is possible in ketones with at least a single hydrogen on the γ-carbon atom, allowing the formation of a six-membered cyclic intermediate.[53] Both reactions result in chain scission, leading to a decrease in the molecular weight of the polymer. Guillet et al.,[52] working with (ethylene-carbon monoxide) copolymers, showed the temperature-independent Norrish II reaction to be the dominant one at ambient temperatures.[54,55] Ethylene copolymers containing ~1% carbon monoxide comonomer are used in commercial applications (such as six-pack yokes) where enhanced photodegradability under exposure to sunlight is desired.

While hydroperoxides may be mainly responsible for photoinitiation during early photooxidation of polyolefins, ketones are believed to be the dominant initiator during the later stages. As shown above, photolysis of hydroperoxides yields carbonyl functionalities as a major reaction product. Consequently, carbonyl group concentration builds up exponentially on exposure of polyethylene to UV light. Quantum efficiency for the (ethylene-carbon monoxide) copolymers irradiated at 285 nm and 313 nm in N_2 has been reported.[56] Carlsson and Wiles[42] studied the photolysis of the predominant ketone species formed during oxidation of polypropylene and found that they undergo Norrish I or II reaction depending upon their structure, with a quantum yield of about 0.08.

An indirect mechanism where the photoexcited triplet carbonyls are quenched by ground-state oxygen to yield singlet oxygen has also been suggested.[57] The singlet oxygen so formed can diffuse freely in the polymer matrix and may react with vinyl end groups formed in Norrish II reactions or even with the hydrocarbon itself to yield hydroperoxides. Polypropylene photooxidized in the presence of singlet oxygen, however, did not yield hydroperoxides.[58,59] Perhaps the short lifetime of the excited oxygen species (about 10^{-5} sec) in the polymer makes this reaction a difficult one,[60] and singlet oxygen apparently plays only a minor role in the photooxidation of polyolefins.

CONSEQUENCES OF EXPOSURE TO UV RADIATION

With diverse chemical pathways available for utilization of photon energy, polymeric materials undergo a wide range of changes in physical and chemical properties as a result of exposure to UV radiation. Radiant energy absorbed by a macromolecular chromophore often results in main-chain bond scission, yielding a polymer of lower average molecular

Table 3 A Simplified Scheme Showing the Effects of Photodegradation of Macromolecular Substrates

Site of Reaction	Type of Reaction	Change in Property
Main chain	Scission	Loss of extensibility and/or strength
		Increased solubility
		Decreased average molecular weight
	Cross-linking	Increased brittleness, loss of strength and/or extensibility
		Decreased or loss of solubility
		Increased average molecular weight
Side chain	Scission	Formation of volatiles
		Changes in color and/or other physical and mechanical properties
		Change in average molecular weight
	Cyclization	Changes in most physical and mechanical properties
		Change in average molecular weight

weight and a broader molecular weight distribution. Alternatively, the polymer may cross-link to form a total or partial gel. The scission reactions may also be localized at the side chains of the polymer, resulting in the formation of low-molecular-weight species which are often volatile. Table 3 summarizes these possibilities, indicating the changes in physical and mechanical properties of the polymer that most often accompany them. These reaction pathways are not mutually exclusive; concurrent processes are the rule rather than the exception.

Discoloration

The mechanisms which lead to discoloration of different polymers on exposure to UV radiation are varied and are best discussed separately for each class of polymer. As a general rule, however, shorter wavelength UV-B (and where available, UV-C) is much more efficient in generating these chromophores. Action spectra relating to yellowing of common polymers, summarized in Table 4, illustrate this general trend. Activation spectra, indicating the wavelength intervals which are most effective in bringing about yellowing or discoloration in a polymer exposed to terrestrial solar radiation, are also given in the table. This is often not the shortest wavelength region in the sunlight spectrum, as the discoloration due to a waveband in the spectral irradiance distribution is a function of both the wavelength of radiation and its intensity. While the 320 nm to 340 nm spectral interval is not as efficient as the shorter wavelengths in causing yellowing, the associated photon fluence is relatively higher, making this wavelength interval a common maximum in the activation spectra for yellowing of several polymers by solar radiation.

Table 4 Reported Data on Spectral Sensitivity of Commodity Thermoplastics to Yellowing and Strength Variations, on Exposure to Solar Radiation

Material	Formulation	Wavelength Range (nm)[b]	Degradation	Action Spectrum	Ref.
PVC	Rigid, white polymer	310–325	Yellowing	Yes	62,63
		320	Yellowing	No	64
PC	Clear sheet	308–329	Yellowing	Yes	65
	Clear sheet	310	Yellowing	No	66
	Clear sheet	300–320	Yellowing	Yes	149
PP	Molded sheet	315–330	Strength	No	149
PE[a]	Laminate	<330	Extensibility	No	150
PS[a]	Foam sheet	320–345	Yellowing	No	150
ABS	Sheet	300–380	Yellowing	No	151
PMMA	Sheet	260–300	—	—	
Wood pulp (Pinus taeda)	Newsprint	335–355	Yellowing	Yes	150

[a] Enhanced photodegradable material. The polymer was modified chemically or a prodegradant was used to accelerate the photodegradation.
[b] Wavelength interval most effective in bringing about degradation.

Poly(vinyl chloride)

Structural features of polymers such as poly(vinyl chloride) (PVC) allow facile dehydrochlorination upon exposure to UV radiation, resulting in the formation of conjugate unsaturated centers in the macromolecule. These polyene structures absorb ultraviolet radiation in the wavelength range of 230–400 nm, depending on the length of the conjugated sequence. Once the sequence length exceeds about $n = 8$, the absorption spreads into the visible region of the spectrum,[61] resulting in discoloration. As might be expected, the hydrogen chloride evolution and the increase in UV absorbance of photodegrading PVC films follow similar kinetics.[61]

This "yellowing" of PVC by light is a well-known phenomenon, and it occurs readily with exposure to sunlight.[67] Titanium dioxide[68-71] (rutile grade at levels of 10–13% by weight) is used in most rigid PVC formulations intended for routine outdoor use in the U.S. Andrady et al.[72] showed that the yellowing efficiency of photons decreases logarithmically with the wavelength in the region 280 nm to 400 nm, for rigid PVC compounds (Figure 4). They also[73] identified the region of the solar spectrum particularly damaging to these compounds in terms of discoloration: 310–325 nm (Figure 5). These results are consistent with previous qualitative observations on uncompounded, unprocessed PVC substrates, where the shorter wavelength UV radiation was found to be

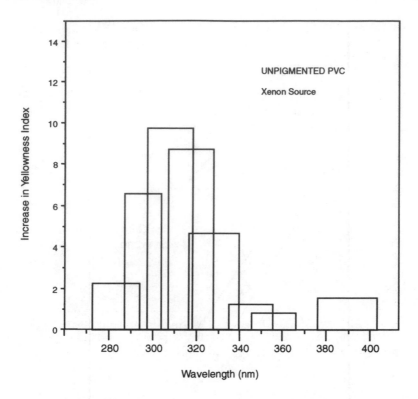

Figure 4 Wavelength sensitivity of some polymeric materials to UV-induced yellowing.

faster and more effective in bringing about yellowing of PVC. Generally, quantum yields for the dehydrochlorination were independent of intensity, typically 0.015 Einstein^{-1} for polymer films irradiated in oxygen at $\lambda > 254$ nm,[74] and much lower when irradiation was carried out under nitrogen.[75] The rate of reaction was first order with respect to the intensity of light,[76,77] a result consistent with the linear dependence of yellowing on the intensity of light, suggested by action spectra reported for rigid PVC formulations by Andrady et al.[63]

Formation of a polyene-rich surface layer which is only a few microns thick[75] on the surface of the polymer has two important consequences for further photodegradation. Shorter sequences of polyenes formed during early photodegradation may absorb UV radiation more effectively, promoting faster discoloration.[74,78] Excited polyenyls may easily dissociate to yield several different radical types. The longer polyenes, however, generally have high extinction coefficients[61] but are able to dissipate the energy without causing further photodegradation,[79] thus imparting a degree of protection from further photodegradation to the polymer. The orange-red polyene layer formed on extended photodeg-

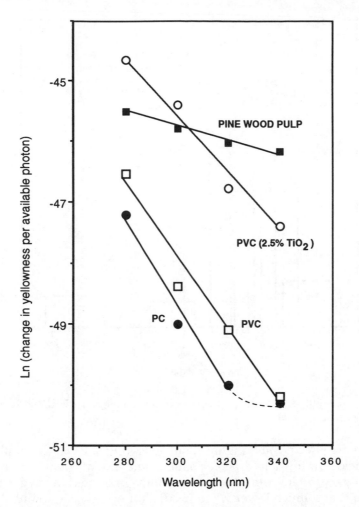

Figure 5 Activation spectra for yellowing of a compounded extruded PVC
laminate with no TiO$_2$ exposed to filtered xenon source radiation.

radation may absorb infrared radiation, contributing to heat buildup in
the material,[80] thus accelerating the dehydrochlorination reaction,[81] which
has a temperature coefficient of 8–18 kJ mol^{-1}.[82]

$$\left(CH_2-\underset{\underset{Cl}{|}}{CH}\right) \xrightarrow{h\upsilon} \left(CH=CH\right) + HCl$$

$$\left(CH=CH\right)_n \underset{\underset{Cl}{|}}{CH}-CH_2 \text{\Large\textasciitilde} \xrightarrow{h\upsilon} \left[\left(CH=CH\right)_n \underset{\underset{Cl}{|}}{CH}-CH_2\right]^*_n$$

n>2

a) $\overset{\bullet}{Cl} +$ \text{\textasciitilde}$\left(CH=CH\right)_n \underset{\bullet}{CH}-CH_2$\text{\textasciitilde}

b) $\overset{\bullet}{H} +$ \text{\textasciitilde}$\left(CH=CH\right)_n \underset{\bullet}{CCl}-CH_2$\text{\textasciitilde}

c) $\left(CH=CH\right)_n \overset{\bullet}{CH_2} + \overset{\bullet}{CHCl}$\text{\textasciitilde}

While radiation at wavelengths λ <400 nm cause yellowing discoloration of PVC materials, at wavelengths λ > 400 nm light of low intensity, in the presence of oxygen, can cause a reduction in coloration or photobleaching. A possible role of hydrogen chloride in bringing about bleaching and eventually adding on to the double bonds has been suggested.[83,84] However, the oxidative reaction also takes place in the absence of light,[74,85,86] when no dehydrochlorination can take place, and is believed to be a result of shortening of the polyene sequences due to reaction with ground-state oxygen. Available experimental evidence supports such a mechanism, as the reduced dehydrochlorination of PVC in air (as opposed to nitrogen) seems to be the result of reduced light absorbance by the polymer rather than the decrease in photon efficiency.[74,87,88] Druesdow and Gibbs[89] and Nagy et al.[90] suggested that quenching of polyenyl radicals by oxygen, yielding in-chain cyclic peroxides, may lead to the bleaching. Further reaction of resulting polyenyl-cyclic peroxide may lead to further peroxidation with reduced polyene sequence length. However, the peroxides may also decompose into alkoxy radicals, increasing the free-radical concentration of the system, as evidenced by increased spin concentrations in PVC/oxygen systems compared to PVC/nitrogen,[91] promoting further free-radical-mediated dehydrochlorination.

While the mechanism of photobleaching remains unclear, there is little doubt that adequately filtered solar radiation can effect such bleaching, which can be seen with samples slightly yellowed due to processing operations or yellowed by previous exposure to light.[73] The discoloration obtained under solar exposure is therefore the net result of competing yellowing and bleaching reactions promoted by the shorter and the longer wavelengths of the solar spectrum, respectively.

Polycarbonate

Polycarbonates, such as that derived from bisphenol-A (BPA), are used in window glazing as a replacement for glass. Any discoloration or surface damage of polycarbonates leading to reduced transparency to visible light is therefore of interest. Exposure of BPA polycarbonate to sunlight over extended periods of time can lead to yellowing.[93] Andrady et al.[65] studied the wavelength sensitivity of the yellowing process and found the change in yellowness index per available photon to be logarithmically dependent upon the wavelength of monochromatic light of wavelength, 280 nm to 400 nm. In a more recent study[92] the activation spectrum for discoloration under natural and simulated solar radiation was reported. The maximum changes in yellowing were observed in the wavelength interval of 310 nm to 340/350 nm. A second discoloration process having a different quantum efficiency was observed at wavelengths below 300 nm. The different photochemistries in these regions were suggested by the distinct separation of the effects of the spectral regions, indications of differences in quantum yields, and the differences in extent of yellowing promoted. The activation spectrum of the same material generated using outdoor solar exposure, however, showed only the 310–350 nm spectral region to be responsible for the actinic effects. In the study using monochromatic radiation,[65] photobleaching of existing low levels of chromophores were obtained at $\lambda = 500$ nm and $\lambda = 600$ nm exposures.

Two major reaction pathways are invoked to explain the photodegradation of BPA polycarbonate; most early work considered the photo-Fries reaction to be the key light-induced process, while the recent work suggests photooxidation reactions to be equally, if not more, important in the degradation process. The latter processes include ring oxidations suggested by several recent experiments. None of these pathways clearly indicate the origins of yellow reaction products; no such products have been isolated and identified completely.

Yellowing has been attributed to photo-Fries reaction products,[94] particularly to the o-dihydroxybenzophenones.[95] However, the products of photo-Fries reactions are themselves readily oxidizable, making it difficult to identify them. Evidence for this mechanism in photodegradation of polycarbonate is for the most part based on exposure to very short λ < 280 nm UV radiation in oxygen-poor or inert atmospheres.[96,97] The significance of photo-Fries reactions in photodegradation of solid polycarbonates to solar radiation in air is not clear; if the process occurs at all it is reasonable to expect that the mechanism is significant only in regions of the polymer away from the surface, where oxygen concentrations are low.

It is now believed that the oxidative reaction brought about by longer wavelength UV radiation in sunlight is the key mechanism in photodegradation of polycarbonates in air.[98-100] Irradiation ($\lambda > 290$) in nitrogen, however, results predominantly in the photo-Fries reaction.[101] Oxidation of the polymer, including aromatic ring oxidation, can yield products which are colored. While quinones and salicylates are believed to be formed in the oxidation,[102] the identity of yellow products has not been unambiguously established.[101]

CH₃ ... hυ ... OH ... CH₃ ... OH ... HO

(Chemical degradation scheme of polycarbonate under UV radiation, showing photo-Fries rearrangement to hydroxy-substituted ester and further to dihydroxy product)

Polystyrene

Polystyrene has a strong UV absorption spectrum due to the presence of phenyl groups in the structure. It readily undergoes light-induced yellowing when irradiated with certain wavelengths of monochromatic radiation,[103] solar radiation,[104] or radiation from filtered xenon sources.[105] Change in the yellowness index of expanded extruded polystyrene foam sheets exposed outdoors in air and while floating in seawater under marine conditions was recently reported by Andrady and Pegram.[106] Extensive yellowing was observed as a surface phenomenon, with the depth affected increasing with the duration of exposure. Embrittlement of the affected surface layer and its subsequent removal by wind, abrasion, or water might have determined the kinetics of the photodegradation process. Due to removal of the yellowed brittle layer, the yellowness index values measured at longer durations of exposure 8–12 months decreased from that for 6 months of exposure.

The structure of the yellow material and the mechanisms leading to its formation are not known. Under exposure to 254-nm UV radiation, Grassie and Weir[107] found the yellowing to occur faster in nitrogen than in air. They attributed the coloration to the formation of conjugate systems from terminally unsaturated polymer fragments. Conjugated systems of several double bonds in the polymer backbone may form.

$$CH_2{=}\underset{\underset{C_6H_5}{|}}{C}{-}CH_2\text{\Large$\wedge$} \quad \xrightarrow{h\upsilon} \quad CH_2{=}\underset{\underset{C_6H_5}{|}}{C}{-}CH{=}\underset{\underset{C_6H_5}{|}}{C}{-}CH_2\text{\Large$\wedge$}$$

However, the colored compounds formed on exposure to UV ($\lambda = 254$ nm) may not be the same as those obtained on exposure to sunlight. Savides et al.,[108] for instance, found the relative amounts of yellowing and the concentrations of carbonyl functionalities formed to be different for the two exposures. This led them to suggest that the yellowing under solar wavelengths is due to production of oxygenated species such as ketones rather than polyenes. The possibility of yellow product formation due to oxidative reactions involving ring opening has also been suggested.[109] In spite of the wide variety of chromophores proposed as being responsible for coloration,[106,110-114] the phenomenon remains poorly understood, and it may be the result of several photochemical processes occurring in concert to yield a complex mixture of products.

Changes in Molecular Weight

Radiant energy absorbed by a macromolecular chromophore often results in main-chain bond scission, yielding a polymer of lower average molecular weight and a broader molecular weight distribution.

Detailed studies have been carried out on (ethylene-carbon monoxide) copolymers, where the main-chain carbonyls absorb short-wavelength UV radiation. Chain scission during photoinitiation of aliphatic ketones was studied by Norrish and is believed to occur by the following mechanisms.[116]

$$\left[\sim\!CH_2-\overset{\overset{\displaystyle O}{\|}}{C}-CH_2-\!\sim\!\!\sim \right]^* \xrightarrow{\quad I \quad} \sim\!CH_2-\overset{\overset{\displaystyle O}{\|}}{C}\!\cdot \; + \; \cdot CH_2\!\sim\!\!\sim$$

$$\Big\downarrow \text{II}$$

$$-CH_2-C\underset{CH_2-CH_2}{\overset{O}{\diagup}}\!\!\diagdown\!\overset{H}{\underset{\diagup}{\diagdown}}\!CH\!-\!\!\sim\!\!\sim \;\longrightarrow\; \sim\!\!\sim\!C\underset{CH_3}{\overset{O}{\diagup}} \; + \; \overset{CH-\!\!\sim\!\!\sim}{\underset{CH_2}{\overset{\|}{C}}}$$

The Norrish type I reaction is a temperature-dependent free-radical-mediated scission reaction of low quantum efficiency,[52] while the Norrish II reaction is essentially a temperature-independent photoelimination which yields methyl ketone and vinyl unsaturation due to chain scission. While both reactions contribute to scission in most instances, the type II reaction amounts for a major part of the chemical reaction under ambient temperature conditions.[52] The type I process yields radicals[115] which in air can readily react with oxygen, eventually yielding macromolecular hydroperoxides. Initiation of autoxidation by hydroperoxides will also contribute to the chain scission on extended exposure. The quantum efficiency of scission for these copolymers was shown to be about 0.035 at 80°C for solution and solid-state irradiation,[52] and the activation energy for the scission process has been reported.[116] The rate of chain scission increases with the chromophore concentration (at constant thickness), allowing the design of controlled lifetime polyethylenes based on this approach. Figure 6 shows the loss in ultimate elongation of the (ethylene-1% carbon monoxide) copolymer under outdoor exposure in Miami, FL, both in air and while floating in seawater.[117] The lower rate of disintegration in seawater was attributed to the lack of heat buildup in the polymer exposed while floating in water as opposed to that exposed in air.

Copolymers of ethylene with vinyl ketone have carbonyl functionalities on side chains adjacent to the backbone of the polymer. These too undergo photolysis via Norrish I and II processes.[118,119] Unlike the main-chain carbonyls, these can initiate rapid photodegradation, and the quantum yield for the loss of carbonyl groups from these copolymers is higher by about a factor of four for irradiation in nitrogen, in solid phase.[115]

Polyethylenes (as well as other polyolefins) undergo chain scission during photooxidation as evidenced by a decrease in average molecular weight. Figure 7 shows the change in average molecular weight, M_w, as a function of outdoor exposure for the (ethylene-carbon monoxide)

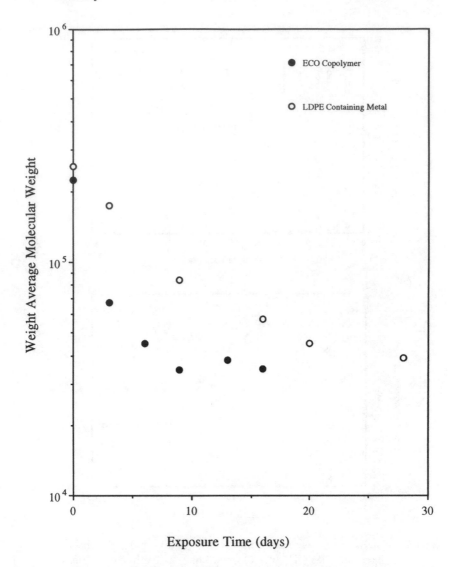

Figure 6 Change in tensile elongation at break of ethylene-carbon monoxide copolymer (1% CO) film and a control polyethylene film of the same thickness exposed (a) outdoors in Miami, Florida, in air and (b) while floating in seawater in Miami, Florida.

copolymer and for polyethylene containing metal pro-oxidants. The exact mechanism leading to main-chain scission is not clear, but it is probably associated with the propagation cycle of the auto-oxidative process. Alkoxy radicals undergo disproportionation reactions (also called β-scission) yielding terminal aldehyde groups and alkyl radicals in a propa-

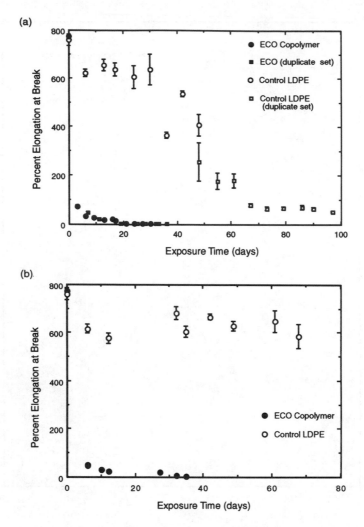

Figure 7 Change in average molecular weight of (a) ethylene-carbon monoxide
copolymer (1% CO) and (b) low-density polyethylene containing metal
compound pro-oxidants.

gation reaction. As such, the scission is a consequence of thermooxidative reactions, the contribution of UV radiation being to assist in the
initiation process, which is unlikely to be the primary scission reaction.
Exposure of polyolefins to ultraviolet radiation is well known to result
in decreased molecular weight, mechanical properties,[35,120] and viscosity.[121] These changes are strictly due to light-initiated thermooxidative
processes. However, oxidative reactions are obtained in most instances
of solar irradiation and in experiments where oxygen is not rigorously

excluded. Assuming random main-chain scission, it can be shown that the total number of bond scissions during irradiation, N, is

$$N = [(\overline{M}_{n,o}/\overline{M}_{n,t} - 1) \, m]/M_{n,o}$$

where   m is the mass of polymer irradiated
        $\overline{M}_n$ is the average molecular weight of polymers
        the subscript o refers to initial condition

Using a viscosity average molecular weight in the above equation Dan and Guillet.[122] calculated N and the quantum yield, φ, for chain scission in several copolymers containing vinyl ketone comonomer:

$$\Phi = \{[(\eta_o/\eta)^{1/\alpha} - 1]m\}/\overline{M}_{n,o}$$

where   η is the limiting viscosity number of polymer solution
        α is a constant

Concurrent with chain scission, photodegradation and photoinitiated oxidation of polyolefins may cause cross-linking of the polymer. The macro-alkyl radical product of the Norrish I reaction, for instance, may form *trans*-vinylene groups via hydrogen loss and subsequently react with another alkyl radical to form a cross-link.[41] A similar reaction by allylic-oxy radicals with a *trans*-vinylidene group may also lead to a cross-link via an ether bond. The observed rapid increases in the gel content of photodegrading polyethylene suggest that cross-linking reactions are significant.[35,36]

In any free-radical-mediated reaction sequence the very reactive macro-alkyl radicals can combine in a cross-linking termination reaction.[123] The ability of the macroradicals to in effect move within even a solid-phase system via a series of hydrogen abstraction reactions increases the chances of a radical pair encounter. This can take place even more readily in the absence of oxygen and is the basis of free-radical curing or vulcanization processes used in rubber chemistry. In the case of polyolefins such as polypropylene, where the relevant alkoxy radical is a stable tertiery radical, cross-linking via a peroxy bond is also possible.

In most polymer systems undergoing photodegradation, both chain scission and cross-linking processes take place concurrently, the effect on the properties of the material being determined by the scission to cross-linking ratio. The main consequence of overall cross-linking of a polymer is the decrease or loss in solubility. Complete cross-linking converts an ensemble of linear chainlike molecules into a three-dimensional network with each macromolecule associated to it by at least one terminal. The resulting single "network molecule" cannot be solvated and will only respond by swelling when placed in a good solvent for the polymer. Concurrent cross-linking and scission in a polymer on irradiation results in the decrease of soluble fraction S of the polymer. Charlesby[124] and Saito[125] have presented analyses of the change in S due to simultaneous scission and cross-linking. A knowledge of the variation of S as a function of the radiation dose (Einsteins per gram) allows the determination[126] of the scission to cross-linking ratio as well as the quantum yield of cross-linking, provided the weight-average molecular weight of the starting polymer is known.

$$S + S^{1/2} = p/q + 1/\Phi_c M_w \gamma)$$

where   p/q is the scission to cross-linking ratio
       γ is the radiation dose

This ratio p/q, however, may vary with the extent of photodegradation; as in the case of photooxidation of poly(vinly chloride) the scission-dominated early degradation may change to a cross-linking process with insolubilization of sample on extended degradation.[127]

Macroradical species obtained on irradiation of poly(vinyl chloride) include polyene radicals and the β-chloro macroradicals. These could undergo termination via combination, resulting in cross-linking. The polyenyl radical may undergo β-scission, yielding a radical and chain-terminal unsaturation.[128] Irradiation of PVC at λ < 254 nm is well known to result in decreased molecular weight of the polymer.[127,129,130,131] The quantum yield for random main-chain scission of the polymer can be estimated using gel permeation chromatographic data on the change in the average molecular weight. A value of 1.7×10^{-4} scissions per absorbed photon has been reported.[74] The polydispersity of the polymer also increased on irradiation and was attributed[132] to concurrent cross-linking reactions.[127,133,134] In systems where irradiation promotes concurrent scission and cross-linking, the determinations based on molecular weight will seriously underestimate the quantum yield.

Irradiation of polystyrene with ultraviolet radiation results in chain-scission reactions as well as cross-linking.[104] Alkoxy radicals in polystyrene may undergo α-cleavage, yielding a terminal ketone and an alkyl radical. The change in molecular weight of polystyrene on exposure to sunlight, outdoors, was recently reported.[106,135] The rate of degradation in terms of decrease in average molecular weight was found to be faster for polystyrene foam samples exposed floating in seawater compared to those exposed in air. The difference was attributed to the removal of surface yellow-colored protective layer by seawater during exposure. The gel fraction formed during irradiation of polystyrene was reported by Torikai et al;[136] a plateau value of gel content (~20–50% depending on temperature) was obtained. Alkoxy radicals in polystyrene may undergo α-cleavage, yielding a terminal ketone and an alkyl radical.

Changes in Mechanical Properties

The useful mechanical properties of polymers, such as tensile strength, extensibility, good impact resistance, and solvent resistance, are consequences of their macromolecular structure. Reduction in molecular weight due to chain scission affects these properties drastically. Cross-linking during ultraviolet degradation is desirable and leads to improved properties (particularly modulus and strength) up to a point; extensive cross-linking renders the polymer too brittle for many applications. Most reported data on changes in mechanical properties due to UV exposure understandably relate to outdoor or laboratory weathering data. Estimating with a high degree of reliability the service life of plastics under outdoor exposure conditions is important in design of products.

Tensile properties of polymers are sensitive to even low extents of photodegradation and can be measured conveniently with an acceptable degree of precision.[137] Both the tensile strength and ultimate extension of the material invariably decrease with irradiation. Cross-linking reactions, depending on the type of polymer and the compound used, may result in increased modulus. Data on relative change in the tensile properties of different types of plastics under similar exposure conditions are reported in the literature,[40,103] but are of limited value since many variables other than the chemical nature of the polymer may determine the susceptibility of the samples to weathering. It is of interest to determine the tensile property, which is particularly sensitive to photodegradation-related changes in polymers. Andrady has reported data on polyethylenes (ethylene-carbon monoxide copolymer, and low-density polyethylene containing added metal pro-oxidants) which show the ultimate extension and the energy to rupture to be significantly more sensitive to degradation than the tensile strength or the low extension modulus of the polymer.[138] The data of Davis and Sims[139] on the change in tensile properties of polycarbonate under exposure to tropical conditions also support this conclusion. Ultimate extension of irradiated polyethylene was found to correlate well with the increase in carbonyl index in the samples.[16,138,140]

Tensile elongation at the breaking point varies logarithmically with the during of exposure provided the available sunlight increases linearly with duration. The gradient of a semilogarithmic plot of the data might be used as an empirical measure of the rate at which the material disintegrates (see Figure 6). Polyethylene undergoes a ready loss in extensibility on irradiation with UV ($\lambda = 290$ nm)[141] or with solar radiation.[142] The rate of degradation obtained varies with location of exposure due to differences in the spectral quality of light, the ambient temperature, and other climatic factors. With enhanced photodegradable polyethylene film samples, the loss in ultimate extension correlated well with the total global solar radiation. More importantly, the color of polyethylene formulations also affects the rate of loss in mechanical properties; outdoor exposure studies in Australia[139,143] and in the U.S.[139] indicate that the darker-colored formulations containing carbon black or iron oxide show superior weatherability compared to natural polymer or lightly colored formulations.

Other mechanical properties such as the flexural strength,[137,144] tear strength,[145] shear strength,[146] and hardness[147,148] are also reported to change as a result of irradiation of polymers with UV-visible radiation. The extensive amount of reported data on the variation of numerous mechanical properties on irradiation with UV radiation or solar radiation cannot be adequately reviewed here. The reader is directed to several excellent reviews on the subject.[19,20,136,138]

REFERENCES

1. Srinivasan, R. and B. Braren. *Chem. Rev.* 89:1303–1316 (1989).
2. Turro, N. *Modern Molecular Photochemistry* (Menlo Park, CA: Benjamin/ Cummings, 1978).
3. Andrady, A. L. and A. R. Shultz. *J. Appl. Polym. Sci.* 33:1389 (1987).
4. Feedasova, G. T., L. D. Strelkova, E. O. Krats, V. P. Lebedev, and K. S. Minsker. *Int. Polym. Sci. Technol.* 8:T1 (1981).
5. Kubelka, A. and F. Munk. *Z. Tech. Physik.* 12:593 (1931).
6. Andrady, A. L. and A. R. Shultz. *J. Polym. Sci.* 33:1389 (1987).
7. Shimada, S., Y. Hori, and H. Kashiwabara. *Polymer* 22:1377 (1981).
8. Garton, A., D. J. Carlsson, and D. M. Wiles. *Makromol. Chem.* 181:1841 (1980).
9. Winslow, F. H., M. Y. Hellman, W. Natreyek, and S. M. Stills. *Polym. Eng. Sci.* 6:1 (1966).
10. Hawkins, W. L. *SPE Trans.* 1964:187 (1964).
11. Neiman, M. B., G. I. Likhtenshtein, V. S. Konstantinov, V. S. Karpets, and J. G. Urman. *Vysokomol. Soedin.* 5:1706 (1963).
12. Benachour, D. and C. E. Rogers, in *Photodegradation and Photostabilization of Coatings*, S. P. Pappas and F. H. Winslow, Eds. (Washington, D.C.: American Chemical Society, 1981), p. 263.
13. Allen, N. S. *Degradation and Stabilization of Polyolefins* (London: Applied Science Publishers, 1983), p. 337.
14. Bolland, J. L. *Q. Rev. Chem. Soc.* 3:1 (1949).
15. Ashby, G. E. *J. Polym. Sci.* 50:99 (1961).
16. Scott, G., Ed. *Ultraviolet Light Induced Reactions in Polymers* (Washington, D.C.: American Chemical Society, 1976), p. 340.
17. Carlsson, D. J. and D. M. Wiles. *J. Macromol. Sci. Rev. Macromol. Chem. C* 14:155 (1976).
18. Carlsson, D. J. and D. M. Wiles. *J. Macromol. Sci. Rev. Macromol. Chem.* C14:65 (1976).
19. Allen, N. S., Ed. *Development in Polymer Photochemistry, Vol. 1* (London: Applied Science Publishers, 1980).
20. Allen, N. S., Ed., *Develoment in Polymer Photochemistry, Vol. 2* (London: Applied Science Publishers, 1981).
21. Rugg, F. M., J. J. Smith, and L. H. Waterman. *J. Polym. Sci.* 11:1 (1953).
22. Amin, M. U., L. M. K. Tillakeratne, and G. Scott. *Eur. Polym. J.* 11:85 (1976).
23. Chakraborty, K. B. and G. Scott. *Eur. Polym. J.* 13:731 (1977).
24. Amin, M. U., G. Scott, and L. M. K. Tillekeratne. *Eur. Polym. J.* 11:85 (1975).
25. Allen, N. S. and J. F. McKellar. *Brit. Polym. J.* 9:302 (1977).
26. Cicchetti, O. *Adv. Polym. Sci.*, 7:70 (1970).
27. Cicchetti, O. and F. Gratini. *Eur. Polym. J.* 8:561 (1972).
28. Irick, G. J. *J. Appl. Polym. Sci.* 16:2387 (1972).
29. Kunz, C. O. and A. N. Wright. *J. Chem. Soc. Trans. Faraday* 68:140 (1971).
30. Kaplan, M. L. and P. G. Kelleher. *J. Polym. Sci.* 9(B):565 (1971).
31. Chien, J. C. W. *J. Phys. Chem.* 69:4317 (1965).
32. Carlsson, D. J. and D. M. Wiles. *J. Polym. Sci.* 11(B):759 (1973).

33. Partridge, R. H. *J. Chem. Phys.* 45:1679 (1966).
34. Pivovarov, A. P., Y. V. Gak, and A. F. Lukovnikov. *Vysokomol. Soedin* A13:2110 (1971).
35. Scott, G. *J. Polym. Sci. Polym. Symp.* 57:357 (1976).
36. Scott, G. *Am. Chem. Soc. Div. Org. Coat. Plast. Chem. Prepr.* 35:163 (1975).
37. Benson, S. W. *J. Chem. Educ.* 42:501 (1965).
38. Morison, J. D. and A. J. G. Nicholson. *J. Chem. Phys.* 20:1021 (1952).
39. Ginhac, J. M., J. L. Gardette, R. Arnaud, and J. Lemaire. *Macromol. Chem.* 182:1017 (1981).
40. Carlsson, D. J., A. Garton, and D. M. Wiles, in *Developments in Polymer Stabilization, Vol. 1,* G. Scott, Ed. (London: Applied Science Publishers, 1979), p. 219.
41. Tsuji, K. and H. Nagita. *Rep. Prog. Polym. Phys. Jpn.* 20:563 (1977).
42. Carlsson, D. J. and D. M. Wiles. *Macromolecules* 2:587 (1969).
43. McGill, W. J. *S. Afr. J. Sci.* 73:313 (1977).
44. Gugumus, F. Paper presented at the European Symposium on Polymeric Materials, Lyon, France, September 14–18, 1987.
45. Guillet, J. E. *Adv. Chem. Ser.* 169:1 (1978).
46. Ng, N. C. and J. E. Guillett. *Macromolecules* 11:937 (1978).
47. Gueskins, G. and C. David. *Pure Appl. Chem.* 51:233 (1979).
48. Stewart, L. C., D. J. Carlsson, D. M. Wiles, and J. C. Scaiano. *J. Am. Chem. Soc.* 105:3605 (1983).
49. Bamford, C. H. and R. G. W. Norrish. *J. Chem. Soc.* 1504 (1935).
50. Davis, W. and W. A. Noyes. *J. Am. Chem. Soc.* 60:2153 (1947).
51. McMillan, G. R., J. G. Clavert, and J. N. Pitts. *J. Am. Chem. Soc.* 86:3602 (1964).
52. Guillet, J. E., J. Dhanaraj, F. J. Colemba, and G. H. Hartley. *Adv. Chem. Ser.* 85:272 (1968).
53. Rice, F. O. and E. Teller. *J. Chem. Phys.* 6:489 (1938).
54. Golemba, F. J. and J. E. Guillett. *Macromolecules* 5:63 (1972).
55. Hartley, G. H. and J. E. Guillett. *Macromolecules* 1(2):165 (1968).
56. Guillet, J. E. *Pure Appl. Chem.* 52:285 (1980).
57. Trozzolo, A. M. and F. H. Winslow. *Macromolecules* 1:98 (1968).
58. Mill, T., H. Richardson, and F. R. Mayo. *J. Polym. Sci. Part A-1,* 11:2899 (1973).
59. Breck, A. K., C. L. Taylor, K. E. Russell, and J. K. S. Wan. *J. Polym. Sci.* 12:1505 (1974).
60. Rabek, F. and B. Ranby. *Polym. Eng. Sci.* 15:40 (1975).
61. Daniels, V. D. and H. H. Rees. *J. Polym. Sci. Polym. Chem. Ed.* 12:2115 (1974).
62. Andrady, A. L., A. Torikai, and K. Fueki. *J. Appl. Polym. Sci.* 37:935–946 (1989).
63. Andrady, A. L., K. Fueki, and A. Torikai. *J. Appl. Polym. Sci.* 39:763 (1990).
64. Hirt, R. C. and N. Z. Searle. *Appl. Polym. Symp.* 4:67 (1967).
65. Andrady, A. L., K. Fueki, and A. Torikai. *J. Polym. Sci.* 42:2105 (1991).
66. Trubiroha, P. in *Advances in the Stabilization and Controlled Degradation of Polymers,* A. V. Patsis, Ed. (Lancaster, PA: Technomic Publishing Co., 1989), p. 236.

67. Stroud, D. *J. Vinyl Technol.* 5(2):52 (1983).
68. Summers, J. W. and E. B. Rabinovitch. *J. Vinyl Technol.* 5(3):91 (1983).
69. Mathur, K. and K. Kramer. *J. Vinyl Technol.* 5(1):32 (1983).
70. Summers, J. *J. Vinyl Technol.* 5(2):43 (1983).
71. Keefer, M. *J. Vinyl Technol.* 5(2):57 (1983).
72. Andrady, A. L., K. Fueki, and A. Torikai. *J. Appl. Polym. Sci.* 37:935–946 (1989).
73. Andrady, A. L. and N. D. Searle. *J. Appl. Polym. Sci.* 37:2789 (1989).
74. Decker, C. and M. Balandier. *Polym. Photochem.* 15:221 (1981).
75. Decker, C. and M. Balandier. *Eur. Polym. J.* 18:1085 (1982).
76. Owen, E. D. and R. J. Bailey. *J. Polym. Sci. Polym. Chem. Ed.* 10:113 (1972).
77. Braun, D. and S. Kull. *Angew. Makromol. Chem.* 85:79 (1980).
78. Balandier, M. and C. Decker. *Eur. Polym. J.* 14:995 (1978).
79. Gibb, W. H. and J. R. MacCullum. *Eur. Polym. J.* 7:1231 (1971).
80. Rabinovitch, E. B., J. G. Quisenberry, and J. W. Summers. *J. Vinyl Technol.* 5(3):110–115 (1983).
81. Braun, D. and E. Bezdadea. *Angew. Makromol. Chem.* 99:55 (1981).
82. Braun, D. and S. Kull. *Angew. Makromol. Chem.* 86:171 (1980).
83. Owen, E. D. and J. I. Williams. *J. Polym. Sci. Polym. Chem. Ed.* 12:1933 (1974).
84. Owens, E. D. and R. L. Read. *J. Polym. Sci. Polym. Chem. Ed.* 17:2719 (1979).
85. Pochan, J. M., H. W. Gibson, and F. C. Bailey. *J. Polym. Sci. Polym. Lett. Ed.* 18:447 (1980).
86. Gibb, W. H. and J. R. MacCullum. *Eur. Polym. J.* 10:533 (1974).
87. Decker, C. and M. Balandier. *J. Photochem.* 15:221 (1981).
88. Decker, C. and M. Balandier. *J. Photochem.* 15:213 (1981).
89. Druesdow, D. and C. Gibbs. *Natl. Bur. Stand. (U.S.) Circ.* 525:69 (1953).
90. Nagy, T. G., T. Kelen, B. Turcsanyi, and F. Tudos. *J. Polym. Sci. Polym. Chem. Ed.* 15:853 (1977).
91. Gupta, V. P. and L. E. Pierre. *J. Polym. Sci. Polym. Chem. Ed.* 17:797 (1979).
92. Andrady, A. L., N. D. Searle, and L. F. E. Crewdson. *Polym. Degrad. Stabil.* 35:235–247 (1992).
93. Ram, A., O. Zilber, and S. Kenig. *Polym. Eng. Sci.* 25:535 (1985).
94. Gupta, A., A. Rembaum, and J. Moacanin. *Macromolecules* 11(6):1285 (1978).
95. Ong, E. and H. E. Bair. *Polym. Prep.* 20:945 (1979).
96. Bellus, D., P. Hrdlovic, and Z. Manasek. *J. Polym. Sci. Polym. Lett.* 4:1 (1966).
97. Humphrey, J. S. and R. S. Roller. *Mol. Photochem.* 3:35 (1971).
98. Rivaton, A., D. Sallet, and J. Lemaire. *Polym. Photochem.* 3:463 (1983).
99. Rivaton, A., D. Sallet, and J. Lemaire. *Polym. Degrad. Stabil.* 14:1 (1986).
100. Clark, D. T. and H. S. Munro. *Polym. Degrad. Stabil.* 8:195 (1984).
101. Clark, D. T. and H. S. Munro. *Polym. Degrad. Stabil.* 4:441 (1982).
102. Factor, A. and M. L. Chu. *Polym. Degrad. Stabil.* 2:203 (1980).
103. McKellar, J. F. and N. S. Allen. *Photochemistry of Man-Made Polymers* (Englewood, NJ: Applied Science Publishers, 1979).
104. David, C., D. Baeyens-Volant, G. Delaunois, Q. Lu Vinh, W. Piret, and G. Geuskens. *Eur. Polym. J.* 14:501 (1978).

105. Gugumus, F. *Dev. Polym. Stabil.* 1:8 (1979).
106. Andrady, A. L. and J. E. Pegram. *J. Appl. Polym. Sci.* 42(6):1589 (1991).
107. Grassie, N. and N. A. Weir. *J. Appl. Polym. Sci.* 9:987 (1965).
108. Savides, C., J. A. Stretanski, and L. R. Costello. "Light Stabilization of Polystyrene," in *Stabilization of Polymers and Stabilizer Processes,* R. F. Gould, Ed., Advances in Chemistry Series No. 85 (Washington, D.C.: American Chemical Society, 1968), p. 187.
109. Ranby, B. and J. Lucki. *Pure Appl. Chem.* 52:295 (1980).
110. Lawrence, J. B. and N. A. Weir. *Chem. Commun.* 273 (1966).
111. Kubica, J. and B. Waligora. *Eur. Polym. J.* 13:325 (1977).
112. Zapalskii, O. B. *Vysokomol. Soedin.* 7:615 (1965).
113. Rabek, J. F. and B. Ransby. *J. Polym. Sci. Polym. Chem. Ed.* 12:273 (1974).
114. Grassie, N. and N. A. Weir. *J. Appl. Polym. Sci.* 9:975 (1965).
115. Sitek, F., J. E. Guillett, and M. Heskins. *J. Polym. Sci.* 57:343–355 (1976).
116. Guillet, J. E., Ed. *Polymers with Controlled Lifetimes* (New York: Plenum Press, 1973).
117. Andrady, A. L., J. E. Pegram, and S. Nakatsuka. *J. Environ. Polym. Degrad.* 1(1):31 (1993).
118. David, C., W. Demarteau, and G. Gueskins. *Polymer* 8:497 (1967).
119. Guillet, J. E. and R. G. W. Norrish. *Proc. R. Soc. London* A233:153 (1955).
120. Omichi, H., M. Hagiwara, M. Asano, and K. Araki. *J. Polym. Sci. Symp.* 24:2311 (1979).
121. Vink, P. *J. Appl. Polym. Sci. Appl. Polym. Symp.* 35:265 (1979).
122. Dan, E. and J. E. Guillet. *Macromolecules* 6:230 (1973).
123. Kujirai, C., S. Hashiya, and H. Furuno. *J. Polym. Sci. A1* 6:589 (1968).
124. Charlesby, A. *Atomic Radiation and Polymers* (Oxford: Pergamon Press, 1960).
125. Saito, O. *J. Phys. Soc. Jpn.* 13:198 (1968).
126. Charlesby, A. and S. H. Pinner. *Proc. R. Soc.* 249A:367 (1959).
127. Kamal, M. R., M. M. Ell-Kaissy, and M. M. Avedesian. *J. Appl. Polym. Sci.* 16:83 (1972).
128. Decker, C. and M. Balandier. *Makromol. Chem.* 183:1263 (1982).
129. Kwei, K. *J. Polym. Sci. Polym. Chem. Ed.* 7:1075 (1969).
130. Mori, F., M. Koyama, and Y. Oki. *Makromol. Chem.* 64:89 (1977).
131. Kwei, K. P. S. *J. Appl. Polym. Sci.* 12:1543 (1968).
132. Scott, G. and M. Tahan. *Eur. Polym. J.* 11:535 (1975).
133. Rabek, J. F., G. Canback, J. Lucky, and B. Ranby. *J. Polym. Sci. Polym. Chem. Ed.* 14:1447 (1976).
134. Ranby, B., J. F. Rabek, and G. Canback. *J. Macromol. Sci. Chem.* 12:587 (1978).
135. Osawa, A., F. Konoma, S. Wu, and J. Cen. *J. Polym. Photochem.* 7:337 (1986).
136. Torikai, A., A. Takeuchi, and K. Fueki. *Polym. Degrad. Stabil.* 14:367 (1986).
137. Suzuki, S., H. Kubota, O. Nishimura, and T. Tsurue. *Kokkaido Kogyo Kaihatsu Shikensho Hokoku* 24:153 (1981).
138. Andrady, A. L. Unpublished data (1993).
139. Davis, A. and D. Sims. *Weathering of Polymers* (New York: Applied Science Publishers, 1983), p. 155.
140. Gugumus, F. *Polym. Dev. Stabil.* 8:239 (1987).

141. Vink, P., in *Degradation and Stabilization of Polyolefins,* N. S. Allen, Ed. (New York: Applied Science Publishers, 1983), p. 215.
142. Dolezel, B. *Die Bestardigkeit von Kunstoffen und Gummi* (Munich: Carl Hansar, 1978), p. 58.
143. Dunn, P. and E. J. Hill. Department of Supply, Def. Standard Lab Report No. 421, Australia (1971).
144. Mathey, R. G. and W. J. Rossiter. *Durabil. Build. Mater.* 2:59 (1983).
145. Carr, C. M. and I. H. Leaver. *J. Appl. Polym. Sci.* 33:2087 (1987).
146. Gan, L. M., H. W. K. Ong, and W. C. Feist. *Durabil. Build. Mater.* 4:35 (1986).
147. Welch, M. J., P. J. C. Counsell, and C. V. Lawton. *J. Oil Colour Chem. Assoc.* 63:137 (1980).
148. Crowder, J. R. and M. A. Ali. *Durabil. Build. Mater.* 3:115 (1985).
149. Andrady, A. L. and N. D. Searle. Unpublished data.
150. Andrady, A. L. Unpublished data.
151. Searle, N. D. et al. Unpublished data.

8

Tropospheric Air Quality

Michael W. Gery

INTRODUCTION AND BACKGROUND

As noted in earlier chapters, a decline in stratospheric ozone concentrations will allow UV-B radiation to penetrate deeper into the atmosphere, causing tropospheric UV-B to become more intense. Because UV-B radiation is a principal energy source driving tropospheric chemistry, increased UV-B near the earth's surface is expected to result in increased chemical reactivity. The increased reactivity could adversely affect tropospheric air quality, since most undesirable compounds (e.g., ozone, peroxides, and acids) are not emitted, but formed through chemical reaction. This degradation of tropospheric air quality would exacerbate or create new pollution problems related to human health and welfare and could increase stress in the biosphere.

This chapter first describes the physical-chemical processes linking tropospheric air quality with stratosphere ozone loss. Possible changes to tropospheric chemistry will vary depending on local concentrations of oxides of nitrogen (NO_x), volatile organic compounds (VOC), and other trace gases.[1,2] Therefore, the discussion of potential air quality impacts is separated into sections describing regions of similar chemical conditions. The final sections present a summary and discussion of future research.

0-87371-911-5/93/$0.00 + $.50
© 1993 by Lewis Publishers

CHEMICAL RESPONSE TO INCREASED UV-B

In the troposphere the rates of some chemical reactions depend directly on the amount of available UV-B.[3,4] Atmospheric measurements have shown that the reaction rate of ozone photodissociation:[5,6]

$$O_3 + h\upsilon \ (UV\text{-}B) \longrightarrow O(^1D) + O_2$$

is inversely related to the amount of overhead ozone. Calculations indicate that this rate would increase significantly (perhaps by between 20 and 25%) at mid-latitude, sea-level locations for a 10% loss of stratospheric ozone.[7] Any significant increase in this rate could affect tropospheric chemical conditions because the rapid reaction of $O(^1D)$ with water vapor is the major source of tropospheric hydroxyl radical (OH).[8]

$$O(^1D) + H_2O \longrightarrow 2 \cdot OH$$

OH is the primary oxidizer of virtually every trace gas found near the earth's surface.[9] It is a member of a chemically related family of extremely reactive molecules known as odd-hydrogen radicals (OH, H, and HO_2). Hence, increased UV-B should increase odd-hydrogen production rates and, therefore, the "chemical reactivity" or "oxidizing potential" of the troposphere.[1]

Although the photolysis rates of other tropospheric trace gases will not be as directly affected by increased UV-B as will the ozone, some important species also photolyze to odd-hydrogen products upon absorption of UV-B.[7] In particular, formaldehyde, which is an oxidation product of almost all organic compounds, can form two hydrogen atoms that quickly convert to hydroperoxy radicals in the troposphere:

$$HCHO + h\upsilon(UV\text{-}B \text{ and } VIS) \longrightarrow 2 \text{ H} \cdot + CO$$
$$H \cdot + O_2 \longrightarrow HO_2 \cdot$$

Increased reactivity caused by enhancement of these photolysis rates has been demonstrated in smog chamber experiments, where controlled increased UV-B led to greater production of oxidized products.[10]

POTENTIAL CHANGES TO TROPOSPHERIC CHEMISTRY

Effects on Areas Distant from Anthropogenic Influence

Most portions of the elevated troposphere and remote regions of the lower troposphere receive little direct impact from human activities. Less populated land areas and oceans comprise over three quarters of the earth's surface. Typical concentrations of VOC (excluding methane) and

Predicted Surface O3 Changes
(as a function of NOx and latitude)

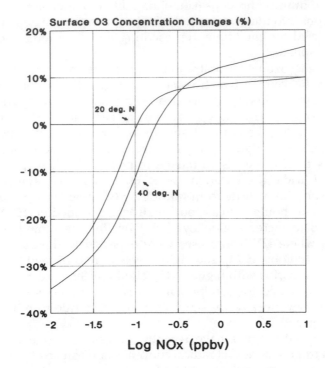

Figure 1   Model-predicted surface O_3 concentration changes due to 20% reduction in column O_3 as a function of NO_x concentration; calculations
were for summer conditions at 20°N and 40°N. (Reprinted from Reference 1. With permission.)

NO_x are extremely low. Therefore, ozone production cannot be *sustained*
(as is the case for urban smog production) and typical ozone concentrations are also low. Analysis of such a relatively simple chemical system
suggests that the effect of increased UV-B should be to decrease tropospheric ozone concentrations by increasing the photochemical destruction of ozone. In essence, the added reactivity (odd-hydrogen production) caused by enhanced UV-B cannot be efficiently used to produce
new ozone because VOC and NO_x precursors are lacking.

Calculations by Liu and Trainer suggested that a 20% loss of stratospheric ozone at northern mid-latitudes could induce a 10 to 35% decline
in remote tropospheric ozone for NO_x levels between 0.10 to 0.01 ppb
(Figure 1).[1] Further investigations employed computer models to investigate the impact of increased UV-B in different types of chemically
coherent regions of the troposphere. Thompson et al.[2,11,12] used a one-

dimensional photochemical model and Isaksen et al.[13] a two-dimensional model to calculate the effects of 10 and 15% stratospheric ozone decreases for projected future conditions (combining different increases of CO and CH_4 emissions into the next century). Tropospheric ozone depletion was again predicted for conditions representing the more remote portions of the troposphere.

Besides using ozone concentrations to indicate the potential consequences of enhanced UV-B on tropospheric air quality, the concentration of hydrogen peroxide (H_2O_2) has also been studied in computer modeling investigations. H_2O_2 is known to be a chemical reservoir for odd-hydrogen radicals. Therefore, it should be a more direct indicator of calculated changes to odd-hydrogen concentrations. In addition, potential changes to H_2O_2 levels would be interesting with respect to the formation of acidic precipitation, since H_2O_2 is usually the principal oxidizer of sulfur dioxide (to form sulfuric acid) in cloud water.[14] Because increased UV-B should increase odd-hydrogen production, H_2O_2 levels are projected to increase globally.[2,11,12] Even for the remote scenario calculations where UV-B increases were expected to diminish surface ozone concentrations, H_2O_2 (and $HO_2\cdot$) levels were projected to increase slightly. For scenarios with higher NO_x, significantly larger increases in H_2O_2 were calculated for continental and rural conditions (NO_x of 0.2 and 1.4 ppb) beyond already significant increases due to other global climate changes.[2,12]

Madronich and Grainer have recently suggested that evidence for increases in tropospheric OH radical concentration (caused by increased UV-B and ozone photolysis) might be found in methane measurements taken over the past 15 years.[15] They point out that trends in methane concentration growth have slowed in the past few years, coinciding with a decline in stratospheric ozone and an anticipated increase in tropospheric UV-B and OH. Since reaction with OH is the main sink for methane, the authors suggest that the decreased methane growth may be due to increased methane loss through reaction with additional OH. While the measurements and trends data are not yet significant enough to conclusively isolate this particular process and determine its impact, the calculations do indicate that atmospheric linkages between radiation, chemistry, and transport are probably far more complex than have yet been investigated and will require more detailed modeling in the future.

Surface Ozone Measurements in the Antarctic

The occurrence of stratospheric ozone loss in the Antarctic springtime is now a well-documented phenomenon. One characteristic of the ozone hole is very enhanced UV-B observed near the surface (see Chapter 2 of this text and references therein). The model simulations summarized above predict that enhancement of UV-B in remote tropospheric regions should induce a coincidental loss of surface ozone. Thompson showed this in more detail with the simulation of an extreme case of increased UV-B over the southern ocean (48°S) during the December breakup of the 1985 ozone hole.[16] An air mass of extremely low ozone (<204 Dobson units) was calculated to cause nearly twice the rate of surface ozone photolysis [to $O(^1D)$] as would occur for the average December overhead ozone column. Simulation results projected a decrease in surface ozone of nearly 30%, with a concurrent increase of surface OH (30%) and hydrogen peroxide (15%).

Recent measurements at the South Pole seem to provide the first observational confirmation of surface ozone loss in remote regions.[17] A decrease of 17% in surface ozone concentrations was reported for the periods during the austral spring and summer from 1976 through 1989. Schnell and co-workers further calculated that enhanced photochemistry could account for the surface ozone depletion if a decrease of about 10% of the overhead ozone column was assumed.[17] Such ozone column changes compare well with observed trends in total ozone from the total ozone mapping spectrometer (TOMS) on the Nimbus 7 satellite.[18]

Effects of Increased UV-B on Rural and Continental Regions

Rural and continental regions of the lower troposphere exhibit greater NO_x and VOC concentrations due to both local emissions and atmospheric transport from more densely populated areas. These regions often constitute a transition regime with chemical characteristics between those of the remote and urban troposphere. Such NO_x and VOC conditions can usually sustain ozone production, but not at levels considered deleterious to human health over a few hours. However, since most agricultural production occurs in rural areas, further degradation of air quality could adversely affect food production, forest yield, and other areas of the biosphere.

The above discussion of remote tropospheric chemistry suggested that, for some combination of higher NO_x and VOC precursor concentrations, an increase in UV-B and an accompanying increase in chemical reactivity would cause net tropospheric ozone production to be greater than for current UV-B conditions. For the mid- and lower-latitude calculations shown in Figure 1, this occurs where the lines cross into positive ozone response with increasing NO_x, for NO_x concentrations between 0.1 and 0.2 ppb.[1] This NO_x range, however, is scenario dependent and should only be taken to indicate the order of magnitude. Nevertheless, many rural regions and all urban areas have NO_x concentrations that place them in the positive response region of Figure 1.

Because continental and rural regions encompass a wide range of chemical conditions and include competition between a number of equally important chemical and physical processes, computer modeling requires a more complete representation of these processes than has yet been attempted. Nevertheless, preliminary information is available from a number of recent studies that have focused on typical portions of these regions. Besides investigating increased UV-B effects for remote regions of the troposphere, the earlier-noted studies of Thompson et al. and Isaksen et al. also studied chemically coherent regions of the global troposphere ranging from pristine to urban influenced.[2,11-13] These model calculations suggest that, for regions of the troposphere directly or even indirectly influenced by human emissions, the chemical response to increased UV-B may be quite different from the response in remote regions.

Given added UV-B, photochemical activity is expected to be enhanced and operative for longer periods of time. Principally, this is thought to be due to higher concentrations of oxides of nitrogen (NO_x). The model results for all regions showed, or were consistent with, increases in H_2O_2 and the free radicals OH and HO_2. In urban-influenced regions, tropospheric ozone was also predicted to increase beyond present levels. However, absolute comparison of results should be avoided at this time because the model construction is relatively simple and the specific impact of increased UV-B could not be directly determined since many of the scenarios combined future stratospheric ozone loss and global warming effects.

The Urban Troposphere and Ozone Control Measures

Urban and surrounding areas record high NO_x and VOC concentrations due to large anthropogenic emissions. This leads to very reactive chemistry that generates high concentrations of ozone and other oxidized compounds through the process commonly known as photochemical smog formation. When such large amounts of VOC are oxidized, the chemistry of the oxidation products also becomes important. Formaldehyde and other oxidized organics are primary reaction products of many different VOCs and are formed at relatively high rates in the urban troposphere. As described earlier, some of these oxidized organics can produce odd-hydrogen radicals upon absorption of UV-B, providing additional chemical channels that could contribute to increased urban reactivity with future increases in UV-B.[3,4,7,19]

In urban areas with present conditions reactive enough to form significantly harmful levels of ozone without using all ozone precursors (NO_x and VOC), the additional energy from increased UV-B radiation could produce even higher levels of urban ozone. In other urban regions, almost all precursors react away during an ozone episode. Since the amount of NO_x and VOC limits ozone production, increased UV-B will probably not significantly alter the present *maximum* ozone concentrations. However, depending on the amount of UV-B increase, precursors

Additional NMOC Control
vs. % Loss of Column Ozone

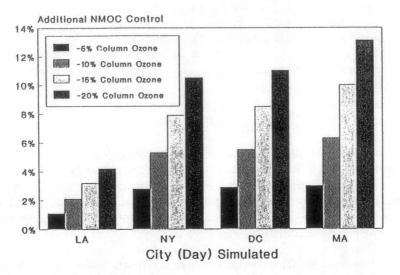

Figure 2   Model predicted VOC controls (in addition to existing controls) for
test days in four United States cities (Los Angeles, CA; New York,
NY; Washington, D.C.; and Springfield, MA). Each bar represents a
successive 5% column O_3 decrease up to -20%. (Reprinted from
Reference 20.)

could react faster and produce potentially harmful concentrations of
ozone earlier in the day and nearer to emission sources and population
centers.[7]

Throughout the world various emission control strategies are being
planned and implemented to limit production of urban ozone. These
strategies are based on the control of VOC and NO_x emissions. Until
recently, no change in stratospheric ozone was expected and, therefore,
pollution control stategies do not address a future with increased UV-B.
Unfortunately, because chemical reactivity in urban smog systems depends on the amount of UV-B, the ozone reductions anticipated in these
strategies could be less than planned if significant stratospheric ozone
destruction occurs.

Preliminary test cases using data from four U.S. cities (with present
maximum hourly ozone concentrations ranging between 0.380 and 0.135
ppm) suggested that *additional*, unanticipated VOC emission controls,
ranging linearly from 0.3 to 0.8% per percent stratospheric ozone loss,
might be needed to maintain the national ozone standard.[20] The extra
VOC control is shown in Figure 2 for these cases, with the lower rates
for cities which presently have the highest ozone levels and already

require the most emission control. Hence, these results imply that additional expenditures (for emissions control) may be needed to maintain the same measure of human health protection from air pollution if stratospheric ozone is depleted. Finally, since maximum urban H_2O_2 concentrations occur late in the day, peroxide concentrations could rise dramatically with loss of stratospheric ozone.[7] However, future control of urban emissions to limit ozone levels should have a similarly strong effect of lowering H_2O_2.

SUMMARY

If stratospheric O_3 levels decrease, the resulting increase in UV-B near the earth's surface should increase the production of some very reactive radical molecules, potentially increasing the chemical reactivity of the troposphere. Changes to tropospheric chemical processes caused by stratospheric ozone destruction suggest the following future directions for tropospheric air quality:

- *Remote Ozone.* (1) Increased levels of UV-B have been calculated to lead to tropospheric ozone depletion in remote regions. Recent measurements of decreases in Antarctic surface ozone provide support for model predictions of increased destruction of remote tropospheric ozone.
- *Rural and Continental Ozone.* (2) Most rural areas have sufficient NO_x levels such that increases in UV-B would increase ozone levels. In addition, air transported to rural areas from urban airsheds may be more polluted with increased UV-B. Such changes, perhaps combined with global climate changes, could affect plant stress and agricultural productivity and increase long-term human exposure.
- *Urban Ozone.* (3) For urban areas which presently utilize most precursor (NO_x and VOC) emissions during an ozone episode, an increase in UV-B would probably not increase the maximum ozone levels for the most extreme cases. However, higher ozone levels could be reached earlier in the day, exposing more of the urban population to hazardous short-term levels and possibly increasing long-term human exposure. (4) For urban cases where a significant amount of emitted NO_x and VOC remains at the end of the day, the added UV-B energy could induce even higher ozone levels throughout the day in the future. (5) Increased UV-B should make the urban troposphere more reactive and less responsive to planned emission control measures. Presently planned emission controls may not be adequate to achieve air quality goals. Specific VOC and NO_x emission control strategies, based on present conditions, may not be the most effective approaches for future UV-B.
- *Hydrogen Peroxide.* (6) It is possible that a future increase in UV-B could significantly increase urban production of H_2O_2. However, a large percentage of this increase could be offset if pollution control

measures to reduce ozone are implemented. (7) Remote and rural H_2O_2 concentrations are projected to increase globally if UV-B increases. This could exacerbate cloud water acidification, since that process is often limited by the availability of H_2O_2.

- *Global Distribution of Polluted Areas.* (8) Because increased UV-B would make the lower troposphere more reactive, the percentage of areas with remote tropospheric conditions may decline, and some rural regions may become more urban-like.
- *Direct Influences of Changes to Global Climate.* (9) Added cloud cover could attenuate UV-B to the surface, diminishing the changes to tropospheric air quality. However, increased water vapor concentrations could counter this by providing more odd-hydrogen radicals from ozone photodissociation. (10) It is possible that increased tropospheric reactivity could lead to increased global aerosol production, providing additional condensation nuclei to the lower stratosphere. Heterogeneous ozone destruction processes could then become more important in nonpolar regions.

CONTINUING CONCERNS AND FUTURE RESEARCH

Although the observed decline in South Pole surface ozone seems to confirm model calculations under the relatively simple conditions of the Antarctic troposphere, additional observations of both UV-B and tropospheric chemical species must be initiated to assess potential effects and evaluate the atmospheric models. This might best be attempted in regions where the impacts should be most easily observed. The TOMS observations indicate statistically significant negative ozone trends extending outward from both poles (see the discussion in Chapter 2 of this text). Episodes of air depleted of stratospheric ozone have been observed to persist for days to weeks over southern Australian and, occasionally, South American cities after the breakup of the ozone hole. Thompson has suggested that it may be possible to detect tropospheric ozone losses in the southern hemisphere through suitable surface and balloon measurements.[21] Such studies must be carefully designed, however, because it will be far more difficult to uniquely correlate stratospheric ozone loss with tropospheric changes at lower latitudes, where the stratospheric ozone loss is less dramatic and the tropospheric chemistry is complicated by the influence of human emissions.

A second item that requires immediate improvement is the level of detail in mathematical models used to describe the chemical and physical processes of the troposphere. It is probable that the current models and scenarios do not yet consider all important effects caused by potential changes in water vapor levels, cloud cover, temperature, and flow and dilution patterns. Even the more recent calculations presented above must be taken in the context of global-scale models. Because these calculations focused on decoupled, chemically similar regions of the entire troposphere (from 0 to 15 km), the results are probably most valid for the more homogeneous regions of the troposphere (marine, remote, and nonsurface regions). More complete calculations than are currently available are now needed to: (1) improve the algorithms for deposition, emission, mass transfer, radiative transfer, and the complex chemical processes that occur in the surface layer, and (2) expand the vertical linkages between surface, free troposphere, and stratosphere, as well as the transfer of mass between different regions in the horizontal direction.

Much of the emission and air quality information for the planet is estimated. To define the current conditions and assess future changes to air quality, better emissions inventories and tropospheric measurements are needed (especially for VOCs, NO_x, sulfur-containing species, and greenhouse gases of both biogenic and anthropogenic origin). In addition, new model calculations of the potential tropospheric effects due to stratospheric ozone loss must include the probable future conditions of trace gas and emissions increases caused by population growth and the effects of changing global climate.

Improved modeling studies are needed to advance our understanding of potential effects to the emissions-dominated photochemistry of urban and continental regions. Although such surface regions are a low percentage of the entire tropospheric volume, accurate description of the impact in such regions would be very important for determining exposures to humans and other portions of the biosphere. Methods to analyze exposure statistics could be coupled with analysis of existing and alternate emissions control strategies to determine the effect of future increases in UV-B.

Finally, it may be necessary to more fully investigate the effect of increased UV-B on condensed phase processes. In areas with significant cloud cover there exists the possibility of enhanced photocatalytic processes and increased source strengths for dissolved free radicals and excited state molecules.[22]

REFERENCES

1. Liu, S. C. and M. Trainer. Responses of the Tropospheric Ozone and Odd Hydrogen Radicals to Column Ozone Change, *J. Atmos. Chem.* 6:221 (1988).
2. Thompson, A. M., M. A. Owens, and R. W. Stewart. Sensitivity of Tropospheric Hydrogen Peroxide to Global Chemical and Climate Change, *Geophys. Res. Lett.* 16:53 (1989).

3. Marx, W., P. B. Monkhouse, and U. Schurath. "Kinetics and Intensity of Photochemical Processes in the Atmosphere," ISSN 0176/0777, Report prepared for Bundesministers fur Forschung und Technologie, Bonn, Federal Republic of Germany (1984).

4. DeMore, W. B., M. J. Molina, S. P. Sander, D. M. Golden, R. F. Hampson, M. J. Kurylo, C. J. Howard, and A. R. Ravishankara. "Chemical Kinetics and Photochemical Data for Use in Stratospheric Modeling, JPL Publ. 87-41, NASA, Pasadena, California (1987).

5. Bahe, F. C., W. N. Marx, W. Schurath, and E. P. Roth. Determination of the Absolute Photolysis Rate of Ozone by Sunlight O_3 + hυ → $O(^1D)$ + $O_2(^1-g)$, at ground level, Atmos. Environ. 13:1515 (1979).

6. Dickerson, R. R., D. H. Stedman, and A. C. Delany. Direct Measurements of Ozone and Nitrogen Dioxide Photolysis Rates in the Troposphere, J. Geophys. Res. 87:4933 (1982).

7. Gery, M. W., R. D. Edmond, and G. Z. Whitten. "Tropospheric Ultraviolet Radiation, Assessment of Existing Data and Effects on Ozone Formation, EPA/600/3-87/047, United States Environmental Protection Agency, Research Triangle Park, North Carolina (1987).

8. Crutzen, P. J. and J. Fishman. Average Concentrations of OH in the Troposphere and the Budgets of CH_4, CO, H_2, and CH_3CCl_3, Geophys. Res. Lett. 4:321 (1977).

9. Logan, J. A., M. J. Prather, S. C. Wofsy, and M. B. McElroy. Tropospheric Chemistry: A Global Perspective, J. Geophys. Res. 86:7210 (1981).

10. Winer, A. M., G. M. Breuer, W. P. L. Carter, K. R. Darnall, and J. N. Pitts, Jr. Effects of Ultraviolet Spectral Distribution on the Photochemistry of Simulated Polluted Atmospheres, Atmos. Environ. 13:989 (1979).

11. Thompson, A. M., M. A. Huntley, and R. W. Stewart. Perturbations to Tropospheric Oxidants, 1985–2035. 1. Calculations of Ozone and OH in Chemically Coherent Regions, J. Geophys. Res. 95:9829 (1990).

12. Thompson, A. M., M. A. Huntley, and R. W. Stewart. Perturbations to Tropospheric Oxidants, 1985–2035. 2. Calculations of Hydrogen Peroxide in Chemically Coherent Regions, Atmos. Environ. 25A: 1837 (1991).

13. Isaksen, I. S. A., T. Berntsen, and S. Solberg. Estimates of Past and Future Tropospheric Ozone Changes from Changes in Human Released Source Gases, in Ozone in the Atmosphere, R. Bojkov and P. Fabian, Eds., 1989, pp. 576–579.

14. Calvert, J. G., A. Lazarus, G. L. Kok, B. G. Heikes, J. G. Walega, J. Lind, and C. A. Cantrell. Chemical Mechanisms of Acid Generation in the Troposphere, Nature 317:27 (1985).

15. Madronich, S. and C. Grainer. Impact of Recent Total Ozone Changes on Tropospheric Ozone Photodissociation, Hydroxyl Radicals, and Methane Trends, Geophys. Res. Lett. 19:465 (1992).

16. Thompson, A. M. Perturbations to UV Incident on Southern Hemisphere Oceans Following the Breakup of the Antarctic Ozone Hole, in Effects of Solar UV Radiation on Biogeochemical Dynamics in Aquatic Environments, N. V. Blough and R. G. Zepp, Eds., Woods Hole Oceanographic Institution Note 90-09 (Woods Hole, MA: Woods Hole Oceanographic Institution, 1990), pp. 22–26.

17. Schnell, R. C., S. C. Liu, S. J. Oltmans, R. S. Stone, D. J. Hofmann, E. G. Dutton, T. Deshler, W. T. Sturges, J. W. Harder, S. D. Sewell, M. Trainer, and J. M. Harris. Decrease of Summer Tropospheric Ozone Concentrations in Antarctica, *Nature* 351:726 (1991).
18. Stolarski, R. S., P. Bloomfield, R. D. McPeters, and J. R. Herman. Total Ozone Trends Deduced from Nimbus 7 TOMS Data, *Geophys. Res. Lett.* 18:1015 (1991).
19. Whitten, G. Z. and M. W. Grey. The Interaction of Photochemical Processes in the Stratosphere and Troposphere, in *Effects of Changes in Stratospheric Ozone and Global Climate, Volume 2, Stratospheric Ozone,* UNEP, USEPA (1986).
20. Gery, M. W. Tropospheric Air Quality, in *UNEP Environmental Effects Panel Report,* J. C. van der Leun, M. Tevini, and R. C. Worrest, Eds. (Nairobi, Kenya: United Nations Environment Programme, November, 1989), pp. 49–54.
21. Thompson, A. M. New Ozone Hole Phenomenon, *Nature* 352:282 (1991).
22. Graedel, T. E. UV Effects on Atmospheric Chemistry in Condensed Phases, in *Effects of Solar UV Radiation on Biogeochemical Dynamics in Aquatic Environments,* N. V. Blough and R. G. Zepp, Eds., Woods Hole Oceanographic Institution Note 90-09 (Woods Hole, MA: Woods Hole Oceanographic Institution, 1990), pp. 5–6.

Index

absorption cross section, 21, 23
absorption spectra, 2, 173
Acartia, 179
action spectra, 19, 97, 102, 111, 164, 175, 207
activation spectra, 207
adaptive mechanisms, 142
aerosols, 17, 83
air pollutants, 145
air quality, tropospheric, 229–240
  chemical response to increased UV-B, 230
  potential changes to tropospheric chemistry, 230–236
    effects of increased UV-B on rural and continental regions, 233–234
    effects on areas distant from anthropogenic influence, 230–232
    surface ozone measurements in Antarctic, 232–233
    urban troposphere and ozone control measures, 234–236
albedo, 25, 34
  influence of, 82
  isotropic surface, 41
  ultraviolet, 40
allergen, sensitization to, 113
altitude effect, 84
amino acids, mycosporine-like, 177
Amphidinium, 171
amplification factor, overall, 107
anchovy larvae, 179
Antarctic
  ozone hole, 49, 155, 232

phytoplankton in, 160, 172
principal producer of DMS in, 181
species, most abundant, 177
surface ozone measurements in, 232
anthocyanins, 10, 135
artificial radiation sources, 160
Astasia, 168
atmosphere, UV radiation in natural and perturbed, 17–69
  calculations of spectral irradiance, 21–26
    illustrative results, 25–26
    methods, 21–25
  measurements of UV trends, 55–60
  radiometric definitions, 18–21
  trends in atmospheric composition and implications for UV radiation, 47–55
    clouds, aerosols, and oxides of sulfur and nitrogen, 54–55
    ozone, 47–54
  UV distributions and sensitivities, 26–47
    geographical and seasonal distributions, 26–28
    sensitivity to atmospheric aerosols, 41–47
    sensitivity to atmospheric ozone, 28–32
    sensitivity to clouds, 35–41
    sensitivity to surface reflections, 33–34
    sensitivity to urban pollutants, 47
attenuation coefficient, 46
autoimmune disease, 114

241